THE CONCEPTS OF

SIGMUND FREUD

The
Concepts
of
SIGMUND FREUD

BY BARTLETT H. STOODLEY

The Free Press of Glencoe, Illinois

TO HELEN,

BARRY

AND RONNY

PREFACE

THIS STUDY was undertaken to explore the hypothesis that the theory of Sigmund Freud is not biological theory in the sense and to the degree that has been supposed. When I say biological theory I refer to a view that holds that gross somatic processes, ontogenetic or phylogenetic, are decisively involved in psychic phenomena. Such a view places prime importance on drives, instincts, mechanisms. Freud's theory started out as biological theory pure and simple. And it is quite clear that Freud was never unequivocally convinced in his own mind that it ceased to be biological theory. Freud depended on the biological frame of reference for his own scientific "security." His concepts, therefore, retained their *biological flavor* long after they had lost their strict biological reference.

Freud was a stubborn genius. He sensed very early, certainly around the time of the hoax in the "thirteen cases of hysteria," that there was a strong input in personality coming from outside the organism—from interpersonal experience. He tried, long and brilliantly, to take account of this interpersonal experience without radical change in his frame of reference. I, on the other hand, have made it explicit and have indicated what changes in Freud's thought I think it requires. I hope these suggestions may throw some light on the interrelations of that important triumvirate—culture, social organization and personality.

I should make it completely clear that this is a study of a system of changing theory, not a study of psychoanalytic technique nor a critique of psychotherapy. I have no idea which period of Freud's thought is most useful to the practitioner of psychoanalysis, but I have strong convictions that his last period is the most fruitful for personality theory. It was the most valiant too, as Freud, with unfailing insight, tried to correct the recurrent weaknesses in his theory.

When I undertook this study in its earliest form I was interested in the convergence of thought between Sigmund Freud and Emile Durkheim. I am still interested in this convergence—which was first suggested to me by Talcott Parsons. But I think this study should be done first, and by itself. If the reader accepts a generous number of the suggestions made here he will feel, I am sure, that Freud and Durkheim have rather "backed" into one another.

A word about the reading of this study. It has been arranged for the reader who does not have a detailed familiarity with Freud's work. The "expert" however should note that the concluding chapter presents a full summary of the implications for personality theory that have been developed.

In larger prospective this study alters considerably what has been generally considered the Freudian image of man. This image is merely one of the latest and most pervasive of the recurrent images man has had of himself. And it is a far departure from the time when Martin Luther posted his famous demands on the door of the church in Wittenberg, and Pascal composed his *Mystère de Jesus*. In those days we recognized the blossoming of Reason. In these days we recognize its blight. The Enlightenment was confident, indeed enthusiastically confident, that Reason could solve the major problems in which people are interested and which indeed serve as the basis for their values, their standards and their norms. In religion it was considered that the existence of God could be proven on a "reasonable" basis. Thus there was no need to truck with the idea of faith. The working minds of men could affirm the divine nature of man, the divinity of God. The power of Reason did not stop at this point. It was also able to furnish pretty specific rules and standards for practical living and in this regard it came to largely supplant the formerly dominant theological standards for right conduct. I do not mean that these rules were considered different, but that the justifications for these rules changed. The law of nature supplanted the law of God. The concept of natural law was of course a very old one, going back even to the Greek philosophers, Anaximander and Heracleitus. But it became a sovereign force in the Enlightenment. Jean Bodin used it to explain, justify and delimit political power. Althusius used it in 1603 as the set of assumptions on which his *Politics* was based.

Reason, then, furnished assumptions that supplanted those of the Medieval period and served as a base for standards of judgment in politics, religion and other fields. However, a steady attack upon those assumptions and upon the law of nature which supported them opened within a short time and has continued to the present.

There was an investigation of Reason. The English Empiricists examined its premises and found them insufficient to sustain it. Thus the force that had sought to limit God became in turn limited. Its claims to transcendental knowledge were denied. Diderot and the other Encyclopedists used it to break down the tottering traditionalism in religion, manners and ideas, but it was already powerless to produce the new rallying cry, the new affirmation.

The logical results of an event take a long time to happen. Yet, on a long range view, our modern inability to establish a set of assumptions that can sustain our standards of judgment in practical affairs is related to the deflation of Reason and the law of nature. The rules of logic and the methods of statistics are ill-designed to furnish standards for judgment.

It would be folly to assert that people have not been disappointed in the history of Reason. It played tricks that were beyond any call of duty. Reason doffed the garb of the seer and the prophet and donned the humble garb of the scientist. Having given up trying to prove those things man was interested in seeing proven, it perversely inquired into the ways of the physical world. Its inquiries seemed to show that the ideas people kept on having about themselves and their destiny could not be right. Thus if Reason could not affirm, it seemed to deny.

These upsetting blows rained upon the Victorian world. Two of the most devastating were natural selection and biological determinism. For a time, it is true, a current of thought endowed these ideas with moral significance. Spencer, Comte and Condorcet, to name but a few, tried to attach some kind of progressive improvement to them. Utopia appeared for a brief period to emerge at the end of the process. But the grounds for this kind of thinking did not prove sound. There was a growing scepticism in the latter part of the nineteenth century and the first half of the twentieth century.

Sigmund Freud formulated his theory during the period of disenchantment. Thus, in a way he is a part of the tradition of disillusionment. And he thought in terms of the basic scientific assumptions of his time, the principal one being biological determinism. He reaped the hostility that surrounded the tradition in which he worked. But his own contributions were well designed to increase this hostility. For one thing he had specific reasons for thinking that man was going to find it difficult to create a perfect society. The views that he expressed in *Civilization and Its Discontents* might influence people, but they could hardly win friends. Freud's apparent emphasis on sex outraged tradition. It was biological determinism with a vengeance! Darwin's researches may have resulted in some unpleasant conclusions. There is evidence that even Darwin looked upon them as unpleasant. However, the principle of natural selection in itself was nothing to be exercised about. Quite the contrary was true of the sex instinct. As we look back upon the attempts to get at basic causative factors during the last century or two we observe a curious turn of events. People with strong commitments to free will and human moral significance were furnished, in evolutionary theory, a doctrine of biological determinism mixed in equal proportion with the laws of chance. And, with the advent of the Freudian view, these same people discovered that this determinism which was foreign to their hopes was triggered by sex which was anathema to their souls!

The Freudian image has persisted. It has even become "institution-alized" and "routinized." Yet, underneath such a mighty image the smaller views of man have been changing. The nineteenth century bound man into a biological matrix. *The twentieth century, however, is binding man into a sociological matrix.* Determinism now strikes from two directions.

Are there more sociological—as distinct from purely biological—insights in Freud's work than have been made manifest either by Freud himself or his followers? The writer feels that there are, and that some of them are brought out in this study. When they are isolated and freed of the biological mechanisms that disguise them they require some changes in the famous Freudian typologies and in his classic views on the allocation of psychic energy. The systematic theory that emerges seems to cut clearly between the two determinisms mentioned above. And in its emphasis on the dynamic qualities of mental life it offers an alternative to the passivity that is attached to these two de-terminisms. Thus, in this study, Freud is proposed as a possible solu-tion to a dilemma which, in the general view, he largely created.

CONTENTS

xi

PART THREE
THE SOCIAL STRUCTURE IN THE MIND

Part One

SOMATIC
REDUCTION

Chapter I

THE PURPOSE,

METHOD AND SCOPE

OF THIS STUDY

MODERN SOCIAL SCIENCE has a rather different picture of personality than has traditional Freudian psychology. The social scientist is not disposed to accept "organic" views of personality. He is likely to feel that such views are as outdated as the views of Lombroso and his students with reference to criminal behavior. For, to the social scientist it is clear that certain important aspects of personality derive from the social experience of the individual. It is on this assumption that he has been able to indicate similarities in the personalities of individuals within the same cultural tradition, to work out with some degree of success ideas of basic personality. Doubtless, at times the social scientist is unduly "sociologistic" in his approach. Having discovered a social influence affecting personality, his enthusiasm may lead him to conclude that this is the *only* type of influence that affects personality. Still, he may be pardoned for some degree of enthusiasm and even for some degree of error. For the concept of culture as a system of "designs of living" which is communicated from generation to generation through learning has been a most useful concept in the fields of anthropology and sociology. Culture, then, must have an "internalized" aspect. It must be related to the ideas, the emotions, the self-other orientations, the goal attitudes of the individual. The "social self" must be an important part of personality. The sociologist or anthropologist who feels that Freud is bound up in a system of "organic" causation is likely to conclude that no *rapprochement* is possible between the "cultural" approach to personality and the Freudian approach. The social scientist is likely to complain of Freud's "instinct hypotheses," his "mysticism," his "pseudo-anthropology."[1]

Yet Freud's conceptualization has been most useful in the treatment of personality strains, particularly what Freud called the "transference neuroses." It appears likely then that his organic conceptualization in some manner takes into account the effects of interpersonal experience upon the individual. The aim of this study is to discover precisely how this is done and to what degree it is done. It is obvious, of course, that some Freudian concepts, notably the super-ego, are related to interpersonal experience. These concepts, however, invariably rest on some kind of organic base and select only certain aspects of social experience for theoretical treatment. Our study shows that Freud was "sensitized" to much broader areas of social influence on the individual, but the theoretical treatment of these areas has been concealed by the emphasis on organic processes and organic mechanisms. In many cases the "instinct hypotheses," the "mysticism" and the "pseudo-anthropology," to say nothing of the mythology of Freud, are but masks for his very real concern with important dimensions of interpersonal experience. I have tried to sort and order such concepts and to subsume them under a general "social" category. Inevitably this has resulted in certain suggestions for alterations in the more general theory. It is hoped that in this manner Freud's concepts may become more available and more congenial to the social scientist, and that some of the dynamism that is the very essence of Freudian analysis may be imparted to the social scientist's thinking about the "social self."

Our "universe" then consists of Freud's "work," of his monographs, papers, lectures, etc. And in this universe we are concerned not only with the formulation of theory but also with the wealth of data presented by Freud. Sometimes this data furnishes evidence for a particular point of view; this is largely true of the data produced in *The Interpretation of Dreams*. On the other hand, it may constitute a core of hard fact that challenges the application of theory. An example of this is the case of "little Hans." I do not question the reliability of Freud's data in this study.

The method of approach has been dictated by the general nature and usefulness of theory as such. We ask such questions as the following:

    a. What aspects of the data are chosen for theoretical elaboration?

    b. How do the concepts account for empirical processes? That is, what causal relations do they establish?

c. What degree of integration exists between the concepts that constitute the "conceptual system"?

d. How do the concepts contribute to the "system"? Do they refer to an empirical entity? In Freud's thought libido-quantum is such a concept. Do they refer to an empirical process? Freud employed the concept cathexis in this manner. Do they fill a gap in the system of concepts? Freud employed the concept "unconscious formations" for this purpose. Or do the concepts "legitimize" some significant alteration in the theoretical system? The assumption of the "cathexis of the ego" performed such a function for Freud.

e. To what extent do certain concepts require other concepts to sustain them and make them work in the system? An example of such a sustaining concept is "erotogenicity." It followed on the heels of the concept "ego-cathexis." Ego-cathexis made libido available to energize ego processes, but ego processes were continuous and therefore they required a continuous source of energy. Freud, however, had not thought of libido as being a continuous source of energy. Rather, he viewed it as erratic since it was produced by excitation of the sexual organs. The assumption of erotogenicity attributed libido-producing power to many organs of the body and thus furnished the ego with continuous energy.

f. Do the data "fit" the theory? Does the theory illuminate the data? These questions may be tested in part by application of the rule of parsimony and in part by the degree to which the concepts "tie in" with other concepts—not necessarily in the particular theoretical system—and direct attention to other significant data—not necessarily under direct consideration. In this regard Freud's concept of "aim-inhibited instincts" is quite unsatisfactory. In this study we indicate that this concept relates to a component of social experience. But in the form Freud used it, it neither integrates with other concepts nor points the way to other significant data.

In most general terms our investigation has disclosed that Freud's theory was in fact "shot through" with concepts having direct or indirect relation to "social" data. However, because of the organic "frame of reference" in which his theory was set the full sociological significance of many of these concepts has been at least partially overlooked. We refer here to such concepts as repetition-compulsion, death-instincts, Eros, etc. In addition, we think that the study indicates that a major source of Freud's difficulty with concepts and their relationships, and the general "closure" of his theoretical system, lies in the fact that (a) he either disregarded the influence of some important dimension of interpersonal experience on the personality, or (b) he compensated for this influence by the assumption of processes and concepts that introduced fundamental disequilibrium into the general theory.

When one is concerned with the relations of concepts and the dimensions of the empirical world which they subsume one must pay close attention to the morphology of these concepts. This has required us to analyze Freud's thought in chronological sequence in order to be present at the invention of concepts and to be sensitive to their definition and re-definition. It has also been important to observe precisely what data gave rise to the inventions or the re-definitions. Fortunately, this procedure has not resulted in random approaches to Freud's theory for Freud himself was immensely orderly in his development. It is for this reason that his theoretical development breaks down logically into chronological periods. The first period runs to about 1900 and the production of *The Interpretation of Dreams*. Here we see the most concerted attempt to formulate theory in terms of some kind of somatic reductionism. Freud's thought changed most radically during this period, becoming ever more complex. The second period carries us to *The Ego and the Id,* a period in which Freud endeavored to establish a workable systematic theory built around the two categories of the ego and the unconscious. The principal focus was the form of the ego and its dynamic relations with the unconscious. In the last period Freud turned more definitely to the sociological component of personality. His concept of Eros indicated one important aspect of social motivation and the death instinct indicated another. These major alterations pointed the way to important changes in the systematic theory. Freud did not live, however, to carry out the new lines of inquiry.

Our investigation has amply confirmed the general suspicion that Freud was wedded to his concepts, that they frequently appeared to him in the form of "primal" mental or physical processes and that as concepts they appeared to have a kind of organic life. To Freud they were not so much defined as observed. They were not supplanted by other concepts. They tended to pine away and die. And one could never be certain that they were dead. They might rise again at a magic sign from their master. The frank rejection of concepts was quite foreign to Freud. Such a rejection must have seemed like an amputation. The result is that in Freud's thought we find a bewildering assortment of biological structures and processes in varying states of Freudian repute.

When one operates as Freud did with organic constructs it is extremely difficult to adhere to the idea of the heuristic value of concepts.

When concepts are mechanisms they become part of the data and so may require the formulation of more concepts and thus more mechanisms. As Freud's system of thought enlarged so did the biological mechanisms that he was observing or thought he was observing. This is especially true of Freud's study of dreams. The rattling of assumed mechanisms in the psyche did much to support Freud's view that the dream was a regressive, hallucinatory process. This view was, of course, in violent and significant contradiction with another view—also held by Freud—that the dream had great functional significance in the psyche.

Libido theory furnishes another example of the tyranny of a "fact." The concept of libido as such grew out of the earlier concepts, libido-quantum and ego-libido. In early thinking libido-quantum represented the excitation-potential of the genital organs. Ego-libido represented this energy when it was translated into the mind. Libido as such emerged as an energy concept applied to mental processes. It was also a reductive concept for it was a sign of mental energy originating in sexual somatic congestion. Thus libido was an energy concept, an origin concept and a theory all in one. Wherever it went it carried its theoretical assumptions with it. The well-known "thirteen cases of hysteria" convinced Freud that quite possibly mental dynamics could in fact be reduced to quantities of somatic energy that had representation in the mind. So the libido theory was promising. It soon developed, however, that there was no strict parallel between mental processes and somatic sexual processes. In line with what we have already pointed out, however, the libido was now a datum. Its quantities were assumed to *cause* psychic events even when these quantities could not be determined, nor could the quantities of the somatic states which they were held to represent. Freud then came to assume such a state of the libido as would "cause" the events in question. The quantity of libido was explained by the events which libido was supposed to explain. In "Mourning and Melancholia" we see him involved in such a case of circular reasoning. Libido became a jack-of-all-trades. It cathected ego and object alike. A "homosexual" component of it cathected the ego-ideal. Although supposedly of sexual origin it could be gratified by hallucination in dreams, a process that was looked upon as peculiarly regressive. It was the "cause" both of egoism and altruism, it was the dynamo behind concupiscence, yet it was in another form the creative power of the artist and the central element in de-sexualized love. Indeed, Freud's use of the concept of libido reminds us of the use of the concept of phlogiston at the time Lavoisier published his memorable reflection on it. We think that what Lavoisier said at that time has application to the libido theory as it was developed by Freud in his middle period. "All these reflections," said Lavoisier, "confirm what I have advanced, what I set out to prove, and what I am going to repeat again. Chemists have made phlogiston a vague principle, which is not strictly defined and which consequently fits all the explanations demanded of it. Sometimes it has weight, sometimes it has not; sometimes it is free fire, sometimes it is fire combined with earth; sometimes it passes through the pores of vessels, sometimes these are impenetrable to it. It explains at once causticity, and non-causticity, transparency and opacity, color and the absence of color. It is a veritable Proteus that changes its form every instant!"[2]

The ideas that are suggested in this study are in many cases the "non-institutionalized" thoughts of Freud himself. For Freud was one of his own severest critics. In his works can be found many of the ideas that may be used to attack the fundamentals of his own systematic thinking. This fact has proved invaluable in the formulation of the present study. Freud's theoretical advances consisted of sudden intuitive perceptions and subsequent painstaking integration and "routinization." The concept of Eros was one of these sudden flashes of intuition. Eros represented the internalized motivations for altruistic action in the individual. The formulation of Eros indicated that Freud had definitely given up the idea of reducing all motivation to libidinal motivation. Thus Eros represented liberation from the confines of the libido theory. Yet this great advance resulted in the rather sterile attempt to integrate the concept with the systematics of libido theory. And Freud resorted to the strained formulations of the aim-inhibited instincts—a formulation which required Freud to surrender some of the classic generalizations set forth in "Three Contributions to a Theory of Sexuality." This is the essence of Freud's progress, vivid illumination plus painstaking after-articulation. The nature and source of the illumination has given us in many cases the key to the theoretical divergences which we suggest. The words which Einstein has written with reference to Newton can be applied equally well to Sigmund Freud, "I must insist that Newton himself was better aware of the weaknesses inherent in his intellectual edifice than the generations of scientists which followed him. This fact has always roused my respectful admiration. . . ."[3]

Chapter II

THE PUZZLE

IN THE CASE

OF LITTLE HANS

IN THE YEAR 1909 Freud published a paper called "Analysis of a Phobia in a Five Year Old Boy." This is the case that has become famous as the case of "little Hans." The history is fully reported in the paper and furnishes us the invaluable opportunity of checking Freud's diagnosis against the evidence. By 1909 Freud was already well embarked on his study of personality. The histologist and brain anatomist had given way to the physical therapist, the hypnotist, the free associationist and finally the psycho-analyst. Early theory, as we shall see, reflected early influences. Freud was searching to understand not merely the diseased mind but the normal mind. And when he studied the case of little Hans he probably felt that he had arrived at a fairly stable theoretical position. At this time Freud had already made many changes in his theories. And many more were still to come. So the case of little Hans is a strategic point of entrance to our analysis. We are going to report the evidence to the reader just about as Freud presented it in his paper. When we measure Freud's diagnosis against this evidence I think we shall be able to make out a number of "puzzles" which will guide our quest into the main stream of Freudian thought. After the consideration of this case we shall consider the clinical and theoretical experiences leading Freud to the position that he took in the Hans case; then we shall follow Freud through his later development and observe his attempts to isolate and correct the weaknesses in the Hans analysis.

The reports on little Hans were furnished Freud by one of his "adherents" who was the father of the ailing boy. The first reports date from a period when Hans was not quite three years old. These reports tell of the flood and ebb of the phobia. The reader will, I think, find Hans a precocious and amusing child. It should be explained that Hans had already developed a great interest in his penis, which he described as his "widdler," and this had led to a generalized interest in all varieties of the genus.

THE FACTS IN THE CASE
OF LITTLE HANS

Hans asked his mother if she had a widdler too. She said that she had. When he went into a cow-shed and saw a cow being milked Hans said, "Oh, look! There's milk coming out of its widdler!"

At the age of three and one-half his mother found him with his hand to his penis. She said: "If you do that, I shall send for Dr. A. to cut off your widdler. And then what'll you widdle with?" Hans answered: "With my bottom."

Standing in front of the lions' cage at Schonbrunn he called out in a joyful and excited voice: "I saw the lion's widdler." When he was at the station (at the age of three and three-quarters) he saw some water being let out of an engine. "Oh, look," he said, "the engine's widdling. Where's it got its widdler?" After reflection he added: "A dog and a horse have widdlers; a table and a chair haven't."

Hans asked his father if he had a widdler. His father answered that he had. Upon being asked why he was staring at his mother when she undressed he said he was looking to see if she had a widdler. His mother said, "Of course. Didn't you know that?" And Hans answered: "No. I thought you were so big you'd have a widdler like a horse."

Hans's little sister Hanna was born when Hans was three and one-half. During childbirth he heard his mother groaning from an adjoining room. He asked why his mother was "coughing" and added: "The stork's coming today for certain." (He had been told during the last few days that the stork was going to bring a little girl or a little boy.) When he was called into the bedroom he did not look at his mother but at the basins and other vessels, filled with blood and water, that were still standing about the room. Pointing to the blood-stained bedpan, he observed in a surprised voice: "But blood doesn't come out of my widdler."

Hans was jealous of the new arrival and when she was praised as a lovely baby he said, "But she hasn't got any teeth yet." About this time he was taken ill with a sore throat and was heard saying, "But I don't want a little sister." In about six months he seemed to have gotten over his jealousy. His brotherly affection was equalled only by his sense of his own superiority.

When the baby was a week old he watched her being given a bath. "But her widdler's still quite small. When she grows up it'll get bigger all right." At the same age, about three and three-quarters, Hans gave his first account of a dream. "Today, when I was asleep I thought I was at Gmunden with Mariedl." When Hans heard his father telling his mother about the dream Hans corrected him: "Not with Mariedl, but quite alone with Mariedl." Six months earlier Hans and his parents had spent part of the summer in Gmunden, a summer resort, and Hans had played with the landlord's children, Marie, Berta, Olga and Fritz. To the parents' surprise Hans had been glad to move back to town. During the last month, however, Hans had been having phantasies connected with Gmunden and his playmates there. After Hanna was born he called Berta and Olga his children. Once he said, "My children, Berta and Olga, were brought by the stork too."

Hans and his father walked past a horse that was urinating and Hans said, "The horse has got its widdler underneath like me." When his sister was three months old he watched her being given a bath and said, "She *has* got a tiny little widdler." He was given a doll to play with and he undressed it and said, "Her widdler's ever so tiny."

Hans invented a game of widdling. He called a dark storeroom near the lavatory "my W.C." When his father went in there to see what he was doing Hans showed "his parts" and said, "I'm widdling." He was in fact only pretending to widdle.

Just prior to his fourth year his father took Hans to a skating rink where he met two girls about ten years of age. They paid no attention to him but he admired them and afterward called them "my little girls." When Hans was four, a five-year-old cousin visited him. Hans constantly put his arms around him and once said, "I *am* so fond of you."

At four and one-half the family moved to Gmunden for the summer holidays. Hans played with the landlord's children and with some of the neighbors' children. His favorite was Fritz. When asked which of the girls he was fondest of he said, "Fritzl." He often hugged him and made protestations of his love. He also embraced and kissed the girls heartily, particularly Berta. Mariedl was now fourteen. One night he wanted to go and sleep with Mariedl. When told that he could not do this he said that Mariedl should sleep with Mummy or with Daddy.

He was told that she must sleep with her own father and mother. Hans then proposed to go down and sleep with Mariedl again, took his clothes and went toward the staircase but was brought back.

Hans had seen a pretty little girl of about eight in a restaurant. He "blushed scarlet" when she looked at him. Although he treated the girls at home aggressively, on this occasion he was a "platonic and languishing admirer." Once he said, "I say, I *should* so like to sleep with the little girl."

At the age of four and one-quarter Hans had been given a bath by his mother and she was powdering around his penis, taking care not to touch it. Hans said, "Why don't you put your finger there?" "Because that'd be piggish." Hans answered: "What's that? Piggish? Why?" "Because it's not proper." Hans then said, laughing, "But it's great fun."

At the same age Hans reported the following dream: "I say, last night I thought: Some one said, 'Who wants to come to me?' Then some one said, 'I do.' Then he had to make him widdle." During the few days prior to the dream Hans had been playing "forfeits" with the land-lord's children. When he repeated the dream to his father he used the same words except for one sentence. Hans now said, "Then *she* said, 'I do.' " The father's report to Freud mentions at this time something that is fairly obvious, that widdling was a pleasurable process for Hans. It consisted of having his knickers unbuttoned and his penis taken out.

When his father was helping Hans do "number one" Hans asked for the first time to be taken to the back of the house so that no one should see him. He added: "Last year when I widdled, Berta and Olga watched me."

At four and one-half Hans was watching his little sister being given a bath. He began to laugh and said, "I'm laughing at Hanna's widdler." "Why?" "Because her widdler's so lovely."

At the age of four and three-quarters Hans woke up one morning in tears. Asked why he was crying he said to his mother, "When I was asleep I thought you were gone and I had no Mummy to coax with." Earlier, at Gmunden, he was frequently in a very sentimental state in the evening. Once he had said, "Suppose I was to have no Mummy," or "Suppose you were to go away." When he felt like this his mother used to take him in bed with her. One morning he climbed into his mother's bed and said, "Do you know what Aunt M. said? She said, 'He *has* got a dear little thingummy.' " This aunt had said these words to Hans's mother while she was giving him a bath. On January 7th, just prior to his fifth birthday, Hans went to the Stadtpark with his nurse-maid as usual. In the street he began to cry and asked to be taken home, saying that he wanted to "coax" with his Mummy. At home he was asked why he had refused to go any farther and had cried, but he would not say. Till the evening he was cheerful, as usual. But in the evening he grew visibly frightened. He cried and could not be separated from his mother, and wanted to "coax" with her again. Then he grew cheerful again, and slept well.

On January 8th Hans's mother decided to go out with him herself. They went to Schonbrunn. Again he began to cry, did not want to start, and was frightened. He finally went, but was frightened in the street. On the way back from Schonbrunn he said to his mother, after much internal struggling: "I was afraid a horse would bite me." That evening he wanted to be "coaxed" with. He said, crying: "I know I shall have to go for a walk again tomorrow." And later he said: "The horse'll come into the room."

On the same day his mother asked: "Do you put your hand to your widdler?" and he answered, "Yes. Every evening when I'm in bed." The next day, January 9th, he was warned, before his afternoon sleep, not to put his hand to his widdler. When he woke up he was asked about it, and he said that he had put it there for a short while all the same.

In reporting this case in his paper Freud states: "I arranged with Hans's father that he should tell the boy that all this business about horses was a piece of nonsense and nothing more. The truth was, his father was to say, that he was very fond of his mother and wanted to be taken into her bed. The reason he was afraid of horses now was that he had taken so much interest in their widdlers. He himself had noticed that it was not right to be so very much preoccupied with widdlers, even with his own, and he was quite right in thinking this."

After the above information had been given to Hans a fairly quiet period followed during which he could be induced to go for his daily walk in the Stadtpark. His fear of horses became transformed more and more into an obsession for looking at them. He said, "I have to look at horses, and then I'm frightened."

After an attack of influenza which kept him in bed for two weeks, his phobia increased and he could not be induced to go out, or at most on to the balcony. On Sunday he would go to Lainz because there was not much traffic in the streets. Once, on the way to the station bound for Lainz his father tried to explain to him that horses do not bite. Hans said, "But white horses bite. There's a white horse at Gmunden that bites. If you hold your finger to it, it bites." He told the following story purporting to have occurred at Gmunden: "When Lizzi had to be away, there was a cart with a white horse in front of her house, and the horse turned its head round [to touch Hans] and he said to Lizzi, 'Don't put your finger to the white horse or it'll bite you.' " Hans's father said to him, "I say, it strikes me that it isn't a horse you mean but a widdler, that one mustn't put one's hand to." Hans said a widdler doesn't bite and tried eagerly to prove that it was really a white horse.

Hans's father told Hans that his feeling about horses had got worse because his illness had kept Hans from going out. Hans said, "Oh no, it's so bad because I still put my hand to my widdler every night."

At this time a new maid came to Hans's house. She let him ride on her back and he called her "my horse." About March 10th he said to this maid, "If you do [a certain thing not specified in the report] you'll have to undress altogether, and take off your chemise even." She said, "And what'd be the harm? I'd just say to myself I haven't got any money to spend on clothes." And Hans answered, "Why, it'd be shameful. People'd see your widdler."

On March 13th his father said to Hans, "You know, if you don't put your hand to your widdler any more, this nonsense of yours'll soon get better." Hans said, "But I don't put my hand to my widdler any more." "But you still want to." Hans answered, "Yes, I do. But wanting's not doing, and doing's not wanting." Then his father said, "Well, but to prevent your wanting to, this evening you're going to have a sack to sleep in." They then went in front of the house. Hans said, "Oh, if I have a sack to sleep in, my nonsense'll have gone tomorrow." He was much less afraid of horses and was fairly calm when vehicles drove past.

On the next Sunday, March 15th, Hans and his father went to Lainz. There was not much traffic and Hans said, "How sensible! God's done away with horses now." His father explained that little girls and women have no widdlers like the one Hans had. Towards evening he became depressed and seemed to be afraid of horses.

A few days later he awoke about six o'clock in the morning in a fright. When asked what was the matter he said, "I put my finger to my widdler just a very little. I saw Mummy quite naked in her chemise, and she let me see her widdler. I showed Grete, my Grete, what Mamma was doing, and showed her my widdler. Then I took my hand away from my widdler quick."

On Sunday March 22nd Hans and his father went to Schonbrunn. There, he showed signs of fear toward animals which on other occasions he had looked at without any alarm. He refused to go into the house in which the giraffe was kept and would not visit the elephant which used to amuse him. He was afraid of all the large animals but was entertained by the small ones. His father said to Hans that he was afraid of big animals because they had big widdlers. Hans said: "But I've never seen the big animals' widdlers yet." His father answered: "But you *have* seen a horse's and a horse is a big animal."

Hans admitted that he had seen horses' widdlers frequently at Gmunden. His father said that big animals have big widdlers and little animals have little widdlers. Hans said: "And every one has a widdler. And my widdler will get bigger as I get bigger, because it does grow on to me."

During the night of the 27th and 28th Hans came from his room to sleep with his parents. The next day he explained why he had come into the bedroom. "In the night there was a big giraffe in the room and a crumpled one; and the big one called out because I took the crumpled one away from it. Then it stopped calling out; and then I sat down on the top of the crumpled one." Hans said he had not dreamed this. He had "thought" it. He . . . "had taken hold of the crumpled one with my hand." Hans noticed his father taking notes and his father told him he would send them to a Professor who could take away his nonsense. Hans said, "Oho! So you've written down as well that Mummy took off her chemise, and you'll give that to the Professor too." His father asked him why he came in to the parents' bedroom in the night. He said, "I don't know." His father asked him to tell what he was thinking of. Hans said, "Of raspberry syrup . . ." and ". . . a gun for shooting people dead with." He said he didn't want to tell his mother about what he had thought ". . . because I felt ashamed with Mummy at first."

Explaining the above phantasy the father furnished more facts about Hans. "Hans," he explained, "always comes in to us in the early morning, and my wife cannot resist taking him into bed with her for a few minutes. Thereupon I always begin to warn her not to take him in bed with her, and she answers now and then, rather irritated, no doubt, that it's all nonsense, and that one minute is after all of no importance and so on. Then Hans stays with her a little while."

The father explained to Hans that he (the father) was the big giraffe, and that its long neck had reminded him of a widdler. He also explained the phantasy by pointing out to Hans how he liked to get in bed with his mother. The mother was the crumpled giraffe. Hans said, "Yes, that's right."

On Monday March 30th Hans had another "thought." "I was with you [his father] at Schonbrunn where the sheep are; and then we crawled through under the ropes, and then we told the policeman at the end of the garden, and he grabbed hold of us." His father explained in his reports that at Schonbrunn a space in the gardens was shut off by a rope. "Hans was very much astonished that the space should be shut off only with a rope, which it would be quite easy to slip under. I told him that respectable people didn't crawl under the rope. He said it would be quite easy; whereupon I replied that a policeman might come along and take one off. There is a life-guardsman on duty at the entrance of Schonbrunn, and I once told Hans that he arrested naughty children."

About this time Hans reported still another "thought." He told his father, "I went with you in the train, and we smashed a window, and the policeman took us off with him."

Hans and his father visited Freud. It was disclosed that Hans was particularly bothered by ". . . what horses wear in front of their eyes" and ". . . by the black around their mouths." Freud reports: "I asked Hans jokingly whether his horses wore eyeglasses, to which he replied that they did not. I then asked him whether his father wore eyeglasses, to which, against all the evidence, he once more said no. Finally, I asked him whether by the "black round the mouth" he meant a moustache; and then disclosed to him that he was afraid of his father, precisely because he was so fond of his mother." Freud then told Hans that his father was not angry with him on that account and he might admit everything to him without any fear. Hans's father interrupted to ask Hans why he thought his father was angry with him. ". . . have I ever scolded you or hit you?" Hans said his father had hit him that morning and his father then remembered that Hans had unexpectedly butted his head into his stomach so that he had given him as it were a reflex blow with his hand.

"Does the Professor talk to God?" Hans asked on his way home.

Freud comments: "It was not to be expected that he should be freed from his anxiety at a single blow by the information I gave him; but it became apparent that a possibility had now been offered him of bringing forward his unconscious productions and of unfolding his phobia."

On April 2nd the father reported the "first real improvement." Hans stayed in front of the street door for an hour—even while carts were driving past. ". . . there is only a trace of the anxiety left."

On April 3rd in the morning Hans went into bed with his father. Hans explained that he got into bed with him because he was frightened. He said, "Why did you tell me I'm fond of Mummy and that's why I'm frightened, when I'm fond of you?" Hans added, "When you're away, I'm afraid you're not coming home." After breakfast he said to his father, "Daddy, don't trot away from me!" His father replied, "Oho! So you're afraid of the horse trotting away from you." Hans laughed.

Hans's father commented that Hans was specially frightened when carts drove into or out of the yard across the street which involved going around a corner. In explanation of this Hans said, "I'm afraid the horses will fall down when the cart turns." His father reported that

". . . Hans is more frightened of large dray-horses than of small horses, and of rough farm-horses than of smart horses such as those in a carriage and pair. He is also more frightened when a vehicle drives past quickly than when the horses trot up slowly."

There was a loading dock across the street. Hans said, "I'm afraid of standing by the cart and the cart driving off quick, and of my standing on it and wanting to get onto the board (the loading dock) and my driving off in the cart." He said he was not afraid if the cart stood still. Hans did not know why he was afraid but said, ". . . the Professor will know." Hans gave these as his reasons for wanting to get on the loading dock: "Because I should like to load and unload the packages, and I should like to climb about on the packages there. I should so like to climb about there. D'you know who I learnt the climbing from? Some boys climbed on the packages, and I saw them, and I want to do it too." Hans did not do this, however, for he was afraid to cross the street.

It developed that Hans was afraid of horses with a "black thing" on their mouths. His father concluded this was a thick piece of harness that dray-horses wear over their noses. And Hans was "most afraid of furniture-vans too." He said, "I think when furniture-horses are dragging a heavy van they'll fall down." He was also afraid of a bus and it was discovered that he had seen a horse in a bus fall down. "When the horse in the bus fell down, it gave me such a fright, really! That was when I got the nonsense." His father called to Hans's attention that formerly Hans had been afraid a horse would bite. Now he was afraid the horse would fall down. "Fall down *and* bite," answered Hans. The father asked, "Why did it give you such a fright?" Hans said, "Because the horse went like this with its feet . . ." He lay down on the ground and showed how the horse kicked. "It gave me a fright because it made a row with its feet."

Hans's mother confirmed this experience and also the fact that the anxiety broke out immediately afterwards. Describing the horse that had fallen, Hans said it was big and fat. It was black in color. "When the horse fell down did you think of your daddy?" Hans answered, "Perhaps. Yes. It's possible."

The father reports that ". . . for some time Hans has been playing horses in the room; he trots about, falls down, kicks about with his feet, and neighs. Once he tied a small bag on like a nose-bag. He has repeatedly run up to me and bitten me." Hans also took to defying his father ". . . in the most decided manner, not impudently, but in the highest spirits."

On April 6th his father asked Hans if the black around the horse's mouth reminded him of a moustache, and Hans answered, "Only by its color." When a cart drew up at the door he became frightened and ran into the house because the horse began pawing with its feet.

But Hans was now showing definite improvement. He would even cross the street. "All the fear that remains," reported the father, "is connected with the bus scene."

On April 9th Hans came to his father while he was washing and said, "Daddy, you *are* lovely! You're so white. . . . The only black thing's your moustache. Or perhaps it's a black muzzle."

Hans's father told him he had informed the Professor on what occasions Hans made a row with his feet. Hans said, "Oh, yes! when I'm cross, or when I have to do 'lumf' and would rather play." By doing "lumf" Hans meant doing "number two." The father adds: "In very early days, when he had to be put on the chamber, and refused to leave off playing, he used to stamp his feet in a rage, and kick about, and sometimes throw himself on the ground."

Hans's mother was showing his father some purchases she had made and among them was a pair of yellow ladies' drawers. Hans made exclamations of disgust when he saw them, threw himself on the ground and spat. He had done this two or three times previously when he had seen drawers. Hans was often with his mother when she went to the W.C.

The same day Hans and his father went out in front of the house. Hans pranced like a horse and said, "I'm a young horse." During the period when Hans's anxiety was at its height he was frightened at seeing horses frisking. His father had said: "These are young horses . . . and they frisk about like little boys. You frisk about too, and you're a little boy." Since then when Hans saw horses frisking he said, "That's right; those are young horses!"

Hans told his father that he had played horse at Gmunden. He never had fallen down when he was the horse. Fritzl was the horse once and ran so fast that he hit his foot on a stone and bled. Fritzl did not fall down. "I think that was how I got the nonsense," Hans said. As explanation he added, "Because they kept on saying '. . . 'cos of the horse.' "

Hans said he used to widdle in the garden where the radishes were and Berta stood outside the front door and looked at him. She widdled in the W.C. and he used to go in there with her. Hans's father reported: "The servants told us about it once, and I recollect that we forbade Hans to do it." Hans explained: "I went in alone and because Berta let me. There's nothing shameful in that."

Concerning the drawers Hans said: "I spit because the black drawers are black like lumf and the yellow ones like widdle, and then I think

I've got to widdle." He said he liked very much to be in the W.C. with Mummy when she widdled or did lumf.

On April 11th he said: "Daddy, I thought something. I was in the bath, and then the plumber came and unscrewed it. Then he took a big borer and stuck it into my stomach." Then he related a second idea. "We were travelling in the train to Gmunden. In the station we put on our clothes: but we couldn't get it done in time and the train carried us on."

Hans said he had seen a horse doing lumf, that it made a loud row when it did lumf, ". . . like when lumf falls into the chamber."

At Gmunden he was always taken to the public baths— " . . . a proceeding against which he used to protest with passionate tears." In Vienna, too, he screamed if made to sit or lie in the big bath. He must have his bath kneeling or standing. Hans said he was afraid of falling in. He said he was afraid of his Mummy's ". . . letting go and my head going in." He didn't know why he thought this. His father said to him: "Perhaps it was because you'd been naughty and thought she didn't love you any more." To this Hans replied, "Yes." His father added: "When you were watching Mummy giving Hanna her bath, perhaps you wished she would let go of her so that Hanna should fall in." Again Hans answered, "Yes."

On April 12th Hans associated lumf with the black upholstery of the seats in a second class carriage, and on April 13th with a piece of liver in the soup.

The same day Hans had been put out on the balcony and had said: "I thought to myself Hanna was on the balcony and fell down off it." His mother asked him if he would rather Hanna were not there and he said, "Yes."

On April 14th Hans's father reported that the theme of Hanna was uppermost. "He has already several times expressed a wish that the stork should bring no more babies and that we should pay him money not to bring any more out of the big box where babies are. . . . Hanna screams such a lot, he says, and that's a nuisance to him." Drays now cause him less alarm. He called out with joy, "Here comes a horse with something black on its mouth!" It was a horse with a leather muzzle. Hans was not afraid of this horse.

Dwelling on Hanna, Hans said that Hanna had travelled to Gmunden in a box like the one in the front hall. Mummy had the box at home in the attic. Hans described how the stork brought Hanna and said he was very fond of Hanna but would prefer that she weren't alive because she screamed so loud. His father said to him: "That was why you thought when Mummy was giving her her bath, if only she'd let go, Hanna would fall into the water. . . ." Hans added, ". . .

and die." Hans's father said: "A good boy doesn't wish that sort of thing, though." Hans answered, "But he may think it. . . . If he thinks it, it is good all the same, because you can write it to the Professor."

On April 16th Hans finally went across into the courtyard opposite the house. On the 17th he would not do it since there was a cart standing at the loading dock. "When a cart stands there," he said, "I'm afraid I shall tease the horses and they'll fall down and make a row with their feet." Under examination by his father he said he had beaten horses at Gmunden and then added, "What I've told you isn't the least true." He said he would like to beat Mummy with a carpet-beater. He explained that buses, furniture-vans, and coal carts were stork-box carts.

In front of the house in the afternoon Hans suddenly ran indoors as a carriage with two horses came along. "The horses are so proud," he said, "that I'm afraid they'll fall down." His father asked him who it really was that was so proud. Hans answered: "You are, when I come into bed with Mummy." "So you want me to fall down?" "Yes." He added, "You've got to be naked [his father says this means "barefoot"] and knock up against a stone and blood must flow, and then I'll be able to be alone with Mummy for a little bit at all events. When you come up into our flat I'll be able to run away quick so that you don't see."

On April 22nd Hans had another "thought." "A street-boy was riding on a truck, and the guard came and undressed the boy quite naked and made him stand there till next morning, and in the morning the boy gave the guard 50,000 florins so that he could go on riding on the truck." Hans had wanted to ride on a trolley and his father had told him that if he did the guard would be after him.

His father reported that "Hans had been playing all the morning with an india-rubber doll which he called Grete. He had pushed a small penknife in through the opening to which the little tin squeaker had originally been attached, and had then torn the doll's legs apart so as to let the knife drop out. He had said to the nurse-maid, pointing between the doll's legs: 'Look, there's its widdler!' "

Hans said he would like to have a little girl. "I should like to have one, but Mummy mustn't have one; I don't like that." When told he couldn't have a little girl, he said: "Oh yes, boys have girls and girls have boys."

On April 24th his parents told Hans that children grow inside their Mummy and are then brought into the world by being pressed out of her like a lumf and that this involved a great deal of pain. In the afternoon he went out in front of the house, ran after carts, but would not venture away from the neighborhood of the street-door.

On April 25th Hans butted his father in the stomach. During the discussion over this Hans was playing with a little toy horse. The horse fell down and Hans shouted: "The horse has fallen down! Look what a row it's making!" Hans admitted he was jealous of his father. He didn't know why.

Hans admitted under questioning that he often got into bed with Mummy at Gmunden and used to think to himself he was Daddy. His father asked, "And then you felt afraid of Daddy?" Hans answered, "You know everything, I didn't know anything." His father continued: "When Fritzl fell down you thought, 'If only Daddy would fall down like that!' And when the lamb butted you you thought, 'If only it would butt Daddy!' Can you remember the funeral at Gmunden?" "Yes, what about it?" "You thought then that if only Daddy were to die you'd be Daddy." Hans answered, "Yes." Hans said he was afraid of buses because there was so much luggage on the top. His father said: "When Mummy was having Hanna, was she loaded full up too?" Hans said: "Mummy'll be loaded full up again when she has another one, when another one begins to grow, when another one's inside her." "And you'd like that?" Hans answered, "Yes." His father continued: "You said you didn't want Mummy to have another baby." Hans said: "Well, then she won't be loaded up again. Mummy said if Mummy didn't want one, God didn't want one either. If Mummy doesn't want one she won't have one." Hans then said he wished for Mummy to have a baby. His father said this must be because he would "like to be Daddy." Hans said, "Yes, how does it work?" "How does what work?" And Hans continued: "You say Daddies don't have babies: so how does it work my wanting to be Daddy?" His father answered: "You'd like to be Daddy and married to Mummy; you'd like to be as big as me and have a moustache; and you'd like Mummy to have a baby." Hans said: "And, Daddy, when I'm married I'll have only one if I want to, when I'm married to Mummy, and if I don't want a baby, God won't want it either, when I'm married." "Would you like to be married to Mummy?" "Oh yes."

On April 26th Hans said he had always imagined that Berta and Olga and the rest were his children, that he got them from himself, that when he sat on the chamber and a lumf came he thought to himself he was having a baby. His father said: "You know when the bus-horse fell down? The bus looked like a baby-box, and when the black horse fell down it was just like. . . ." Hans, finishing for his father, added, ". . . like having a baby."

Hans's father reported: "All day long to-day Hans has been playing at loading and unloading packing-cases. He used to call the doors of the Head Customs House shed 'holes.' But now, instead of hole, he says, 'behind-hole.' "

The anxiety had almost completely disappeared.

On April 30th his father said to Hans: "You know quite well a boy can't have any children." Hans said: "I know. I was their Mummy before, now I'm their Daddy." "And who's the children's Mummy?" Hans answered: "Why, Mummy, and you're their Grandaddy." His father said, "So then you'd like to be as big as me and be married to Mummy, and then you'd like her to have children." Hans answered, "Yes, that's what I'd like, and then my Lainz Grandmamma [his father's mother] will be their Grannie."

On May 1st Hans came to his father at lunch-time and said: "D'you know what? Let's write something down for the Professor." "What shall it be?" Hans said: "This morning I was in the W.C. with all my children. First I did lumf and widdled, and they looked on. Then I put them on the seat and they widdled and did lumf, and I wiped their behinds with paper. D'you know why? Because I'd so much like to have children; then I'd do everything for them—take them to the W.C., clean their behinds, and do everything one does with children."

That afternoon Hans pointed out a bus as a stork-box cart.

On May 2nd Hans said to his father: "I thought something to-day. The plumber came; and first he took away my behind with a pair of pinchers, and then gave me another, and then the same with my widdler."

In a postscript the father reports that Hans's disorder survives only in the normal instinct for asking questions. Hans refers to his illness as a matter of history: ". . . at the time when I had my nonsense."

FREUD'S ANALYSIS

Our greatest aid in the reconstruction of Freud's analysis is the understanding that, in his view, only certain repressions were of major importance in this case. These major repressions were concerned with Hans's hostile and jealous feelings toward his father and sadistic feelings, "premonitions, as it were, of copulation," towards his mother. Other repressions were of minor importance. "We have seen how our little patient was overtaken by a great wave of repression and that it caught precisely those of his sexual components that were dominant. He gave up onanism, and turned away in disgust from everything that reminded him of excrement and of looking on at other people performing their natural functions. But these were not the components which were stirred up by the exciting cause of the illness (his seeing the horse fall down) or which provided the material for the symptoms, that is, the content of the phobia."[1]

The real foundation for the phobia was the Oedipus complex. "These aggressive propensities of Hans's found no outlet, and as soon as there came a time of privation and of intensified sexual excitement, they tried to break away with reinforced strength. Then it was that the battle which we call his 'phobia' burst out."[2]

If other components appeared to be involved in the phobia they were not truly causal but part of the manifestation of deeper forces. "During the course of it [the phobia] a part of the repressed ideas, in a distorted form and transformed on to another complex, forced their way into consciousness as the content of the phobia. But it was a decidedly paltry success. Victory lay with the forces of repression; and they made use of the opportunity to extend their dominion over components other than those that had rebelled."[3]

The aggressive propensities of little Hans had for their purpose in Freud's view the "seduction" of his mother. In this case the word "seduction" must be taken in something close to its literal sense. Freud mentioned the pleasure that Hans received from cutaneous contact. He pointed out as attempts at "seduction" certain invitations to stroke his penis extended by Hans to his mother. Freud believed that the evidence warranted even stronger conclusions. The bath phantasy, in which the plumber unscrewed the bath and plunged his "borer" into Hans's stomach, the doll episode, where Hans tore open the doll's legs to let the knife fall through, and the giraffe phantasy—in conjunction with the two criminal phantasies—indicate to him that Hans had an unconscious knowledge of coitus and the part played by the male in the production of children. Of the bath phantasy Freud said: "The interpretation that we are obliged to give to the phantasy will of course sound very curious; 'With your big penis you "bored" me . . . and put me in my Mother's womb.' "[4] Freud interpreted the doll episode as follows: "By means of a brilliant symptomatic act, 'Look!' he [Hans] said to his parents, 'this is how I imagine that a birth takes place.' "[5] The giraffe phantasy and the two criminal phantasies (crawling through under the ropes at Schonbrunn, and breaking a window in a train), were ". . . symbolic phantasies of coitus, and it was no irrelevant detail that his father was represented as sharing in his actions; 'I should like,' he seemed to be saying, '. . . to do something with my mother, something forbidden; I do not know what it is, but I do know that you are doing it too.' "[6]

In the light of these interpretations Freud obviously thought that Hans's instinctual impulses of sexual sadism toward his mother and hostility toward his father found their roots not in any social situation but in unconscious and truly seductive desires.

And these laid the groundwork, the motivational basis, for later developments. Somehow motivations became distorted, anxiety appeared, and symptoms were formed. The appearance of the anxiety furnished a stumbling block which Freud was quick to acknowledge. Why did the anxiety develop and what is the relation of repression to it? Freud found Hans's earliest manifestation of anxiety in a dream. In this dream Hans's mother had left him. "The child dreamed of exchanging endearments with his mother and of sleeping with her; but all the pleasure was transformed into anxiety, and all the ideational content into its opposite. Repression had defeated the purpose of the dream-mechanism."[7] Freud felt that the origin of the anxiety must, however, be sought earlier and he traced it to intensified sexual excitement with reference to Hans's mother. "The intensity of this excitement was shown by his two attempts at seducing his mother (the second of which occurred just before the outbreak of his anxiety); and he found an incidental channel of discharge for it by masturbating every evening and in that way obtaining gratification. Whether the sudden exchange of this excitement for anxiety took place spontaneously or as a result of his mother's rejection of his advances, or owing to accidental revival of earlier impressions by the 'exciting cause' of his illness . . . this we cannot decide . . . The fact remains that his sexual excitement suddenly changed into anxiety."[8]

Freud suggested a further possibility for the origin of anxiety. When neurotic content was attached to a horse Freud suggested an automatic formation of anxiety. ". . . the pathogenic material was remodelled and transposed on to the horse-complex, while the accompanying affects were uniformly turned into anxiety."[9] Still another possibility was that the anxiety was a symptom resulting from repression. It was related to a longing for his mother. The repression acting on the longing made it pathological. "It was this increased affection for his mother which turned suddenly into anxiety—which, as we would say, succumbed to repression."[10] Thus the anxiety was repressed longing. Freud added: "But it was not the same thing as the longing: the repression must be taken into account too. Longing (as such) can be completely transformed into satisfaction if it is presented with the object longed for. Therapy of that kind is no longer effective in dealing with anxiety. The anxiety remains even when the longing can be satisfied. It can no longer be completely retransformed into libido; there is something that keeps the libido back under repression."[11] That repression had taken place in the case of Hans was shown by the fact that even when he went to walk with his mother, the object of his longing, the anxiety still persisted. ". . . his anxiety had stood the test" [i.e., even in the presence of his mother it was not reconverted into libido]; "and the next thing for it to do was to find an object."[12]

But what was the source of this repression? Freud suggested that "Perhaps it was merely the result of the intensity of the child's emotions, which had become greater than he could control . . ."[13] He also presented an alternative explanation. Although speaking warmly of Hans's "excellent and devoted mother," Freud admitted that there was some justice in her husband's accusation that she was responsible for the outbreak of the child's neurosis, on account of her "excessive display of affection for him." [14] Freud then added an accusation of his own: "We might as easily blame her for having precipitated the process of repression by her energetic rejection of his advances ('that'd be piggish'). But she had a predestined part to play, and her position was a hard one."[15] This last allusion doubtless reflected Freud's conviction that Hans's mother had her inevitable role to play out in the Oedipus trilogy.

In his analysis to this point Freud stressed four variables: (a) longing, (b) sexual excitement, (c) repression, (d) anxiety. To him these variables are not only crucial in this case but persist as key variables in all of his clinical experience. What are their relations to each other? It is clear that repression occurred and that, in some sense, the repression "caused" the anxiety. But what caused the repression? Freud suggested what are really two alternative solutions but he combined them in such a fashion that the distinction between them is not clear. On the one hand he suggested that the cause of the repression was sexual excitement. This sexual excitement may have intensified from organic causes, or it may have been increased by the mother's caresses. On the other hand, the repression may have been somehow caused by the mother's rejection of the boy. The first solution assumed that sexual excitement may turn "naturally" into anxiety. The second solution assumed that some unfavorable development in interpersonal relations could produce anxiety symptoms.

Hans's "desire" for his mother was broken down by Freud into several unconscious wishes, (a) the desire to see his mother's "widdler," (b) the desire that his mother should have no more children, (c) the desire to possess her, (d) the desire to get rid of his father as a preliminary to possessing his mother. These wishes were held to be manifest in the symptoms. Only their direction and object had changed. Thus Freud felt that all of the repressions, both major and minor, were repressions of sexual desires. In the symptoms, however, they appeared in an entirely different manner. In the case of the minor repressions there was loathing and disgust for the very things that had formerly been an object of sexual interest. In the major repressions there is no such loathing and disgust. The sexual interests are maintained but they are displaced.

Hans's reactions to animals at the zoo is an example of the shame and disgust associated with the minor repressions. He would not visit the elephants. Also, packages in vans reminded Hans of "lumf" and so shared the disgust he felt for "lumf." Generally, items associated with "widdlers" or with "lumf" caused disgust in Hans because these interests had fallen into minor repression.

However, Hans like to tease and beat horses at least in his phantasies. This, Freud maintained, is because the horse was, in one aspect, his mother, and teasing and beating the horse is an outlet for his sexual, sadistic designs upon his mother. These designs have not been influenced by disgust or shame. They exist as before but they have been displaced from the mother onto the horse.

Freud described the mechanics of the phobia as follows: There was repression of the intense sexual excitement directed toward the mother as object. There also must have been some repression of the hostile feelings toward the father which would be expected in the "normal" Oedipus. In the first instance, the horse was the symbol of the father and therefore the repression must have taken place. This displacement was easy because Hans had played horse with his father at Gmunden. The displacement did not immediately take place because Hans had easy access to his mother there and his father was frequently away. Furthermore, there was an outlet for Hans's sexual excitement in his association with the landlord's children. However, when the family returned to Vienna, Hans's father was home more of the time and therefore Hans's hostile feelings were intensified. Furthermore, he no longer had any playmates to act as safety valves for the sexual excitement mounting up within him. Now Fritzl, when he was making believe he was a horse at Gmunden, had stubbed his toe until it bled and also had fallen down. Since Hans's father had played at being a horse it was possible for Hans to treat Fritzl as a father substitute. It was then but a short step for Hans to displace onto the horse the feelings he harbored against his father. When Hans became afraid of a horse biting him, he was really afraid of his father's punishing him for his hostile feelings. In Freud's view the black around the horses' mouths and what they wore in front of their eyes—things that made Hans afraid—were displacements from the father's eyeglasses and moustache. Everything therefore seemed to point to the horse as a displacement from the father.

However, the fear of a *falling* horse was not so easily explained. What was the significance of the fall? and what was the source of the fear? To answer these questions Freud had recourse to many of the repressions at work in Hans. Since the original displacement was from the father to the horse, the falling horse must represent in some manner Hans's hostile feelings toward his father. The falling horse probably symbolized a dying horse. The falling horse was therefore Hans's dying father. Furthermore, we remember that at Gmunden "a father" had said to Lizzi, "Don't put your finger to the white horse or it'll bite you." This was an indication that the repression applying to "widdlers" also had application to horses. "Don't put your finger to . . ." was reminiscent of what Hans's mother had told him in warning him against touching his penis. Freud said: "When repression had set in and brought a revulsion of feeling along with it, horses, which had till then been associated with so much pleasure, were necessarily turned into objects of fear."[16] Therefore, the fear that Hans felt concerning the falling horse was in some measure due to the repression of his onanism.

We have not yet exhausted the symbolism of the falling horse. Hans had for some time been evolving solutions to the problem of childbirth. His mind evolved the typical infantile theory that children were born like "lumf." When Hans did not wish to go to the W.C. and do "lumf" he was in the habit of stamping his feet, ("making a row with his feet"), and sometimes throwing himself on the ground. As a result, when the horse fell and made a row with its feet it was no longer merely his father dying, but also his mother in childbirth.[17] This symbolism applied when the horse was pulling a heavily loaded cart, for the cart, in Hans's mind, would be heavy with lumf. The wish that Hans's mother should have no more children could then be easily displaced onto the horse.

These are the main lines of the Freudian diagnosis. There was, in Hans's phobia, great richness in the employment of the lumf and widdler themes. This may be seen in Hans's feeling about giraffes, elephants, loaded carts, packages, liver, sausage, etc. In Freud's view, however, these displacements were servient to the Oedipus themes which furnished the motivating causes of the phobia.

Freud's consideration of dream and phantasy supported his main view. Most of the interpretations add depth to the mother desire by attributing to Hans some sort of unconscious knowledge of childbirth and the role of the penis in procreation. Freud also supposed some kind of rational conjecture in Hans about these things. Hans surmised that ". . . his father not only knew where children came from, he actually performed it—the thing that Hans could only obscurely divine. The widdler must have something to do with it, for his own grew excited whenever he thought of these things—and it must be a big widdler too, bigger than Hans's own. If he listened to these pre-monitory sensations he could only suppose that it was a question of some act of violence performed upon his mother, of smashing something, of making an opening into something, of forcing a way into an enclosed space—such were the impulses that he felt stirring within him."[18]

The phantasy in which his mother showed her "widdler" to Hans was given a rather different interpretation, however. Freud said: "I had expressed a suspicion that Hans's repressed wish might now be that he wanted to see at all costs his mother's widdler. As his behavior to a new maid fitted into this hypothesis, his father gave him his first piece of enlightenment, namely, that women have no widdlers. He re-acted to this first effort at helping him by producing a phantasy that he had seen his mother showing her widdler. This phantasy, and a remark made by him in conversation, to the effect that his widdler did grow on to him, allow us our first glimpse into the patient's unconscious mental processes. The fact was that the threat of castration made to him by his mother some fifteen months earlier was now having a de-ferred effect upon him. For his phantasy that his mother was doing the same thing as he had done . . . was intended to serve as a piece of self-justification; it was a protective or defensive phantasy."[19]

Freud indicated that the resolution of the phobia occurred when there was a resolution of the Oedipus. This took place in a "triumphant phantasy" in which Hans became married to his mother, had children and tended them, and his father was married off to Hans's grand-mother. To cap the climax, there was another phantasy in which a plumber came and gave Hans a bigger behind and a bigger widdler so that he could properly perform the functions of his new office. "With this phantasy," says Freud, "both the illness and the analysis came to an appropriate end."

The resolution of the Oedipus did not involve somatic discharge, i.e., true libidinal gratification. What then had taken place? Freud ex-plained it this way: ". . . the only results of the analysis were that Hans recovered, that he ceased to be afraid of horses, and that he got on to rather familiar terms with his father, as the latter reported with some amusement. But whatever his father may have lost in the boy's respect he won back in his confidence; 'I thought,' said Hans, 'you knew every-thing, as you knew that about the horse.' For analysis does not undo the *effects* of repression. The instincts which were formerly suppressed remain suppressed; but the same effect is produced in a different way. Analysis replaces the process of repression, which is an automatic and excessive one, by a temperate and purposeful control on the part of the highest mental faculties. In a word, analysis replaces repression by condemnation. This seems to brings us the long-looked-for evidence that consciousness has a biological function, and that with its entrance into the picture an important advantage is secured."[20]

55097

THE PUZZLE IN THE CASE
OF LITTLE HANS

In 1909 when Freud published the record and analysis of Hans he had not developed the imposing theory that came later. However, we know that in 1909 Freud held to a strictly biological system of explanation. He set out, therefore, to "explain" Hans's phobia with that kind of a system. There are fundamental difficulties with this explanation which can be summarized as follows:

a) The role of consciousness, as suggested by Freud, is not consistent with the clinical evidence.

b) The Oedipus complex is not strong enough to explain the symptoms.

c) The manner in which sexual excitation turns into anxiety is not explained.

d) It is not clear how the mother's prohibition against Hans's touching his penis is related to the phobia.

e) At the time of the cure of the phobia the factors alleged to be causes still remain.

These specific difficulties with Freud's views can be supplemented by two suggestions.

1) Hans's symptoms can be generally accounted for by the threat of the deprivation of his mother's love.

2) Hans achieved a cure of his phobia as soon as he was able to create a situation where his interest in widdlers was reconciled with his mother's esteem and love for him.

Let us look at these points a little more closely.

a) The role of consciousness is not consistent with the clinical evidence.

Freud maintained that consciousness performed the function of "condemnation." However, most of the factors that Freud believed caused the phobia were present in consciousness before the phobia set in. Hans was well aware that he loved his mother. If we wish to attach rather extravagant designs to his actions we can maintain that he was set on seducing her into an interest in his penis. When she demurred he told her it was "such fun." An erotic interest could hardly be more artlessly and consciously confessed. Why did consciousness not perform its function of condemnation *before* this 'longing' fell into repression? Why was it necessary for the repression to come about before consciousness exercised its prerogative?

b) *The Oedipus complex is not strong enough to explain the symptoms.*

Freud built up a strong case for the Oedipus but he built it up on the basis of suppositions. He turned a strong affection for the mother into an overwhelming erotic passion. He saw in the father not so much an object of rivalry as an object of deep-seated jealousy and hate. These interpretations were buttressed by dream interpretations indicating that Hans had some kind of unconscious knowledge of sexual intercourse and the process of childbirth. It is quite likely that he had *seen* more of both than his parents admit. But, from the evidence, we would conclude that Hans is much more interested in 'widdlers' and in 'lumf' than he is in seducing his mother. There were times when he expressed some hostility against his mother and upon some occasions he showed real affection for his father. The mildness of the Oedipus symptoms, does not explain the intensity of the neurotic symptoms. It seems likely from the clinical evidence that Freud has exaggerated the Oepidus to give it a plausible relation to the phobic symptoms.

c) *It is not clear how sexual excitation turns into anxiety.*

Hans supposedly suffered from a surplus of sexual excitement. Through some kind of automatic process this surplus was turned into anxiety. The somatic system was overloaded. This overload is not easily inferred from the data, but must be deduced from Freudian assumptions. Out of the strength of the Oedipus desire for the mother, and hate for the father, out of the unconscious imaginings of sexual joys, out of fevered dreams of seduction, and, lastly, out of the caresses of Hans's mother, developed an intolerable somatic strain. This strain caused a sickness that poisoned the mind.

Even if we concede the existence of intolerable sexual tension we note that *Hans's cure was performed without any discharge of this sexual excess*. Hans was, perhaps, not as well off at the time of his cure as in the early days of his phobia. For during the beginning of his phobia he was still "putting his hand to his widdler." Freud assumed that this masturbation would give him some relief. However, at the end of the phobia he had transformed his interest in widdlers to imaginary children and only seldom was he touching his own widdler. In addition, Freud's assumption of excess sexual excitation runs in direct opposition to his assumption of the "condemnation" function of consciousness. He did not indicate that through the process of condemnation some kind of sexual satisfaction was obtained. *He intended the precise opposite.* Condemnation produced some kind of recovery and yet it refused satisfaction to the erotic desires.

Condemnation, as a hypothesis, is based on quite different ground than that of sexual excitation. It is based on a judgment about it. The assumption is that *the right kind of judgment can do away with the anxiety without reduction of the sexual excitation.*

d) It is not explained how the mother's prohibition against Hans touching his penis is related to the phobia.

Hans's mother told Hans not to touch his penis. Freud considered this an important factor in Hans's phobia but he did not make it clear in what respect it was important. On the one hand there is an intimation that this was an aggravating circumstance that increased or heightened Hans's sexual turmoil by depriving him of cutaneous satisfactions formerly furnished by his mother. It also reduced the amount of masturbation that Hans resorted to. This is the view that Freud favored. However, there are intimations that the injunction against touching his genitals meant more to Hans than a sexual deprivation.

e) The "causes" of the phobia remain after Hans is cured.

Hans cured himself by creating a fanciful social situation. He was married to his mother and his father was married to his grandmother. He had children of his own and he tended to their wants with the same interest that he had formerly extended to himself. How did this work to reduce the somatic excitation? How did this satisfy the lust of the little boy for his mother? These points constitute the puzzle of little Hans. Hans cured himself by a fancy. He "condemned" his interest in his widdler and his desire for his mother. None of these things reduced the sexual pressure that Freud felt caused the phobia. Therefore we must conclude that *the sexual pressure was not the cause of the unhap-*

piness that Hans felt. Something new had been added to Hans's outlook on life. And this was the source of Hans's unhappiness.

If we explore this point of view we see that Hans was placed in quite an intolerable position by his mother's stricture against touching his widdler. It deprived him of pleasure. *And this deprivation of pleasure became a condition of his mother's affection.* A new rule was added to Hans's living code. And, from the attitude of his mother, Hans could see that this was not a rule that could be broken at will. It was a rule that announced in sternest terms his mother's policy. Her attitude said unmistakably that she could not love a boy with an exaggerated interest in widdlers.

This constituted a traumatic situation for Hans as it would for most boys and girls of his age. It was necessary to hold on to his mother's love at all costs. The situation was unusually traumatic in Hans's case because his mother had been particularly demonstrative in her affection for Hans and because a signal and sign of her affection had been the cutaneous satisfaction she had furnished him in their play to-gether. This play had heightened Han's sexual sensitivity. But it had also become the symbol of his mother's love. The sudden, and to Hans inexplicable, withdrawal of interest in this play, the disapproval of the very idea of it, could mean only a withdrawal of interest in Hans, a disapproval of the very idea of him. This general interpretation may have been confirmed, in Hans's mind, by the later arrival of Hanna.

The "unpleasure" that Hans felt, then, may have been, not closely related to somatic conditions, but traceable to the fear of the loss of his mother's love.

If this hypothesis is correct it follows that the "cure" of little Hans would occur when he was able to recover the love of his mother or find some satisfactory substitute. However, Hans's interest in widdlers and in lumf was all-consuming. This interest had been increased by tactual stimulation on the part of Hans and of his mother. These erotic sensa-tions and interests were thus well established in Hans. He would re-quire some field for these interests.

Following this line of thinking we can arrive at an idea of what Freud had in mind in his use of the concept "condemnation." It was necessary for Hans to accept the rule of his mother as a rule of his own and to act in accordance with it. He must "condemn" certain interests and acts that formerly had been important to him. It was unpleasant to give up these satisfactions, but *it was doubly unpleasant not to con-form to the pronouncement of his mother.* It thus became Hans's new law of life to indicate to his mother that he had no interest in lumf and widdlers. In this way, albeit with uncertainty and misgiving, he could hope to establish himself again in her love.

While his father was extracting Oedipus confessions for the use of the "Professor," little Hans was in the process of working out a cure for his phobia. While his father was discovering deep sources of Hans's hate for him, Hans was in fact leaning upon his father more and loving him more. The father became a substitute love-object for Hans while his relations with his mother were in jeopardy. Although his mother appeared to have withdrawn her love from Hans, his father appeared to have increased his interest and attention. Furthermore, his father's behavior did not support his mother's attitude toward widdlers but ran directly contrary to that attitude. His father wanted to know of his slightest interest in widdlers. His strictures were of the mildest. Departures from the rules were always "good" in one respect—they gave the "Professor" something to think about.

The drift of Hans's relations with his father indicates that he came to like him more and more. He liked him enough to confess to any kind of deviltry and hate if that would please him. There are times, however, when, without suggestion or leading questions, Hans was free to say what he thought. On April 3rd there was the following conversation:

FATHER: And why have you come [into bed with me] today?
HANS: When I'm not frightened I shan't come any more.
FATHER: So you come in to me because you're frightened?
HANS: Yes. Why did you tell me I'm fond of Mummy and that's why I'm frightened, when I'm fond of you?

On the other hand, while Hans's relations with his father seemed to be improving, his relations with his mother were not. We can assume that he was still dependent in part upon her for his own sense of security. But there appears to be an increase in his hostility toward her. In other words, instead of developing in this case a typical Oedipus, we find that the hostility for the father is progressively muted while the hostility toward the mother is aggravated. The following conversation took place on the 17th of April. There had been some talk about Hans's wanting to beat horses.

FATHER: Which would you really like to beat? Mummy, Hanna, or me?
HANS: Mummy.
FATHER: Why?
HANS: I should just like to beat her.
FATHER: When did you ever see any one beating his Mummy?
HANS: I've never seen any one do it, never in all my life.
FATHER: And yet you'd just like to do it. How would you like to set about it?

HANS: With a carpet-beater. (*Hans's father reported that his mother often threatened to beat Hans with the carpet-beater.*)

The rule about widdlers was compulsive for Hans as long as he was dependent upon his mother. He never became free of this dependence but he lessened it. His continued need for his mother is indicated by his need for "coaxing" with her.

In the "cure" Hans reduced the emotion associated with the rule his mother had made, he reduced the field of its application, and he found a way to get his own interest in widdle and lumf accepted, even by his mother. Then indeed the days of his "nonsense" were gone for good.

The process of his recovery can be seen in his dreams, phantasies, and "thoughts." In the early dreams Hans was preoccupied with the fear of losing his mother's affection. In one of the earliest she actually had gone away from him. In the "giraffe dream" he was successful in gaining his security even in the face of resistance from his father. In the first bath dream, in which the plumber unscrewed the bath and then stuck his big borer into the child's stomach, the father appeared as a substantial threat to the child who was struggling to regain the esteem of his mother and who felt the fright associated with her apparent loss. His father reported to Freud that prior to this last dream Hans had been coming into the parents' room each morning but had been sent away.

Another category of dreams consisted of an attack on the rule that Hans's mother had made. This rule as it appeared to Hans meant that he should not touch his penis. It also meant that his mother would not and should not touch his penis. The reason for all this was general. To do things *of this sort* was "piggish," "not proper." Thereafter Hans tried to avoid widdlers like the plague. Much of his fear of horses, elephants and other animals was associated with a fear that he would see their widdlers. This would be "piggish," "improper" and carried with it the threat that his mother would not love him if he saw such things. One of the most traumatic incidents in the early days of the phobia took place when Hans was out walking with his mother and a horse fell down and "made a row with its feet." In this case there was not only the likelihood that Hans would see the horse's widdler, but the more fateful possibility that his mother would see the horse's widdler too. This would cause in her the same reaction that Hans had seen when he had invited her to touch his own widdler. Thus the anxiety and fear returned with redoubled force. He cried and his mother was forced to bring him home.

Hans's dreams show that he started a course of action *against the rule*. The first dream in this category is the one where his mother showed her own widdler. As Freud said, this dream ". . . was intended to serve as a piece of self-justification."[21] Following the Freudian custom, let us put words into Hans's mouth: "This concern with widdlers," he seems to be saying, "is not really as bad as mother says it is. For here she is showing her widdler herself." Perhaps this dream meant a little more than this. For Hans his mother was the creator of rules. Furthermore, she was an exemplification of them. It would be quite impossible for her to violate a rule. Therefore, if she showed her own widdler Hans must have misunderstood the rule. It must be all right to show one's widdler sometimes. Thus dream and reality become topsyturvy. The dream sets out to show that reality was not really true after all. Mother did not say what she said, or do what she did.

This is all well enough in dreams. But the phobia continued. And the dreams continued to attack the rule. Later they implicated the father. In the first "criminal phantasy" Hans crawled through the ropes at Schonbrunn. In the second he smashed a window on a train. In both cases his father participated in the act and in both cases policemen arrested both Hans and his father. There is, in these dreams, what might be called displacement of the prohibition. The rules are no longer made by the mother. They are made, let us say, by the policemen. And the rules no longer have anything to do with widdlers. They are concerned with crawling under ropes and smashing windows. But they are rules just the same. They are prohibitions that prevent Hans from doing what he wants to do. He does do what he wants to do. *And his father helps him.* Symbolically, this kind of dream announces that Hans's father will help him break the rules. It is therefore all right to touch his widdler even in the face of his mother's rule. And his father will help him do this.

Another dream in this category is reported by Hans as follows: "A street-boy was riding on a truck, and the guard came and undressed the boy quite naked and made him stand there till next morning, and in the morning the boy gave the guard 50,000 florins so that he could go on riding on the truck."[22] Explaining the circumstances around this dream, Hans's father told Freud that the "Nordbahn" ran past opposite the house. "In a siding there stood a trolley on which Hans once saw a street-boy riding. He wanted to do so too; I told him it was not allowed, and that if he did the guard would be after him."[23]

In this dream there was again a criminal act, a violation of a rule. No ally is present, however. Perhaps the absence of his father led Hans to separate himself by a comfortable distance from the action in the dream. He wanted to see how it would come out, this violation of a rule *all by one's self*. Thus, Hans, at least in his imagination, came to a point where he could violate a rule on his own initiative. In the dream 50,000 florins secured immunity from the application of the rule. In real life, however, 50,000 florins would not buy immunity from his mother. This immunity was finally discovered in the form of imaginary children. He could be as interested as he wanted in *their* lumf and widdle and it violated no rule. Thus, by a process of attack from all sides, Hans finally was able to reduce the rule to size, to extract the fear, and to reconcile the rule with his own major interests. Hans's father and the "Professor" formed the supports as this process of healing continued. In the final "triumphant phantasy" Hans did not achieve any libidinous gratification, but he did establish a situation in which his children made sense. You could not have children without being married and if you did not have any children you could not be interested in widdle and lumf because it was "piggish." It was therefore necessary to be married. There was no one available to marry except Hans's mother. That meant that Hans's father would have to be dispensed with. But even then Hans was not big enough to be married. That was taken care of when he was given a new behind and a new widdler. Now he was in a position, not so much perhaps to seduce his mother, but to have imaginary children. And now, on May 1st, Hans can report without fear of criticism or feeling of guilt: "This morning I went to the W.C. with all my children . . . ."[24]

The riddle in the case of little Hans is this; it permits of two explanations. One explanation is based on the idea of a strong Oedipus complex and an overload of sexual somatic excitation. This explanation cannot be dismissed if it cannot be definitely "proved" within the context of Hans's case. The same is true of the other "explanation." It takes the point of view that Hans was not struggling with a sexual overload but with a moral problem intimately associated with the fear of losing his mother's love.

Each explanation permits the acceptance of some elements of the other. The problem is one of primacy but not of exclusion. Freud suggested through his concept of "condemnation" that he accepted some elements of the second explanation. He disapproved the vehemence with which Han's mother refused to touch his penis. And the second explanation admits elements of sexual desire and Oedipus orientation.

These alternative explanations are significant beyond the borders of the case of little Hans. They point to two different "causative" points of view. The first explanation indicates a largely biological way of thinking. It takes the view that processes are generated within the body and that these processes affect the mind. Thus the processes tend to be universal and they tend to be compulsive. They are hard to alter, difficult to deny. This is what Freud has in mind in thinking of the role of Hans's mother. She was bound to be the object of Hans's desire because this libidinal charge was organically preordained in Hans. Maybe she made the situation a little worse then it otherwise would have been. Nevertheless, the hard core of the Oedipus would have made things difficult anyway.

The second explanation does not look upon Hans as the prisoner of his biology. It looks upon his biology as the prisoner of his experience. That is to say, the second explanation takes the view that there were no inevitable organic urges in little Hans producing a strong desire for his mother and a consequent hate of the father. The second explanation does not stress *a biological archetype*. If Hans had desire for his mother it was because he experienced satisfactions with her and wanted to continue them. If he hated his father it was not because of a biological inheritance but because his father prevented these satisfactions or was an object of enmity for other reasons. Thus, Hans's hate, (if he hated) was not a biological inheritance, an inevitable growth, but the result of his social experience.

The first explanation considers that somehow Hans must have achieved a libidinal discharge to affect his recovery, since this libidinal overcharge was the "cause" of his condition. The second explanation takes the view that Hans's "unpleasure" was connected not with his sexual tension so much as with his "social" tension. The direction of recovery was then in the direction of correcting the social situation.

These explanations are relevant to general theories of personality. For if the first explanation is correct we should construct biological concepts for the understanding of personality. We can expect to find a comparatively mechanistic system operating according to its own laws with comparatively little influence from outside forces such as training and experience. On the other hand, if the second explanation is entitled to primacy, we are faced with a rather more complex situation. We shall be required to fashion concepts that show the effect of social experience on physical and mental processes. We shall be faced with the fact that the individual is partly a biological and partly a social entity. We shall be required to investigate how these two entities are related.

It is clear from our discussion of the Hans case that Freud inclined to the first explanation in considering the phobia of Hans. This was in 1909. In the chapters that follow we shall consider the genesis of the positions taken by Freud in this study. We shall then observe the gradual changes in theory that serve to meet the types of objections we have outlined.

IN THE CASE of little Hans we did not try to point out the larger aspects of Freud's thought. It was enough to keep close to the clinical data and concern ourselves with a specific series of explanations. Behind these explanations is a more comprehensive attitude about the nature of mind and personality. This attitude was well developed by the year 1900 when *The Interpretation of Dreams* was published. At that time the broad outlines of a systematic theory are discernible and I would like to sketch in these outlines, leaving to the next chapter the story of their development.

THE DIVISIONS OF THE MIND

In *The Interpretation of Dreams,* Freud suggested three different types of mental process: the Conscious, Preconscious, and Unconscious. (When there is reference to the Unconscious, Preconscious or Conscious as *process* I am going to capitalize. When these words refer only to the psychic state of material, i.e., whether known to the subject or not, I shall not capitalize. In direct quotations I shall accept the translation and leave it to the reader to make the necessary distinction.) We find examples of these different types of process in dream-wishes. Freud considered dreams, for the most part, to be the fulfillment of

38

wishes. First, there was the Conscious wish which might find expression in a dream. As an example Freud cited a dream of his own where the intent was to show that Freud was in error when he said that all dreams were wish fulfillments. Children have dreams that are influenced by Conscious wishes. Freud gave examples of dreams of children in which the Conscious wish was to make an excursion on land or water, or to make up for an omitted meal. There is often expressed in a dream the Conscious wish to sleep. Of this last wish Freud said: "The wish to sleep, to which the conscious ego has adjusted itself, and which . . . represents the ego's contribution to the dream, must thus always be taken into account as a motive of dream-formation, and every successful dream is a fulfillment of this wish."[1]

Another class of wish belongs to the Preconscious system. Preconscious wishes have been rejected by the Conscious mental system and therefore these wishes remain unsatisfied. ". . . there is thus left for the night an unsatisfied but suppressed wish."[2] An example of such a wish is in the dream of a ". . . rather sarcastic lady, whose younger friend has become engaged to be married, [and who] is asked in the daytime by her acquaintance, whether she knows her friend's fiancé, and what she thinks of him. She replies with unqualified praise, imposing silence on her own judgment, although she would have liked to tell the truth, namely, that he is a commonplace fellow—one meets such by the dozen (Dutzendmensch). The following night she dreams that the same question is put to her, and that she replies with the formula: '. . . in case of subsequent orders, it will suffice to mention the reference number.' "[3] Thus, although the wish to say that the fiancé was "run of the mill" was rejected during the day, it found symbolic expression in the dream.

Wishes of the third type belong to the Unconscious. They are incapable of leaving the area where unconscious processes take place. These wishes are largely childhood wishes. ". . . in the lowest stratum," Freud said, "one comes upon the fulfillment of a wish from the earliest period of childhood. . . ."[4] These wishes are not all sexual wishes. Freud mentioned a dream of his own about "my friend R," where the dominant wish was concerned with youthful ambition. Freud denied that all Unconscious motivations are sexual. This was an angry retort to his critics but, as we shall see, not entirely justified by *The Interpretation of Dreams*. "The assertion," said Freud, "that all dreams call for a sexual interpretation . . . is quite foreign to my *Interpretation of Dreams*. It will not be found in any of the eight editions of this book and is a palpable contradiction to the rest of its contents."[5] The exception to sexuality in dreams, namely, some childhood dreams, would hardly silence his critics who, as Freud said, were guilty of an "untiring polemic."

Freud considered the Unconscious process the basic process. ". . . the unconscious must be accepted as the general basis of the psychic life. The unconscious is the larger circle which includes the smaller circle of the conscious; everything conscious has a preliminary unconscious stage, whereas the unconscious can stop at this stage, and yet claim to be considered a full psychic function. The unconscious is the true psychic reality; in its inner nature it is just as much unknown to us as the reality of the external world, and it is just as imperfectly communicated to us by the data of consciousness as is the external world by the reports of our sense-organs."[6]

THE PRIMARY
AND SECONDARY PROCESSES

Although the Unconscious was considered the "true psychic reality" the fact remained that another area of the mind was in constant conflict with it and did not always come off second best. How could this force that emerged from the Conscious and the Preconscious be explained?

Freud observed the similarity between the processes of the Unconscious and the motivations of childhood. He noted that, "A child is absolutely egoistical; he feels his wants acutely and strives remorselessly to satisfy them, especially against his competitors, other children, and first of all against his brothers and sisters."[7] Freud noted that the same characteristic applied to dreams. "All dreams are absolutely egotistical," he said. "In every dream the beloved ego appears, even though in a disguised form. The wishes that are realized in dreams are invariably the wishes of the ego."[8]

The difference between children and adults seemed to be that children expressed their egoism openly while adults expressed it mostly in dreams. In children the egoism is Conscious, while in adults it is Unconscious. In children it finds spontaneous conscious expression in their everyday life, while in adults it finds only disguised expression in their dreams. It seemed likely that some change took place in the mind, during the growth of the organism, with the result that a large part of the childhood personality became part of the Unconscious. An organic development of this nature had been suggested by Meynert, and Freud adopted it as a model. ". . . we may expect," he suggested, "that within the very period of life which we reckon as childhood, altruistic impulses and morality will awake in the little egoist, and that in the words of Meynert, a secondary ego will overlay and inhibit the primary ego."[9] So the total infantile personality fell into the Unconscious with the development of the secondary ego. When the secondary ego develops the childhood ego has not only built up a system of wants and needs, it has also associated these wants and needs with specific objects. In the Oedipus complex the child has associated his sexual or libidinal urges with the person of the mother. The child has "cathected" the person of the mother. All of these objects of needs and wants, all of the "object-cathexes," also sink into the Unconscious with the development of the secondary ego.

Freud thought that the early primary ego of the child might have roots, through inheritance, in the earliest history of the human race. He felt that all dreams show "the mark of the beast"[10] not alone because they are egoistic but because they are deemed to express a primal past. "Behind this childhood of the individual we are then promised an insight into the phylogenetic childhood, into the evolution of the human race. . . ." From this he concluded that ". . . psychoanalysis may claim a high rank among those sciences which endeavour to reconstruct the oldest and darkest phases of the beginnings of mankind."[11] This remark may serve to clear up for us some of the perplexity that we may have felt in Freud's analysis of the case of little Hans. The Oedipus that Freud saw there, the desire for the mother and the hate for the father, was to him an inheritance from a savage past. Its intensity did not have to be verified by the evidence but could be assumed as a phylogenetic characteristic. This also makes clear why Freud felt that the mother had a "prescribed" role to play.

The primary ego of the child became part of the Unconscious as a result of the growth of the secondary ego. In the child mental events were all Conscious or Preconscious (i.e. capable of becoming Conscious). In the child there was ". . . no division and censorship . . . as yet between the Pcs (Preconscious) and the Ucs (Unconscious). . . ."[12] For this reason undisguised wish-dreams may be found in children.

What happens in the case of adults? Freud gave us a number of examples to indicate what takes place. Here are some instances of "guileful dreams." A husband says to his wife, "Oughtn't we to have the piano tuned?" She replies, "It's not worth while, the hammers would have to be rebuffed as well." This dream practically reproduces the events of the preceding day. The husband has asked his wife such a question and she had answered in much the same words. But what is the meaning of the wife's dreaming this event? Freud asked her about the piano and she described it as a "disgusting old box" that had a bad tone and she said that it belonged to her husband before they were married. Freud said that the key to the interpretation of the dream lay in the phrase, ". . . it isn't worth while." This phrase derived from a call paid by the wife on the previous day to a woman friend. She was asked to take off her coat, but declined, saying, "Thanks, it isn't worth while, I must go in a moment." Freud pointed out that, during the analysis, the wife suddenly took hold of her coat, of which a button had come undone. "It was as though she meant to say: 'Please don't look in, it isn't worth while.' The 'box' becomes 'chest,' and the interpretation of the dream leads to the years when she was growing out of her childhood, when she began to be dissatisfied with her figure. It leads us back, indeed, to earlier periods, if we take into consideration the disgusting and the bad tone, and remember how often in allusions and in dreams the two small hemispheres of the female body take the place—as a substitute and an antithesis—of the large ones."[13]

Another example was concerned with the "innocent" dream of a young man. Freud reported: "He dreamt that he was putting on his winter overcoat again; this was terrible. The occasion for this dream is apparently the sudden advent of cold weather. On more careful examination we note that the two brief fragments of the dream do not fit together very well, for what could be terrible about wearing a thick or heavy coat in cold weather? Unfortunately for the innocency of this dream the first association, under analysis, yields the recollection that yesterday a lady had confidentially confessed to him that her last child owed its existence to the splitting of a condom. He now reconstructs his thoughts in accordance with this suggestion: A thin condom is dangerous, a thick one is bad. The condom is a 'pullover,' (*Ueberzieher*), for it is pulled over something: and *Ueberzieher* is the word for a light overcoat. An experience like that related by the lady would indeed be 'terrible' for an unmarried man."[14]

Such dreams appear on their face to be "innocent" but when carefully examined they are not innocent. They are expressions of the primary ego. Yet they have not been able to gain direct expression. They find their outlet in dreams through disguise and subterfuge. This shows us one characteristic of the Unconscious system. At least some of the material in this system does not have direct access to consciousness. It is "suppressed." Suppressed material in the Unconscious can only struggle for expression through some kind of dream symbolism.

These examples indicate how the adult dream differed from the childhood dream and how the Meynert view served as a convenient model to explain the difference.

Was all the dream-forming energy transferred to the Unconscious on the growth of the secondary ego? At first Freud favored a mutuality of influence. "It seems to us probable," he said, "that the source of the dream wish does not affect its capacity to incite a dream. I have in mind the dream of the child who continued the voyage that had been interrupted during the day, and the other children's dreams cited in the same chapter; they are explained by an unfulfilled but unsuppressed — wish of the daytime. . . . At first sight, then, it seems that in respect of dream-formation all wishes are of equal value and equal power."[15] Soon, however, Freud became more cautious. "Children's dreams," he said, "leave us no doubt that a wish unfulfilled during the day may instigate a dream. But we must not forget that this is, after all, the wish of a child; that it is a wish-impulse of the strength peculiar to childhood."[16] And, finally, he took quite the opposite view. "I am of the opinion that unfulfilled wishes of the day are insufficient to produce a dream in adults. I will readily admit that wish-impulses originating in consciousness contribute to the instigation of dreams, but they probably do no more. The dream would not occur if the preconscious wish were not reinforced from another source. That source is the unconscious. I believe that the conscious wish becomes effective in inciting a dream only when it succeeds in arousing a similar unconscious wish that reenforces it. . . . I believe that these unconscious wishes are always active and ready to express themselves whenever they find an opportunity of allying themselves with an impulse from consciousness and transferring their own greater intensity to the lesser intensity of the latter."[17]

THE UNCONSCIOUS

AND THE PRIMARY EGO

In the Meynert view the whole childhood personality became part of the primary ego, on the growth of the secondary ego. Freud, of course, equated the primary ego with the Unconscious after the growth of the secondary ego. Thus the desires of children to complete voyages, to eat pie, and to seduce their mothers, all descended willy-nilly into the Unconscious. On this assumption the dreams of adults would be filled not only with symbolic seduction of mothers but with clandestine eating of pie! This would constitute somewhat of an affront to the dignity of the Unconscious. On the other hand, Freud was reluctant to give up the Meynert model since it furnished him, on the best of authority, with a fine organic model that could preserve the dominant psychic energy in the Unconscious. This was an important point for Freud was quite committed to the dominance of the Unconscious. But he could not very well preserve it if the secondary ego established itself through its own energy. For this gain, however, Freud had to accept the child's personality *in toto,* as I mentioned above. In truth, then, the Unconscious and the primary ego did not present much "goodness of fit." Freud was not one to compromise. He, too, was motivated by a childhood wish, to have his cake and eat it too.

Freud's experience with the psychoneuroses inclined him to exclude some childhood material from the Unconscious. "The theory of the psychoneuroses," he said, "asserts with absolute certainty that it can only be sexual wish-impulses from the infantile life, which have undergone repression (affect-conversion) during the developmental period of childhood, which are capable of renewal at later periods of development (whether as a result of our sexual constitution which has, of course, grown out of an original bisexuality, or in consequence of unfavourable influences in our sexual life); and which therefore supply the motive-power for all psychoneurotic symptom-formation. It is only by the introduction of these sexual forces that the gap still demonstrable in the theory of repression can be filled."[18]

Freud was in doubt about amending the Meynert view in terms of his experience with the psychoneuroses but he gave ample grounds for the "polemic" that irritated him. "Here I will leave it undecided," he said, "whether the postulate of the sexual and the infantile holds good for the theory of dreams as well. . . ."[19] He concluded: "I am not completing the latter [the theory of dreams] because in assuming that the dream-wish invariably originates in the unconscious I have already gone a step beyond the demonstrable."[20]

REPRESSION

AND THE PRIMARY PROCESS

The Meynert view made no provision for repression. But it invited Freud to consider repression an organic development rather than a fluent, dynamic state of opposing energies and processes. Yet the clinical evidence showed that the Unconscious did not stay in place after the growth of the secondary ego. On the contrary it tried to dominate it and often succeeded. This "defect" of the Meynert "overlay" and repression were, then, closely related. The "return of the repressed" seemed to indicate that the secondary ego did not develop effectively. This tendency toward defective process seemed to be confirmed by Freud's work with the psychoneuroses. There also the "return of the repressed" indicated instability.

The trouble started with wish-impulses in the Unconscious. These originated in the infantile life and were "indestructible and incapable of inhibition." Some of them ". . . have come to be in contradiction with the purposive ideas of our secondary thinking."[21] These ideas are of course the "altruistic impulses" and "morality" that Freud attributed to Meynert's secondary ego.

Freud translated that development into terms developed in the study of the psychoneuroses. "The fulfillment of these [infantile] wishes would no longer produce an affect of pleasure, but one of pain; *and it is just this conversion of affect that constitutes the essence of what we call 'repression.'* "[22] Freud did not at this time pursue any further the origin of this process. He leaned gladly on the Meynert crutch. "In what manner and by what motive forces such a conversion can take place constitutes the problem of repression, which we need here only touch upon in passing. It will suffice to note the fact that such a conversion of affect occurs in the course of development (one need only think of the emergence of disgust, originally absent in infantile life), and that it is connected with the activity of the secondary system."[23]

THE USES OF THE MODEL

We have mentioned the major aspects of Freud's system as it appeared at the turn of the century. Although the study of Hans's phobia came nearly a decade later the reader will recognize how these orientations were employed in the Hans case. The secondary ego had enveloped little Hans. But "unfavorable influences" on the "sexual constitution" reenforced infantile wishes leading to the phobia. Since moral principles were a developmental phenomenon leading to "conversion of affect" it was not necessary for Freud to look deeply into the ways Hans's mother may have tinkered with these principles or the ways in which Hans's dreams were related to them.

After we have inquired into the genesis of the major views described here, we shall return to a further study of psychic process as Freud analysed it in *The Interpretation of Dreams*.

The model we have mentioned shows clearly how and where it was patched together. The study of dreams contributed the idea of egoism. But the study of dreams and the work with the psychoneuroses brought out the importance of infantile wishes and sexual wishes, and they have documented the dynamic conflict within the psyche. In a sense, Meynert saved the Unconscious as the true phychic reality by providing a maturational boundary between the Unconscious and the secondary ego or secondary process involving both the Preconscious and the Conscious. Freud definitely posited the sexual basis of the psychoneuroses, but he hedged on the sexual motive as the sole motive in dreams. In any event, it is by far the dominant one.

The price Freud paid for the secondary ego is that he accepted the whole childhood personality in the primary ego or the Unconscious. He was not unwilling to accept the egoism of childhood. Egoism and sexuality can be very closely bound together as he later showed. But the rest of the impedimenta of childhood he proposed to disregard. Yet, by disregarding it he implied that something more than the Meynert overlay was required to picture the areas of the mind. "Conversion of affect" occurred with reference to some material in the Unconscious and not with reference to other material. Repression was then not only a restatement in different terms of the Meynert hypothesis, it was also a radical alteration in it. The authority of Meynert could not sustain this alteration. Freud, therefore, maintained a curious "anaclitic" relation to the Meynert overlay.

There is not much room for "social influence" in this model. The sexual constitution may undergo various vicissitudes which are related to social experience as well as somatic excitation. But generally the varieties of social experience have to be absorbed within rigid categories. Hans was cured of his phobia. But it is likely that his psyche was capable of occasional subtleties not easily handled by the rough, systematic theory of the "Professor."

Chapter IV

THE DEVELOPMENT

OF THE

UNCONSCIOUS

WE HAVE SEEN the outlines of the Freudian way of thinking. Now we must look into earlier Freudian thinking and into earlier Freudian clinical experience. There we will find the factors that led to the views we have discussed. However, we shall find successive formulations that finally lead us to our goal. We can start where Freud picked up the bequest of an earlier, respected, and, we might say, a classical tradition. I am referring to instinct theory. This was the line of thinking represented in Freud's time by McDougall. McDougall had assumed an imposing array of instincts and he made no secret of the fact that Freud and his followers would do well to look it over. As for the Unconscious. Well, ". . . the Unconscious," he said, "is a fraudulent entity that has gravely obstructed the path of progress." Yet, to gain the ears of the psychoanalysts was a vain hope. They were devoted to their own array of concepts. "To cast a sceptical glance upon the universal efficacy of the libido," complained McDougall, "would be to lay sacreligious hands on the ark of the covenant."[1]

Yet Freud did give consideration to instinct theory. It permeated Freud's early thinking but it was soon transmuted into concepts of wider potentiality. Our task now is to trace Freud's thought as it progressed from instinct theory to the formulation of the Unconscious.

EGO-LIBIDO

AND LIBIDO-QUANTUM

In any theory of instinct it is necessary to consider the relation between somatic and mental processes. "By an instinct," said Freud, "we can understand in the first place nothing but the psychic representative of the continually flowing inner somatic source of stimulation which is to be distinguished from a 'stimulus' which comes from combined external excitations. . . . What distinguishes the instincts from one another and furnishes them with specific attributes is their relation to their somatic sources and to their aims. The source of the instinct is an exciting process in an organ, and the immediate aim of the instinct lies in the release of this organic stimulus."[2] This concept, then, indicates a causal relation between certain somatic or physiological processes and certain mental or psychic processes. The mental "representative" is caused by the physiological process and is itself the instinct. There are other "representations" in the mind. They come from physiological stimulations but these are caused in turn by external sources. These representations are not instincts. For example, the body itself sets up a sexual, somatic excitation. This excitation has a mental representative. This representative is an instinct. But suppose a hot iron touches the skin. This sets up a somatic excitation which in turn has a mental representative. This representative is not an instinct since the somatic excitation was set up by an external source.

What organs are we to suppose to be the somatic source of the sexual instinct? Freud made a "provisional assumption" that many organs may be the source of sexual stimulation. He assumed that ". . . from the bodily organs two kinds of excitation arise which are founded upon differences of a chemical nature. One of these forms of overstimulation can be designated as specifically sexual, and the concerned organ, an erogenous zone, while the sexual element emanating from it is a partial impulse."[3] The sexual instinct thus shows a similarity with other instincts and also an important difference. The similarity is in the fact that the sexual instinct, like hunger and thirst, is based on a body state, a special chemism. The difference is that a variety of organs are "erogenous zones," i.e. although they do not have specifically sexual functions they generate sexual impulses. Examples of such erogenous zones are the oral cavity and the anal opening. It should be added that there is another difference between the sexual instinct and other instincts. Sexual excitation may be caused by tactual stimulation of appropriate areas which may be either sexual organs or erogenous zones.

There are both psychic or mental, and somatic signs of "sexual excitation." "The psychic sign consists of a peculiar feeling of tension of a most urgent character, and among the manifold somatic signs, the many changes in the genitals are uppermost. They have a definite meaning—namely, that of readiness, and constitute a preparation for the sexual act, (the erection of the penis and the glandular activity of the vagina)."[4] Tension, therefore, is the psychic representative of excitation. As to tension Freud states that "despite all divergence of opinion regarding it in psychology, I must firmly maintain that a feeling of tension must carry with it the character of displeasure."[5] The sexual instinct triggers the following process: Somatic excitation from sexual organs or erogenous zones causes psychic or mental states of tension which are received as "displeasure" by the individual. The individual is motivated by this feeling of displeasure to act so as to reduce this feeling of mental tension which can be done only by reducing the sexual excitation which causes the mental tension.

Freud's definition of instinct makes it a mental process and distinguishes instinct from a somatic process. This distinction is not ordinarily made in instinct theory. Furthermore, the emphasis is usually placed on the physiological mechanism (as in the case of "reflex") rather than on the mental event. Freud wished to explore the mental dynamics of the representative itself. He therefore proposed a new term for the mental representative of the sexual somatic excitation. Freud described the new term as follows: "We have laid down the concept of libido as a force of variable quantity by which processes and transformations in the sphere of sexual excitement can be measured. This libido we distinguished from the energy which is at the basis of the psychic processes in general as far as their special origin is concerned, and we thus attributed to it also a qualitative character. In separating libidinal from other psychic energy, we give expression to the assumption that the sexual processes of the organism are differentiated from the nutritional processes through a special chemism. We thus formulated for ourselves the concept of libido-quantum, the psychic representation of which we designate as ego-libido."[6] Libido as such, then, is *the total amount of energy created by sexual, somatic processes and available for psychic employment.* Libido-quantum is the quantity of gross sexual excitation. It is the energy potential of this sexual excitation available for psychic use. The psychic representative of the libido-quantum is termed ego-libido. Freud held that ego-libido is so directly related to the libido-quantum that after sexual intercourse the libido-quantum and also the ego-libido subside together.

On the somatic side Freud observed that organs not ordinarily thought of as the sources of sexual excitation may nevertheless display such innervation. The oral cavity is an example. Sexual excitation creates libido-quantum. Therefore, it followed that the organs creating libido-quantum vary in number and in volume of production.

The ego-libido as the mental counterpart of libido-quantum has a number of functions. "The narcissistic or ego-libido appears to us," said Freud, "as the great reservoir from which all object-cathexis is sent out, and into which it is again drawn back, while the narcissistic libido-cathexis of the ego appears to us as the realized primal state in the first childhood, which only becomes hidden by the later emissions of the libido, and is retained at the bottom of it."[7]

Freud, then, visualized the basic process in this manner: (a) A variable number of organic areas—erogenous zones and sexual organs—produce somatic, sexual excitation. (b) This excitation produces a related amount of libido-quantum. (c) The libido-quantum is the sole source from which ego-libido is drawn and the amount of ego-libido is generally proportional to the amount of libido-quantum. (d) The ego-libido being the psychic representative of libido-quantum powers fundamental action in the mind by furnishing the energy for the cathexis of objects and even the cathexis of the ego, itself. The very name, ego-libido, shows us what Freud thought was most important about this type of energy. It cathected or attached itself to the ego. This was a "primal" objective of ego-libido. The ego was a "primal" object. This expresses in libido terms the self-centeredness, the "self-love," the egoism of the basic personality as Freud saw it.

By postulating ego-libido Freud distinguished sexual energy in the psyche from other types of energy that might exist there. And, by assuming libido-quantum he stipulated a somatic base for his ego-libido and invited investigation as to the relation between libido-quantum and ego-libido. These concepts, or constructs, indicate that ego-libido, in terms of its *quantity* and its *power,* is to be understood in terms of libido-quantum and thus in terms of sexual somatic excitation. So ego-libido has a biological source. In this sense Freud reduced mind to body.

A logical conclusion from this "reductionism" is that ego-libido although in the mind is not wholly of it. It is not dependent on the mind. It has "outside" support. *It follows that if ego-libido is excluded from the generalized operation of the mind, as by repression, its activity will not be curtailed.* It is only a step from here to stipulate a mental region or process, the Unconscious, where the translation of libido-quantum into ego-libido may take place.

THE LOCATION AND FUNCTION OF
LIBIDO-QUANTUM

In his "Three Contributions to a Theory of Sexuality" Freud did not make clear to us the precise usefulness of the concept "libido-quantum." It appeared to be merely a signpost indicating the physiological origin of ego-libido. However, in earlier writings, we can find much to indicate that libido-quantum, far from being an empty concept, is actually one of the key concepts in Freud's imposing conceptual array. It is a concept that will lead us to the Unconscious and to the nature of the division between the Unconscious and the Conscious. Our course leads us back from libido-quantum into the psychoneuroses. There we will see what Freud believed to be their causes and how his ideas of their causes led to libido-quantum and the Unconscious.

In Freud's earliest writings we find the proposition that in repression there is a splitting of consciousness. "That the symptom-complex of hysteria, as far as it can be understood, justifies the assumption of a splitting of consciousness with the formation of separate psychic groups, has attained general recognition since P. Janet, J. Breuer, and others have given out their interesting work. Less understood are the opinions concerning the origin of this splitting of consciousness and concerning the role played by this character in the structure of the hysterical neuroses."[8] Janet thought that the splitting of consciousness was the primary feature of the hysterical alteration, and that it was due to a congenital weakness of the capacity for psychic synthesis. Freud and Breuer disagreed with this view. "The splitting of consciousness is secondary and acquired, and originates because the ideas emerging in the hypnoid states are isolated from associative communication with the rest of consciousness."[9] Freud also pointed out that while in some hysterias the splitting of consciousness occurred, in other cases, the pure "retention hysterias," it played no part. He felt therefore that there must be something else in the history of neuroses that was their true cause. He found clues in a type of personality conflict. "In those patients whom I have analyzed there existed psychic health until the moment in which a case of incompatibility occurred in their ideation, that is, until there appeared an experience, idea or feeling which evoked such a painful affect that the person decided to forget it because he did not trust his own ability to remove the resistance between the unbearable ideas and his ego."[10] Freud further found that "Such incompatible ideas originated in the feminine sex on the basis of sexual experiences and feelings."[11]

Freud made a distinction between an "idea" and the "affect" or emotion that is associated with it. The idea may be separated from the affect. Then the idea becomes weak, ". . . but the separated sum of excitement must be utilized in another direction."[12] This affect or excitation may attach itself to other ". . . not in themselves unbearable ideas." On account of this "false" connection these ideas may become obsessions. However, Freud considered that the affect might not join another idea. It might remain free-floating in the mind. Whether the affect attached itself to another idea or remained free-floating, it retained an affinity to the original idea, and it had a marked disposition to rejoin it at the first opportunity. It would succeed in rejoining this earlier idea ". . . as soon as a newly formed similar impression succeeds in breaking through the barrier formed by the will and in adding new affects to the weakened idea, and in forcing for a while the associative union of both psychic groups until a new conversion produces defenses."[13] This explanation, although not clear in detail, gives us the general process. The separation of the emotion from the idea with which it was associated gives the individual some relief. An example would be the emotion in Hans that was attached to the idea of his mother and was concerned with seduction. Hans dissociated the idea from the emotion. Then the emotion attached itself to "widdlers," horses, etc. However, new, similar ideas may bring new emotion into the mind and these re-enforcements may be able to join up with the original ideas and cause a re-attachment of the original separated affect. The new formation, being stronger than the old, requires stronger defenses by the will. In these circumstances, the individual may perform some act against the resistance of the will. He may say that he acted ". . . because something in him was stronger than he was." He may protest that ". . . he couldn't help himself."

Freud felt that the emotion, separated from the idea, could not be disposed of in any "harmless" manner. It bided its time, and in moments of "auxiliary traumatic" excitement it found ways of pressing the individual relentlessly.

In Freud's view, then, emotion triggers this whole process. Ideas by themselves are impotent enough. Freud spoke of "incompatible" ideas, and of "unbearable" ideas as though the ideas might produce the emotion. But the emotion is not caused by the idea, it cathects the idea. The emotion is to be seen as an independent force that invests the otherwise static idea. The peculiar power of the combination is that it presents to the mind a program of action. In the case of Hans there was mental, sexual excitation. By itself it was a vast unrest. In Freud's view this emotion attached itself to the idea of the mother. This union presented to Hans a program for action. He could seek to discharge the emotion upon the mother-object. This, of course, is the central trend of the Oedipus complex in Freud's thought.

It will come to us as no surprise that Freud considered that the source of the psychic unrest, of the emotion or affect, was physical excitation. "The effect of Breuer's cathartic method," he said, "consists in the fact that it consciously reconducts the excitement from the physical into the psychic spheres and then forces an adjustment of the contradiction through intellectual work, and a discharge of the excitement through speech."[14]

We have been quoting here from Freud's paper on "The Defense Neuro-Psychoses" which was published in 1894. It is the first published paper of his own, closely following a paper which was written in association with Breuer called "On the Psychical Mechanism of Hysterical Phenomena." We have now worked our way to the wellsprings of Freud's thought. We see him concerned, as he was for his entire life, with the dynamics of mental events. At this period he saw emotion as the sovereign force, ideas as giving a direction and focus to the emotion. The emotion is based on physical excitation. In many cases, when the physical excitement penetrates the mind, becomes affect, and searches out an idea, the resulting formation is distasteful to the personality. The "will" rejects this association, splitting the affect from the idea. However, new physical excitement may penetrate the mind, force its way through the will to the original idea and its separated emotion. If this association is still distasteful to the will it must take further steps to separate the emotion from the idea. So the process continues. In the "cathartic method" that Breuer used, the growing emotion was quieted by discharge "through speech." Thus a physical process, excitation, that had become tangled up with a mental formation, finally was reduced by another physical process, speech, and the mental symptoms subsided. Freud saw the mental system at this time as largely inert. He saw the physical system as a sea whose waves beat upon the shores of the mind, and he traced the resulting tremors as they disturbed the mind and agitated the will which presided as the agent of the status quo. Of these complex events Freud said: "Perhaps it would be more correct to say that these are not really processes of a psychic nature but physical processes of which the psychic result so presents itself that the expressions 'separation of the idea from its affect and the false connection of the latter,' *seem* actual occurrences."[15] (Italics ours.)

Freud felt sure of the insight that physical excitement turned into mental emotion and somatic pressure turned into mental tension. Everywhere he saw somatic quantities reaching, perhaps disappearing, into the mental regions, and yet reappearing and perhaps disappearing in the process of the physical action involved in cathartic therapy. Little wonder that Freud, in this early time, felt a pardonable enthusiasm, and a deep confidence. "In conclusion," he said in his early paper on the neuropsychoses, "I will mention in a few words the subsidiary idea of which I have made use in this discussion of the defense neuroses. It is the idea that there is something to distinguish in all psychic function (amount of affect, sum of excitement), that all qualities have a quantity though we have no means to measure the same—it is something that can be increased, diminished, displaced, and discharged, and that extends over the memory traces of the ideas perhaps like an electric charge over the surface of the body. This hypothesis, which also underlies our theory of 'abreaction' . . . can be used in the same sense as the physicist uses the assumption of the current of electric fluid."[16] Here we see the germ of the later concept "libido."

Freud's confidence in the somatic base of mental difficulties was enhanced by his clinical work during the decade 1890–1900. This clinical work not only seemed to emphasize the somatic base as crucial in the etiology of mental ills but it also indicated that it was sexual. A great deal of this clinical experience was summarized in his published work with reference to "anxiety" neuroses.[17] He found that anxiety neurosis appeared in women in the following cases: (a) As virginal fear in adults; this anxiety could be evoked in maturing girls at adolescence. (b) As fear in the newly married. This was most noticeable when young women remained "anesthetic" during the first cohabitation. (c) As fear in women whose husbands suffered from *ejaculatio praecox* or from diminished potency. (d) In women whose husbands practiced *coitus interruptus* or *reservatus*. "These [last] two cases go together, for on analysing a large number of examples one can easily be convinced that they only depend on whether the woman attained gratification during coitus or not." (e) As fear in widows and intentional sexual abstainers. (f) As fear in the climacterium during the last marked enhancement of the sexual desire. Anxiety neurosis appeared in men in the following circumstances: (a) As fear in intentional sexual abstainers. (b) As fear in men with frustrated sexual excitement. (c) As fear in men who practised *coitus interruptus*. (d) As fear in men in the *senium*. There were two causes of anxiety neurosis that hold true for both sexes. Freud found that neurasthenics merge into anxiety neurotics in consequence of masturbation, as soon as they refrain from this manner of sexual gratification. The second cause, for both sexes, ". . . seems," he says, "in the first place, really not to be of a sexual nature. Anxiety neurosis originates in both sexes through the moment of overwork, exhaustive exertion, as for instance after sleepless nights, nursing the sick, and even after serious illnesses."[18]

Freud's problem was to find the source of this psychic fear. He reports, "As the *coitus interruptus* is rendered so prominent among the causes of anxiety neurosis, I have thought at first that the source of the continuous anxiety was perhaps the repeated fear during the sexual act lest the technique will fail and conception follow. But I have found that this state of mind of the man or woman during the *coitus interruptus* plays no part in the origin of the anxiety neurosis, that the women who are really indifferent to the possibilities of conception are just as exposed to the neurosis as those who are trembling at the possibility of it, it all depends on which person suffers the loss of sexual *gratification*." (Italics ours.)

Freud also observed that in anxiety neurosis there was a diminution of psychic desire, or ego-libido. So it seemed that this ego-libido could not be causally related to the neurosis. Yet all the evidence pointed to a sexual cause of the neurosis. Since "all qualities have a quantity" the neurosis must have its quantity and it most probably was a sexual quantity. In most of the reported cases of anxiety there was a marked degree of sexual *abstinence* for one reason or another. It appeared, then, that in anxiety neurosis there was ". . . an accumulation of excitement," and that the anxiety which ". . . probably corresponds to such an accumulated excitement is of somatic origin, so that somatic excitement becomes accumulated, and furthermore that this somatic excitement is of a sexual nature, and that it is accompanied by a decreased psychic participation in the sexual processes." Freud concluded that the ". . . mechanism of the anxiety neurosis is to be found in the deviation of the somatic sexual excitement from the psychic, and in the abnormal utilization of this excitement . . ."[19] He therefore had recourse not to the mind but to the body in explaining the basic process in anxiety neurosis. "In the sexually mature male organism," he said, "the somatic sexual excitement is—probably continuously— produced, and this becomes a periodic stimulus for the psychic life. To make our conception clearer we will add that this somatic sexual excitement manifests itself as a pressure on the wall of the seminal vesicle which is provided with nerve endings. This visceral excitement thus becomes continuously increased, but not before attaining a certain height is it able to overcome the resistances of the intercalated conduction as far as the cortex, and manifest itself as psychic excitement. Then the group of sexual ideas existing in the psyche becomes endowed with energy and results in a psychic state of libidinous tension which is accompanied by an impulse to remove this tension. Such psychic unburdening is possible only in one way which I wish to designate as specific or adequate action. This adequate action for the male sexual impulse consists of a complicated spinal reflex-act which results in the unburdening of those nerve endings, and of all psychically formed preparations for the liberation of this reflex. Anything else except the adequate action would be of no avail, for after the somatic sexual excitement has once reached the liminal value, it continuously changes into psychic excitement; that must by all means occur which frees the nerve endings from their heavy pressure, and thus abolish the whole somatic excitement existing at the time and allow the subcortical conduction to re-establish its resistance."[20] Freud assumed that much the same processes occurred in women in spite of the ". . . stunting of the female sexual impulses." The next question is, what happens if adequate action does not take place and the nerve endings are not relieved of their pressure. "Neurasthenia always originates whenever the adequate (action) unburdening is replaced by a less adequate one, like the normal coitus under the most favorable conditions, by a masturbation or spontaneous pollution; while anxiety neurosis is produced by all moments which impede the psychic elaboration of the somatic sexual excitement. The manifestations of anxiety neurosis are brought about by the fact that the somatic sexual excitement diverted from the psyche expends itself subcortically in not at all adequate reactions."[21]

We saw in the case of little Hans that Freud gave some attention to the idea of "condemnation." Here we find one of the earliest expressions of this idea of psychic resistance. Freud called it the "resistance of the subcortical conduction." He implied that it is an automatic, physical process. It is a valve that admits sexual excitement to the mind only after it has reached a certain pressure point. When the sexual excitement has reached a certain value this resistance is overcome and in most cases the energy flows into the mind. If it is excluded for some reason at this point it results in anxiety as the energy expends itself in inadequate action. If it enters the psyche it may induce the mind to set upon a program of "adequate action" which apparently can consist only of "normal coitus." This reduces the sexual somatic excitation in the genitals with the result that the pressure against the "resistance" falls and the "subcortical conduction" is able once more to exclude sexual energy from the mind. However, if the mind does not preside over a course of adequate action, but resorts to inadequate action ("masturbation" or "spontaneous pollution"), then neurasthenia is very likely to result.

In this early thinking Freud indicated what he felt were the essential differences between four neuroses: anxiety, neurasthenia, hysteria, and compulsion neurosis. Anxiety neurosis had this in common with neurasthenia, ". . . the source of the excitement, and cause of the disturbance, lies in the somatic rather than in the psychic sphere as in the case of hysteria and compulsion neurosis."[22] The contrast between anxiety neurosis and neurasthenia ". . . can be expressed in the catchwords, accumulation and impoverishment of excitement."[23] In comparing anxiety neurosis with hysteria, he states, ". . . we find aspects which make it appear that the anxiety neurosis is really the somatic counterpart to hysteria. Here as there we have accumulation and excitement—on which is perhaps based the similarity of the aforementioned symptoms; here as there we have a psychic insufficiency which results from abnormal somatic processes; and here as there we have instead of a psychic elaboration a deviation of the excitement into the somatic. The difference only lies in the fact that the excitement, in which displacement the neurosis manifests itself, is purely somatic (somatic sexual excitement) in anxiety neurosis, while in hysteria it is psychic (evoked through a conflict)."[24]

I think we can sum up Freud's view here rather simply. In anxiety there is impoverishment of *psychic* excitement. The somatic excitation expends itself subcortically. In neurasthenia there is accumulation of *psychic* excitement because adequate action is not taken and this excitement finally overwhelms the mind. Both of these neuroses are *totally somatic* in their significant etiology. However in hysteria and compulsion neurosis there is a slightly different situation. There is sexual excitation and it is displaced, i.e. not relieved by adequate action. In these last two neuroses, however, the cause of the displacement is to be found in mental conflict.

In the Hans case, as in the more general theory we discussed in *The Interpretation of Dreams,* Freud assumed a mental process that divided into Conscious and Unconscious process. Between these two was some kind of resistance, or "censor," some kind of unamiability, such that the Conscious area, of which the Preconscious was a part, was trying to exercise some dominion over the Unconscious area. In our present discussion we discover the germ of just this kind of system in Freud's early work with neuroses. However, in the early work this system is a physiological system through and through. Mental processes appear as will-of-the-wisps.They change to reflect the somatic situation. In the neuroses, with the partial exception of hysteria and compulsion neurosis, to do work on the neurosis we must do work on the body. We must unburden the nerve endings. We must perform adequate action. Freud came to call the energy value of this sexual excitation, "libido-quantum." He termed the psychic representative of this libido-quantum "ego-libido." As the system now stands the libido-quantum struggles to gain a liminal point where it flows over the "resistance of the subcortical conduction" and becomes ego-libido. *The disposition of the libido-quantum is the critical factor in normal and neurotic mental states.*

The necessity for the use of the term, libido-quantum, was then indicated to Freud by his work with neurotics and by his conviction that sexual somatic processes were crucial in neuroses. But it might seem he could have used the term "sexual excitation" and observed the rule of parsimony. The point was, however, that a given quantum of sexual excitation could result in different mental manifestations. The individual might be normal, or neurotic. Thus the quantum of excitation was not diagnostic. By employing the concept, libido-quantum, Freud indicated his intention to follow the sexual energy to the "resistance" and from the resistance he could follow it over into the mind or back into subcortical processes. It was the relation of the libido-quantum to the "resistance" which was an important diagnostic element, not the mere quantum of sexual excitation. However, it appeared that libido-quantum did not act the same outside and inside the mind. For one thing the amount of libido-quantum might be great, yet the amount of libido in the mind might be small. This happened in anxiety. A new concept was required and Freud employed the term "ego-libido." Now, in view of the way things happened in the neuroses, libido-quantum and ego-libido were "real" things. In anxiety libido-quantum turned into anxiety. Therefore it had mental significance. In neurasthenia libido-quantum overflowed the resistance and as ego-libido it again caused mental events.

Although we are anticipating, this is a good place to indicate the considerations leading Freud toward the formulation of the Conscious and the Unconscious categories. The first consideration is that libido-quantum is a useful concept but it is neither somatic nor psychic. The somatic aspect of libido-quantum is sexual excitation. The mental aspect of libido-quantum is ego-libido. Yet libido-quantum is a functionally efficient force. It can "cause" anxiety as in the case of Hans. Through ego-libido it can "cause" neurasthenia. Libido-quantum, then, has a name and a function but it has no habitation. As Freud's thought develops he thinks more and more in terms of mental dynamics. This results in one of the major "displacements" or alterations in Freudian theory. It consists in the removal of an essentially somatic concept from its somatic environment into a mental or psychic environment with a consequent improvement in the level of theory.

The concept "Unconscious" is merely a "displacement" of the concept, "libido-quantum." It means that Freud is going to think about these events in terms of mental dynamics rather than in terms of physiological process. The Unconscious brings the libido-quantum into intimate access to the Conscious and the "resistance."

However, the displacement of libido-quantum from the somatic to the mental was not merely a convenience. It was dictated by the fact that libido-quantum appeared to be actually involved in mental process. We have seen that libido-quantum could cause anxiety. This might be looked upon as a sort of parallel process. Somatic, subcortical action of the libido-quantum was reflected by a parallel mental process, that of anxiety. However, there were other mental phenomena that did not fit this oversimplified point of view. These phenomena are concerned with "ideas" and their "affect" or emotional components. Freud took the point of view, in *The Interpretation of Dreams,* that the ego may either repress the idea and its affect or it may repress the affect leaving the idea in a weakened condition in the ego. The question arises, what is this affect that must be repressed by the ego? The first answer, in view of Freud's definition of terms, would be that it must be ego-libido, for ego-libido is the psychic representative of libido-quantum and furnishes the major energy in the ego. Now there are two psychoneuroses that Freud termed "pure." They are anxiety neurosis and neurasthenia. They are "pure" because it is clear that they are caused by sexual, somatic excitation. In one of these psychoneuroses, however, there is a diminution of ego-libido, i.e. in anxiety neurosis. We would expect then that in anxiety neurosis there would be no important affect connected with ideas. Thus there would be little need for repression. The neurosis would arise simply from the subcortical action of the libido-quantum. But it appears that there is need of repression in anxiety and that the ego defends against the affect-idea complex. This repression was clearly marked in the Hans case. It follows then, if we can reason as Freud may well have reasoned, that *this affect is not derived from ego-libido.* However, although there is impoverishment of ego-libido, we know that somatic excitation is increasing. This is represented by an increase in libido-quantum. We therefore must assume that in some manner the libido-quantum has a direct influence on psychic process. The affect that attaches itself to ideas and frequently forms a combination that is repugnant to the ego is then a very intimate representative of sexual somatic excitation. It does not work with, but perhaps against, ego-libido. Its dynamics are its own because the ego frequently must marshal its own forces against this hostile force.

Thus, we suggest that Freud, thinking about his clinical experience in terms of his early concepts, was gradually forced away from his early physical frame of reference. Mental events were too complex to be explained by gross physical process. It was necessary to meet this mental complexity with mental concepts. *The Unconscious then is a concept that has special application to the behavior of the libido-quantum in the mind.* Because the libido-quantum acted in such a manner as to indicate that it was distinct and independent from the rest of the mind, so, too, the Unconscious must be considered to be distinct and independent. Now we can visualize the Unconscious as a system of autonomous impulses arising from a "special chemism," from sexual somatic excitation, that continually impinges on the ego, or the Conscious-Preconscious, often intruding itself as an alien and hostile influence. We can see, in this perspective, that the Unconscious is really a functional system, i.e. it consists of psychic material that has similar "activation." A topological view is especially useful here. It is convenient to visualize a sort of conduit system between the sexual organs and erogenous zones and the mind where mental material is energized with libido-quantum.

DIFFICULTIES WITH FREUD'S
EARLY VIEWS

The reader has probably observed a number of difficulties that attend Freud's slowly crystallizing views. They may be summarized as follows:

a) *The topological tendency in Freud's thought can be a distorting factor as joined to the Unconscious.*

b) *The nature of ideas or images is difficult to explain in terms of libido-quantum.*

c) *Two sexual energies have been introduced to the mind without adequate explanation of their relation to each other, or to the mind.*

d) *"Adequate action" does not appear to be always somatic discharge.*

e) *We are given no explanation of "unpleasant affect."* ,

a) *The topological tendency in Freud's thought*

I have pointed out the heuristic value of viewing the Unconscious as having direct physical connections with sexual somatic excitation. We can imagine that there is a region of the mind where these connections are established. At these points sexual energy in the raw, as it were, is continuously pouring into the mind. This type of physical model is not harmful if it is not "reified," converted into an existential system. However, the model is reified if the sexual conduits are thought to impart sexual energy only to one region of the mind. Further harm may be done if this region is termed the "Unconscious" because it may then be assumed that sexual energy favors one area of the mind and that the material in this area is, by definition, unconscious. These last positions do not necessarily follow from the clinically established position that raw sexual energy is communicated to the mind. In the Hans case we will remember that sexual material was conscious before it was repressed. The clinical evidence has tended to indicate that sexual energy is introduced to the mind at large until repressed and that sexual formations are conscious until repressed.

b) *Images and libido-quantum*

This problem is illustrated by the following case history as reported by Freud. "A young woman who had only one child after five years of married life complained of obsessive impulses to throw herself from the window or balcony, and of fears lest at the sight of a sharp knife she might kill her child. She admitted that the marriage relations were seldom practised and then only with caution against conception; but she added that she did not miss this as she was not of a sensual nature. I then ventured to tell her that at the sight of a man she conceived erotic ideas, and that she therefore lost confidence in herself and imagined herself a depraved person fit for anything. The retranslation of the obsession into the sexual was successful; weeping, she soon admitted her long concealed marital misery, and then mentioned painful ideas of an unchanged sexual character such as the often recurring sensation of something forcing itself under her skirts."[25]

This case is a good example of the kind of evidence drawing Freud to the assumption that libido-quantum is active in the mind. The woman said she was not of a "sensual nature." The ego-libido was diminished. But nevertheless it developed on analysis that there were strong sexual forces at work. Freud indicated to the woman that she had erotic ideas and she finally agreed. One of these was the sensation of something forcing itself under her skirt. The symbolism is easily understood. How did the "idea" and the energy combine? We know that Freud looked with some favor on "primal images." This however was not a primal image. It was indigenous to the time and place. Another possible explanation would be the Meynert overlay which we have discussed. Perhaps images attached to sexual energy were part of the primary ego and descended into the Unconscious. This view is untenable because this image was not a childish image but the "idea" of an adult. The idea is so well-tailored to the sexual interest and desire of the subject that we can hardly imagine it was a childish fancy that was conveniently located in the primary personality. A reasonable view is that this "idea" was part of the secondary system of the subject. The creation of this image must be imagined as the work of the secondary ego. Otherwise we would be forced to the conclusion that pertinent images are manufactured by the libido-quantum, that is, by somatic processes in the genitalia. It seems then that there are not one but two processes here. First, there is the sexual energy in the mind. Second, there is the pertinent image. The former is created by somatic processes. The latter is created in the secondary ego. To that extent the secondary ego has connived with the sexual energy furnishing us the hypothesis that an image-energy formation is the result of cooperation between sexual energy and personality interest.

c) *A redundancy of sexual energies*

Originally Freud had a clear picture of sexual energy. It resulted from somatic process. It was called libido-quantum. It flowed to the "subcortical resistance." Part of it might flow over into the mind as ego-libido. The rest would expend itself in physical action that might be reflected in mental manifestations. This was a clear picture but it was inadequate for reasons that we have seen. So Freud introduced his libido-quantum into the mind. This furnished him with two sexual energies, both in the mind. Originally, he seemed to think that the ego-libido would carry out the general program of the libido-quantum. However, it developed that this was not so. Libido-quantum had to be introduced to do its own work. It thus remains for us to discover what the ego-libido does. At the present point of development it is a vestigial remain in Freud's thinking. We would expect it to be discarded as a result of what I have called the displacement of the libido-quantum. Later we will see that it served very useful purposes. This discussion will aid our later consideration of this concept.

d) *"Adequate action" not always somatic discharge*

By "adequate action," as we have seen, Freud referred to the discharge of somatic sexual excitation. This is the only way the "tension" in the mind can be relieved. The bald conclusion appears, a conclusion from which Freud never quite satisfactorily escaped, that the only "cure" for the "pure" neuroses, anxiety and neurasthenia, was sexual discharge. Freud said, however, that masturbation and spontaneous pollution did not suffice for that purpose. Since both of these actions produce the discharge in question they should both be curative in their effect. Freud did not, at this stage, consider this problem carefully. What answer he gave is curiously evasive. He said of masturbators that ". . . these persons so easily merge into the state of abstinence after they have for long been accustomed to afford a discharge, to be sure an incorrect one, for every little quantity of somatic excitement."[26]

e) No explanation of unpleasant affect

We know that in the Freudian view physical energy or libido-quantum may attach itself to or cathect an idea. The resulting formation may be "intolerable" to the ego. As a result action may be taken to separate the affect from the idea as we have already seen. The attitude about the formation, or the affect connected with it, cannot be inferred from the formation itself. There is nothing in the nature of the formation to cause the unpleasant feelings. These unpleasant feelings therefore appear to be due to other conditions in the mind.

THE SEXUAL BASIS
OF THE EGO "RESISTANCE"

We have mentioned that the "intolerableness" of libido-quantum is quite impossible to understand without introducing some kinds of new conditions into the ego. As we would expect Freud sought for these new conditions in his clinical work with neuroses. The assumption on which he worked is clearly stated in his epochal paper "The Role of Sexuality in the Etiology of the Neuroses." "In a normal *vita sexualis* no neurosis is possible."[27] The technique of psychotherapy was also disclosing the strain for uniformity, the tendency toward consistency, in personality. "The hysterical stream of thought, even if it reaches into the unconscious, may be expected to show the same logical connections and sufficient causations as those that would be formed in a normal individual."[28] And in the case of the neurotic as in the case of the normal individual we make the assumption of sufficient motivation. "If the association of ideas of neurotics, and especially of hysterics, makes a different impression (i.e. seems to be unmotivated), if the relation of the intensities of different ideas does not seem to be explainable here on psychological determinants alone, we know

that such manifestations are due to the existence of concealed unconscious motives. Such secret motives may be expected wherever such a
deviation in the connection, or the transgression from the normally
justified causations can be demonstrated."[29]

In our search for an understanding of the "resistance" we then
assume that neurotics and normal people have the same types of personalities. They are to be understood on the same principles. The basic
cause of personality action is "motivation" and this is true of normal
people and neurotics. However, tracing the sufficient motivations in
neurotics may be more difficult than in normal people because they
may be concealed in the Unconscious. However they *can* be traced.
"It is a fact worthy of reflection that in . . . analysis one can follow
a stream of thought from the conscious into the unconscious (that is,
absolutely not recognized as a reminiscence) thence draw it for some
distance through the consciousness, and again see it end in the unconscious; and still this variation of the psychic elucidation would change
nothing in it, in its logicalness, and in a single part of its connection."[30]

This view does more than undertake to define a system of therapy.
It implies a consistency, a unity of cause in personality events. Since
Freud has established to his own satisfaction the sexual somatic cause
of some mental events it would be natural to assume a sexual somatic
source of all mental events. From the moment that Freud introduced
libido-quantum into the mind he considered it the dominant motivating
force in the mind. The "resistance" deflected it, choked it back, but
in only a negative and temporary manner. Thus it appears that Freud's
"thought history" predisposed him toward "reducing" the "resistance"
to the *vita sexualis* and in preserving its negative and temporary character. This would appear to be quite an undertaking but Freud went
far toward accomplishing it.

The clinical basis for this accomplishment consisted of "thirteen
cases of hysteria." He reported, "Every one of the infantile traumas
which the analysis revealed for these severe cases had to be designated
as marked sexual injuries; some of them were indeed abominable.
Among the persons who were guilty of such serious abuse, we have in
first place nurses, governesses, and other servants to whom children
are left much too carelessly, then in regrettable frequency come the
teachers; but in seven of the thirteen cases we dealt with innocent
childish offenders, mostly brothers who for years entertained sexual
relations with their younger sisters. The course of events always re-
sembled some of the cases which could with certainty be tracked,
namely, that the boy had been abused by a person of the feminine
sex, thus awakening in him prematurely the libido, and that after a

few years he repeated in sexual aggression on his sister the same procedure to which he himself was subjected."[31]

We may disclose now that Freud's interpretation of the clinical evidence in these cases was later altered.[32] Evidence which at first he took at face value he later largely rejected.

In these thirteen cases, which were assumed by Freud to be cases of childhood seduction, an important question was the effect of the sexual injury. In two cases these seductions took place at the ". . . delicate age of one and one-half or two years."[33] In a number of cases ". . . the sexual trauma occurred during the third and fourth year of life."[34] In these circumstances one could hardly imagine the libido to be in such a developed condition as to threaten the mind by its sudden increase. So no augmented libido-quantum could become active. Furthermore, if this had happened we would have cases of anxiety or neurasthenia, rather than hysteria. It seemed, then, that the early age of the subject must be connected in some manner with the essential distinguishing feature of the hysteria and repression. "All the experiences and excitements which prepare the way for, or occasion the outburst of hysteria in the period of life after puberty," suggests Freud, "evidently act through the fact that they awaken the memory remnants of those infantile traumas, which do not become conscious but lead to the liberation of affect and repression. It is quite in harmony with this role of the later traumas not to be subject to the strict limitation of the infantile traumas, but that both in intensity and quality they can vary from an actual sexual assault to a mere approximation of the sexual, such as perceiving the sexual acts of others, or receiving information concerning sexual processes."[35] Thus Freud opened the way to explain resistance in the ego. He also laid the basis for the view that ultimately the roots of neurosis lie in childhood traumas.

Excitements after puberty awaken "memory remnants" of childhood sexual traumas which in turn lead to the liberation of affect and repression. This then is the answer to the question we were raising about the independent conditions causing "intolerable" affect. If there is a "sexual" injury or abuse *before the development of the libido-quantum*, before libido-quantum can be generated, then later sexual stimulation will activate this injury which will produce the "intolerable" affect and repression. The so-called pure neuroses are due to a flood of libido-quantum which expends itself in the two different ways that distinguish these neuroses. The psychoneuroses produce a flood of libido-quantum but also a sum of energy emerging from an early sexual injury. This latter energy finds the libido-quantum idea formations repugnant and represses or condemns them. *This dynamic condition in the mind is automatic*. It is based on sexual excitation and sexual injury. In his paper "The Role of Sexuality in the Etiology of the Neuroses" Freud makes explicit what can be readily inferred. Sexual repression is "organic."[36] *So we see that sexual somatic factors are the causes of both dynamic aspects of mental events.* The simple or pure neurosis is caused by one organic sexual determinant, while the psychoneuroses are caused by two organic, sexual determinants.

Freud doubted whether sexual passivity can be a cause of repression after the child reaches the age of eight or ten unless there are some previous qualifying experiences. "All the experiences and excitements which prepare the way for, or occasion the outburst, of hysteria in the period of life after puberty evidently act through the fact that they awaken the memory remnants of those infantile traumas which do not become conscious but lead to the liberation of affect and repression."[37]

Freud fitted the neuroses into his growing theory in the following manner, "The etiology of both defense neuropsychoses now shows the following relation to the etiology of both simple neuroses, neurasthenia and anxiety neurosis. . . . Both the latter neuroses are the direct results of the sexual noxas alone, while both defense neuroses (hysteria and compulsion neurosis) are the direct results of sexual noxas which acted before the appearance of sexual maturity, that is, they are the results of the psychic memory remnants of the noxas."[38] Freud made a distinction between hysteria and the compulsion neurosis. Hysteria is based on a trauma that was received sexually but passively. The obsessions of the compulsion neurosis refer to a childhood trauma which was "pleasurably accomplished."[39] Behind this, however, is a period in which the sexual trauma was passively accomplished. The passive experience made repression possible, but the pleasant experience made the repression difficult to accomplish. Nevertheless, ". . . after conscious and recollected effort" the repression is accomplished. Then comes a period, evidently generated by the passive experience in which there are "symptoms of scrupulousness, shame and diffidence."[40]

The four principal neuroses have been reduced to sexual events in the physical organism. Shame arises from a type of sexual injury. Shame also is at the base of the attempt of the ego to protect itself, to repress material. It is then logical to assume that *only* sexual material is repressed. Freud explains this on the basis of the somatic process. "A psychological theory of repression," he says, "ought also to inform us why only ideas of a sexual content can be repressed. It may be formulated as follows: It is known that ideas of a sexual content produce exciting processes in the genitals resembling the actual sexual experience. It may be assumed that this somatic excitement becomes transformed into psychic. As a rule the activity referred to is much stronger at the time of the occurrence than at the recollection of the same. But if the sexual experience takes place during the time of sexual immaturity and the recollection of the same is awakened during or after maturity, the recollection then acts disproportionately more excitingly than the previous experience, for puberty has in the meantime incomparably increased the reactive capacity of the sexual apparatus. But such an inverse proportion seems to contain the psychological determination of repression. Through the retardation of the pubescent maturity in comparison with the psychic function, the sexual life offers the only existing possibility for that inversion of the relative efficacy. The infantile traumas subsequently act like fresh experiences, but they are then unconscious."[41]

I think that the "thirteen cases of hysteria" gave a powerful direction to Freud's thought. It may eventually appear that this impetus was, on the whole, unfortunate. In due course we will find that Freud made rather dramatic alterations in his views of the ego. But these alterations were delayed, perhaps, by this early evidence. Although Freud later decided that these "sexual injuries" were fancies of his patients he could not be expected to retract all the theory that had been largely based on the assumption that these injuries took place. Instead, he looked for other evidence that would support much the same point of view. He was incorrect in thinking that changing the testimony of these patients from fact to fantasy did not reduce its support for his theory.

THE RESISTANCE

OF THE "RESISTANCE"

We have seen that Freud favored mechanistic views and physiological was of thinking. His experience and marked competence in histology and neurology influenced him in this direction. It is not to be wondered that he sought to "reduce" mental phenomena to somatic conditions. He wanted to be able to look at, experiment with, and quantify the basic causative factors in mental behavior. In sexual factors he found clear somatic conditions which clearly had considerable mental significance. Sexual factors offered the most promising road to a satisfactory system of somatic theory that would explain mental events. But each provisional system of somatic theory presented a fundamental difficulty.

Could the activity of this "resistance" be reduced to a "special chemism"? Freud presented his strongest case in favor of this position in his paper "The Role of Sexuality in the Etiology of the Neuroses." He said, "I think it worth emphasizing that with all changes my ideas on the etiology of the psychoneuroses still never disavowed or abandoned two points of view, to wit, the estimation of sexuality and infantilism. In other respects we have in place of the accidental influences the constitutional moments, and instead of the pure psychologically intended defense, we have organic 'sexual repression.' "[42] He followed this with an even more definite statement. "We have unexpectedly advanced from the question of the causation of the psychoneuroses to the problem of their essence. If we wish to take cognizance of what we discovered by psychoanalysis we can only say that the essence of these maladies lies in disturbances of the sexual processes, in those processes in the organism which determine the formation and utilization of the sexual libido. We can hardly avoid perceiving these processes in the last place as chemical, so that we can recognize in the so-called actual neuroses the somatic effects of disturbances in the sexual metabolism, while in the psychoneuroses we recognize besides the psychic effects of the same disturbances. The resemblance of the neuroses to the manifestations of intoxication and abstinence following certain alkeloids, and to Basedow's and Addison's diseases, obtrudes itself clinically without any further ado, and just as these two diseases should no more be described as 'nervous diseases,' so will the genuine 'neuroses' soon have to be removed from this class despite their nomenclature."[43]

At times Freud still hoped to read the record of the mental by the clues in the somatic; "The delusional formations of paranoiacs containing the greatness and sufferings of their own ego, which manifest themselves quite typically in almost monotonous forms are universally familiar. Furthermore, through numerous communications we become acquainted with the peculiar organizations by means of which certain perverts put into operation their sexual gratification, be it in fancy or reality. On the other hand, it may sound rather novel to some to hear that quite analogous psychic formations regularly appear in all psychoneuroses, especially in hysteria, and that these so-called hysterical fancies show important relations to the causation of the neurotic symptoms."[44] This method had its draw backs for Freud pointed out the diagnostic problems resulting from the bisexuality of symptoms. "In psychoanalytical treatment," he said, "it is very important to be prepared for the bisexual significance of a symptom. It should not be at all surprising or misleading when a symptom remains apparently undiminished in spite of the fact that one of its sexual determinants is already solved. Perhaps it is still supported by the unsuspected contrary sexual."[45]

The "resistance" was proving highly resistant! Early theory could not come to a workable hypothesis. But in papers written after the turn of the century we find indications that Freud is preparing to attack the resistance from another angle. In his paper on "Hysterical Fancies and Their Relations to Bisexuality" (1908) he said: "Everything that can exert harmful influences in the processes serving the sexual function therefore belongs to the etiology of the neurosis. In the first place we have the noxas directly affecting the sexual functions insofar as they are accepted as injuries by the sexual constitution *which is changeable through culture and breeding.*" (Italics ours.)[46] Sociocultural influence is admitted at precisely the point where Freud has sought to maintain a closed biochemical system. This point of view is largely ignored, however, in the study of Hans (1909). In that case "condemnation" is not so much related to culture and breeding as it is to some automatic effect of the Conscious system.

But the function of the Conscious system, as indicated in the Hans case indicates an increasing interest in this area. A unilinear approach to mental behavior is being abandoned. The cue can be found in Freud's paper "On Psychotherapy" (1904) where he asserted the importance of the Conscious system. ". . . you will understand," he said, "that the interpretation of this unconscious, in patients' psychic life, into the conscious, must result in a correction of their deviation from the normal, and in an abrogation of the compulsion controlling their psychic life. For the conscious will reaches as far as the conscious psychic processes and every psychic compulsion is substantiated by the unconscious. You need never fear that the patient will be harmed by the emotion produced in the entrance of his unconscious into consciousness, for you can theoretically readily understand that the somatic and affective activity of the emotion which becomes conscious can never become as great as those of the unconscious. For we only control all our emotions by directing upon them our highest psychic activities which are connected with consciousness."[47]

Freud has been blocked but not defeated. The great, intuitive mind is on the move. We must wonder, as we see how this mind is always in flux, how Freud ever came to represent for many a closed system of thought. His own system was certainly never closed.

Chapter V

THE DYNAMICS

OF THE CONSCIOUS

AND THE UNCONSCIOUS

WE HAVE INDICATED the general outlines of Freud's thought at about the turn of the century as indicated mainly in *The Interpretation of Dreams* and "Three Contributions to a Theory of Sexuality." We have also explored the roots of these ideas in his earlier thinking and clinical experience. Our purpose now is to examine in more detail than we have yet done mental processes as Freud described them in *The Interpretation of Dreams*.

THE UNCONSCIOUS
AS AN INDEPENDENT REGION

Dream analysis introduced phenomena of such a varied type that Freud's theory, in the form we have examined it, was subject to great strain. We now will see new, ingenious threads in the fabric of Freud's thought. Yet behind the new we find the hard core of the old, zealously maintained. One root idea is that libido-quantum introduces energic impulses into the psychic life at some point. In Freud's mind, no matter how much complexity is introduced into mental events, this fundamental insight must not be lost. And connected with this insight is the twin conviction that organically derived sexual impulses influence the mind mainly through unconscious channels. These basic ideas focused Freud's attention on the Unconscious as the dominant factor in mental events. Our examination therefore properly starts with a close look at Freud's developing views of the Unconscious.

"Everything," said Freud, "points to the . . . conclusion . . . that we need not assume that any special symbolizing activity of the psyche is operative in dream-formation; that, on the contrary, the dream makes use of such symbolizations as are to be found ready-made in unconscious thinking, since these, by reason of their ease of representation, and for the most part by reason of their being exempt from censorship, satisfy more effectively the requirements of dream-formation."[1] Symbolism, then, has an origin beyond the individual. ". . . it should be noted that symbolism does not appertain especially to dreams, but rather to the unconscious imagination, and particularly to that of the people, and it is to be found in a more developed condition in folklore, myths, legends, idiomatic phrases, proverbs, and the current witticisms of a people than in dreams."[2] Freud indicated what some of those symbols were. "The Emperor and the Empress (king and queen) in most cases really represent the dreamer's parents; the dreamer himself or herself is the prince or princess. . . . All elongated objects, sticks, tree trunks, umbrellas (on account of the opening, which might be likened to an erection), all sharp and elongated weapons, knives, daggers, and pikes represent the male member. . . . Small boxes, chests, cupboards, and ovens correspond to the female organ; also cavities, ships, and all kinds of vessels. . . . A room in a dream generally represents a woman; the description of its various entrances and exits is scarcely calculated to make us doubt this interpretation. The interest as to whether the room is 'open' or 'locked' will be readily understood in this connection. . . . The dream of walking through a suite of rooms signifies a brothel or a harem. . . . Steep inclines, ladders, and stairs, and going up or down them, are symbolic representations of the sexual act. Smooth walls over which one climbs, facades of houses, across which one lets oneself—often with a sense of great anxiety—correspond to erect human bodies, and probably repeat in our dreams childish memories of climbing up parents or nurses. 'Smooth' walls are men; in anxiety dreams one often holds firmly to 'projections' on houses. Tables, whether bare or covered, and boards, are women, perhaps by virtue of contrast, since they have no protruding contours. . . . Of articles of dress, a woman's hat may very often be interpreted with certainty as the male genitals. In the dreams of men one often finds the necktie as a symbol for the penis. . . . All complicated machines and appliances are very probably the genitals. . . ."[3]

These symbols are not learned. They may well characterize the dreams of a child of four, and therefore we may conclude that the ". . . dreamer has command of symbolism from the very first."[4] This symbolism is at a lower level than the Preconscious and therefore is in the Unconscious and is subject to the control of the "censor." The dreams of normal persons are simple and transparent, displaying the purest symbolism. In the case of neurotics, however, ". . . owing to the greater strictness of the censorship and the more extensive dream-distortion resulting therefrom,"[5] the dreams are obscured and more difficult to translate, or interpret.

Freud made a three-way association between symbols, sex, and the Unconscious. These were seen as the major characteristics of the mind. As a result of his dream analysis Freud concluded that the Unconscious had other characteristics. He said that an act of judgment in a dream was ". . . merely the repetition of an original act of judgment in the dream-thoughts."[6] The dream-thoughts are latent and unconscious and originate below the censor. Freud assigned critical faculties to these dream-thoughts. "Everything in dreams which occurs as the apparent functioning of the critical faculty is to be regarded, not as the intellectual performance of the dream-work, but as belonging to the substance of the dream-thoughts, and it has found its way from there, as a completed structure, into the manifest dream-content. I may even go farther than this! I may even say that the judgments which are passed upon the dream as it is remembered after waking, and the feelings which are aroused by the reproduction of the dream, belong largely to the latent dream-content, and must be fitted into place in the interpretation of the dream."[7] We see then that this region in which the unconscious, the sexual, and the symbolic are conjoined has functions with reference to judgments. The Unconscious is blossoming forth with a variety of potentialities not dreamed of in the system of libido-quantum and resistance.

But the Unconscious is an even richer system than we have yet disclosed. In it there are also native fantasies. Freud said that the dream process ". . . threads its way progressively from the unconscious scenes or phantasies to the preconscious."[8] This region also is the source of affect, or emotion. "The mortification suffered thirty years ago operates, after having gained access to the unconscious sources of affect, during all these thirty years as though it were a recent experience."[9] Here is the indication of the connection between the Unconscious region and the sexual somatic base. This "affect" is the libido-quantum translated into the mental area, and it lingers in this area, electrifying the material that it touches. We can visualize this area now. It is at the bottom of the mental topology, under the censor, and at the border of the somatic terrain. A thin wall, perhaps, exists between the Unconscious and the somatic. Through this wall somatic sexual energy gets changed into mental energy. An osmosis takes place that locates libido-quantum in the Unconscious. In this same area is the dream-wish. "We have built up the theory of dreams," Freud said, "on the assumption that the actuating dream-wish invariably originates in the unconscious; which, as we ourselves admitted, cannot be universally demonstrated, even though it cannot be refuted."[10]

What is this dream-wish? A "wish" is a concept derived from the behavior of the organism in relation to pleasure and pain. Freud explained it this way: "We . . . discussed the psychic results of experiences of gratification, and were able at this point to introduce a second assumption, namely, that the accumulation of excitation—by processes that do not concern us here—is felt as pain, and sets the apparatus in operation in order to bring about again a state of gratification, in which the diminution of excitation is perceived as pleasure. Such a current, in the apparatus, issuing from pain and striving for pleasure, we call a wish."[11] A wish is the basic initiator of action, and the "pleasure principle" is fundamental. ". . . nothing but a wish is capable of setting the apparatus in motion and . . . the course of any excitation in the apparatus is regulated automatically by the perception of pleasure and pain."[12]

This term "wish" indicates the somatic impulse after it has passed through the wall between the psychic and the somatic. It can be seen that a "wish" is very similar to an "instinct" as Freud used the term and also very similar to "libido-quantum." This search for more and more adequate representations of mental activity resulted in new concepts that trod upon the toes of old ones.

Another characteristic of the Unconscious is that the wish which exists in this region is capable of "cathexis." "The first occurrence of wishing," said Freud, "may well have taken the form of a hallucinatory cathexis of the memory of gratification."[13] We can see more clearly now how the concept, "wish," includes something more in it than the concepts, "libido-quantum" or "instinct." We could say it has a cognitive aspect. It seeks things out that are related to its pleasure.

To summarize, the Unconscious area has the following characteristics: (a) material is in an unconscious state; (b) the source of power is sexual, somatic energy; (c) it contains "primal" symbolism and native fantasies; (d) there is a faculty for making judgments; (e) there is strong affect (libido-quantum) derived from sexual, somatic excitation; (f) the "wish" is the basic impulse to action, a current "issuing from pain and striving for pleasure;" (g) this wish is capable of "hallucinatory cathexis."[14]

There is not much left of the simple somatic view of the Unconscious now. You can't reduce judgments, cognitions, fantasies to somatic excitation. The Unconscious has independent faculties that are used by the libido-quantum. And, as we have seen, all is not well with the Meynert overlay. Perhaps we can say of this rich and confusing region that all that is not sexual is "primal" and all that is not primal is infantile, but all that counts is sexual.

This is not a very good way of putting theory together. But it is the way that Freud proposes to think until he can get his theory in better order. In the meantime he has accepted the operational philosophy of the sentiment—"full speed ahead and damn the torpedoes!"

THE RESISTANCE AS A CONSCIOUS

REGION

This "region" we are now discussing is concerned with that vexatious opposition in individuals to purely sexual reactions. Freud found it necessary to examine this opposition more and more carefully since, like the Unconscious, it was more complex than seemed to be the case at first.

The Conscious area (including the Preconscious), or secondary ego in Meynert's view, has the function of censorship. The psychic force resulting in this censorship is conceived to be different from the psychic force which forms the wish expressed by the dream. The secondary ego also has the power of "secondary elaboration" of the dream, and a single wish-impulse, the wish to sleep. About secondary elaboration Freud states, "It is indisputable that the censoring agency, whose influence we have so far recognized only in the restrictions of and emissions in the dream-content, is likewise responsible for interpolations in and amplifications of this content. . . . Only in the most extreme cases does the psychic function in dream-formation which we are now considering rise to original creation. . . . I do not wish to deny to this . . . factor the faculty of creatively making new contributions to our dreams. But its influence is certainly exerted . . . mainly in the preference and selection of psychic material already formed in the dream-thoughts."[15] The dream-thoughts, as Freud has pointed out, originate below the censor in the Unconscious.

The secondary ego has other, if precarious, functions. It contains

the day residues (memory traces of the day's experiences) which
". . . may be either wishes, or psychic impulses of any other kind,
or simply recent impressions."[16] We must assume, by this use of the
word "wish," that Freud is referring to an ordinary feeling of preference, not to the Unconscious wish. These day residues offer to the
Unconscious something of great importance to it, ". . . the points of
attachment necessary for transference."[17] The Unconscious may use
these day residues to express the Unconscious wish if they can in any
way be put to this use. While the day residues or the day thoughts may
be pressed into service by the Unconscious they may also find the motive power to express a wish of their own. Freud admits that, "It might
even prove possible to explain, on the basis of our train of thought,
those extreme cases in which the dream, continuing the work of the
day, brings to a happy issue an unsolved problem of waking life."[18]

Freud came close to making the admission that the secondary
ego may form its own dream. But he hastily retreated and tried to
take a permanent position upon a razor's edge. In taking this position he first made a needed distinction between a wish and an
"incitement." An "incitement" belonged in the secondary ego. It is a
simple preference. When the secondary ego feels this preference it
is in a state of "incitement." Freud said, "I will admit that there is a
whole class of dreams in which the incitement originates mainly or
even exclusively from the residues of the day . . ." but ". . . the
motive-power needed by the dream had to be contributed by a wish.
. . ."[19] The day residues, then, may contain incitements and these
incitements may in fact find expression in dreams and appear therefore to have caused the dream. In fact, however, these incitements
were picked up and employed by the Unconscious wish which really
furnished the power to form the dream. However, there is evidence
that the secondary ego may, upon occasion, express "incitements"
in dreams that appear unrelated to any dependency on the unconscious
wish. Thus, in dreams that are painful to the secondary ego, the ego
sometimes ". . . reacts with violent resentment to the accomplished
satisfaction of the repressed wish, and even goes so far as to make an
end of the dream by means of anxiety. It is thus not difficult to recognize that dreams of pain and anxiety are, in accordance with our
theory, just as much wish fulfillments as are the straightforward dreams
of gratification."[20] Punishment dreams are even more important in
this connection. ". . . it would be the essential characteristic of punishment-dreams that in them it is not the unconscious wish from the
repressed material (from the system Ucs) that is responsible for dream-
formation, but the punitive wish reacting against it, a wish pertaining
to the ego, even though it is unconscious (i.e. preconscious)."[21]

Freud has stated that a dream ". . . must be furnished by a wish belonging to the unconscious."[22] We know that the "unconscious" to which he referred is *not* the state of unconsciousness. He referred to the Unconscious area where "wishes" lurked along with fantasies and libido-quantum. The "wish" or "incitement" in punishment dreams comes from the Preconscious area of the Conscious and is thus powered by a different force than the Unconscious wish. The fact that this wish is also in an unconscious state does not qualify or alter the important exception that Freud has made here. If "painful" dreams and "punishment" dreams are to be reconciled with the rule requiring an Unconscious wish to form a dream then a more expert method of reconciliation must be devised. (The dialectic we find here is a characteristic "stage" in Freud's encounters with theoretical problems.)

The power of the secondary ego in dream formation may extend even further. ". . . there are persons in whom the retention at night of the knowledge that they are sleeping and dreaming, becomes quite manifest, and who are thus apparently endowed with the conscious faculty of guiding their dream-life. Such a dreamer . . . is dissatisfied . . . he breaks off the dream . . . and begins it afresh, in order to continue it along different lines, just like the . . . author who . . . gives a happier ending to his play. Or on another occasion, when the dream places him in a sexually exciting situation, he thinks in his sleep: 'I don't want to continue this dream and exhaust myself by an emission; I would rather save it for a real situation.' The Marquis Hervey (Vaschide) declared that he had gained such power over his dreams that he could accelerate their course at will, and turn them in any direction he wished. It seems that in him the wish to sleep had accorded a place to another, a preconscious wish, the wish to observe his dreams and to derive pleasure from them. Sleep is just as compatible with such a wish-resolve as it is with some proviso as a condition of waking up (wet-nurse's sleep)."[23]

It appears that a dreamer can *direct* a dream. This is more than the "wish to observe" a dream or "derive pleasure" from it. Freud's comment assumed that the secondary ego had a ringside seat at the spectacle and enjoyed the performance. The evidence in the cited passage shows that the dreamer may continue a dream along different lines, accelerate it, turn it in any direction; in other words, *assume an ascendant position over the wish in the Unconscious.*

Freud encountered a similar problem earlier with relation to the concept "resistance." He avoided coming to grips with it at first but finally reduced it to the somatic by means of the ephemeral insight in the thirteen cases of hysteria. Like a compass needle he comes to rest only when aligned with his magnetic pole—somatic excitation. Other forces set him awhirl.

Clearly, if you assume the predominant power in the Unconscious you are confronted with a most difficult assignment in explaining the secondary ego's role in some dreams. Freud suggested a solution to this problem in *The Interpretation of Dreams*. It aligned him anew with his somatic "pole." The concept employed was "ideal masochism." And again we get back to that illusive term, "sexual constitution." "In the sexual constitution of many persons," Freud suggested, ". . . there is a masochistic component, which has arisen through the conversion of the aggressive, sadistic component into its opposite. Such people are called 'ideal' masochists if they seek pleasure not in the bodily pain which may be inflicted upon them, but in humiliation and psychic chastisement. It is obvious that such persons may have counter-wish-dreams and disagreeable dreams, yet these are for them nothing more than wish-fulfillments, which satisfy their masochistic inclinations."[24] (Here is an idea that will develop into the "death-instinct.")

Freud touched on the question of masochism again and again. He wondered, ". . . how is it possible for a dream to place itself at the service of self-criticism in its conflict with parvenu pride, and to take as its content a rational warning instead of a prohibited wish-fulfillment?"[25] By way of explanation he said, "We may conclude that the foundation of the dream consisted at first of an arrogant phantasy of ambition; but that in its stead only its supression and abasement has reached the dream-content. One must remember that there are masochistic tendencies in mental life to which such an inversion might be attributed. I see no objection to regarding such dreams as punishment-dreams, as distinguished from wish-fulfilling dreams. I should not see in this any limitation of the theory of dreams, hitherto as presented, but merely a verbal concession to the point of view to which the convergence of contraries seems strange."[26]

This "convergence of contraries" does seem strange to the writer. Time and again Freud tried to pass off this kind of convergence as nothing new. Yet he returned to a logical attack on it again and again. It is, of course, a threat to the very heart of his theory. "Ideal masochism" has a stop-gap function like "sub-cortical conduction" and pre-pubescent "seduction." Perhaps the most apposite prior view is in the "reversal of the relative efficacy." This latter phrase developed from a consideration of repression. The "convergence of contraries" emerges not so much to meet the problem of repression as to explain the power of the Conscious system. Obviously both problems are closely related.

The sails of theory were fluttering aimlessly. To catch the wind again Freud needed a new hypothesis and he came up with one.

THE EGO AND THE REPRESSED
—A NEW HYPOTHESIS

As we have seen, Freud's views were threatened by the discovery that various ego "wishes" or "incitements" were fulfilled in dreams. Fears and punishments were the two main types. These fears and punishments had nothing to do with that stream of libido-quantum in the Unconscious which searched for gratification. They ran counter to that search, and were strong enought to prevail. If we were to take a position that accorded with our data we would either consider our Conscious system as stronger and more creative than we had imagined, or we would somehow transfer these strong and creative elements into the Unconscious system. Freud suggested a solution. "The mechanism of dream-formation," he said, "becomes indeed in every way more transparent if in place of the antithesis 'conscious' and 'unconscious' we put the antithesis: 'ego' and 'repressed.' This however cannot be done without taking into account what happens in the psychoneuroses, and for this reason it has not been done in this book. Here I need only remark that the occurrence of punishment-dreams is not generally subject to the presence of painful day residues. They originate indeed most readily if the contrary is true, if the thoughts which are day residues are of a gratifying nature, but express illicit gratifications. Of these thoughts nothing then finds its way into the manifest dream except their contrary. . . ."[27]

In the above manner Freud tried to accommodate the punishment wish in the Unconscious even at the expense of getting the rest of the Unconscious into the Conscious system. Without "painful day residues" the Conscious system had no motive for acting: the distorting influence must come from a lower level.

Freud was sending up a trial balloon. He was facing the knotty problem of explaining punishment-dreams without equivocation and without robbing the Unconscious area of its dominant energy. Both the Preconscious and the Unconscious were seen as existing under repression and struggling against the Conscious system which was now called the "ego." The fear at the base of punishment-dreams was a part of the ego but was repressed. It was repressed into the Preconscious. At the same time it was proper to refer to it as an "ego-fear" or an "ego punishment-wish." But these wishes were also unconscious. So the ego wish and the purely libidinous wish had these common characteristics: they were both repressed and they were both in an unconscious state. But the ego wish was in the Preconscious functional system, while the libidinous wish was in the Unconscious.

Instead of two mental regions we now have three. The punishment-wish did not gain access into the Unconscious only into the unconscious state. The Preconscious system belonged with the "ego" since its wishes were in the ego and came from the ego. Freud's compromise was an admission that the Conscious-Preconscious system can form dreams of its own. But the evidence in the psychoneuroses prevented him from making an explicit admission, and he had no explanation of the wish for punishment.

Freud's tentative categories, ego and repressed, do not at first examination appear to be very helpful. They are artfully devised for the moment but quickly become part of that array of irreconcilable generalizations that make Freud so hard to pin down. But these generalizations must be dovetailed sooner or later if we are to get a fuller understanding of mental events. It does not do to have one generalization (out of an entire stock) ready at hand *for whatever happens.*

It seems to me, however, that there is a strong and valid intuition in Freud's suggestion of the antithesis: ego and repressed. It pointed toward mutually exclusive categories that would sort out mental events into distinct classes. Freud's suggestion could lead us to this: It is not so important whether a mental event is conscious or unconscious. It may not be so important whether a wish is sexual or non-sexual. What may be of great importance is *whether a mental event is repressed or not.* It suggests that the major axis of analysis is repression and non-repression and that other axes are subsidiary. Following Freud's cue we could call the totality of non-repressed events the ego, and the totality of repressed events the repressed. If we take it that the major axis is this distinction then Freud's assimilation of all wishes to repression was a definite advance in his thinking. It puts like with like. It concentrates attention on the dynamics of the relations between repressed material and the ego. Since repression is an act performed by the ego this view would assume that the characteristics of repressed material would be determined by the preferences of the ego which performs the repression.

Freud did not totally commit himself to this line of thought, possibly because the corollaries attached to it did not point to a dominant Unconscious energy. Instead, he harnessed part of the repressed with the secondary ego and maintained the Unconscious as a separate area. The view of the Preconscious as partly repressed came in handy also in analyzing the Unconscious.

THE RELATIONS BETWEEN THE
CONSCIOUS AND THE UNCONSCIOUS

Freud suggested the idea of the "censor" as an expression of the restraints that the Conscious imposed upon the Unconscious. (We have used Conscious to apply to the Conscious-Preconscious functional system. Now Freud is dividing them. When we divide the main system we will refer to the Preconscious and the Conscious sub-system.) Therefore, he placed the censor in that part of the Conscious system that he termed the Preconscious. But we shall see that he had just as much difficulty trying to express the dynamics of the "resistance" in terms of his Conscious-Preconscious categories as he had in "reducing" the resistance to sexual excitation. The Preconscious was considered to ally itself with the objectives of the Conscious. It was on the side of the "resistance." But material in the Preconscious was in the unconscious state. Freud referred to the Preconscious as the "criticizing system." Exciting processes in this system could reach consciousness—when not under repressions as we shall see later—if they attained a definite degree of intensity and a certain ". . . apportionment of the function which we must call attention."[28] Most things which are not "in our minds" but which can be remembered, in time, if we "think hard enough" are, in Freud's view, in the Preconscious. These things may "pop into our minds" without particular concern of our own. We assume then that they come to consciousness through some "intensity" of their own. Or we may search for something in the Preconscious, perhaps an old telephone number or the chemical formula that will help us in an examination, and finally it may come to us "like a flash." Here we have "apportioned" our attention and it has finally ferreted the information out of the Preconscious. The Preconscious is innocuous. It is full of the furniture and trappings of our minds that are not being used at the time. When we want any of these things we can get them although it may take us time and give us trouble. This of course is not at all like the situation in the Unconscious. We cannot get at things in the Unconscious. They have their own meanings and their own vitalities.

Freud put the censor in the Preconscious. He assumed that the Unconscious wish, proceeding toward Consciousness, entered the Preconscious and somewhere along the way was confronted by the censorship to whose influence "it soon succumbs." Under this view the Unconscious wish could become Preconscious at least for a period of time. This made the Preconscious an unsatisfactory "region" since a part of it, the part that admitted the Unconscious wishes, appeared to resemble the Unconscious system. Uncertainty about the nature of this region is indicated by Freud's description of thinking in the Pre-conscious. He said, "We call such a train of thought [one in the Pre-conscious] a preconscious train, and we believe it to be perfectly cor-rect, and that it may equally well be a merely neglected train or one that has been interrupted and suppressed."[29] It does not add much to our understanding to assume that material in the suppressing system is itself suppressed.

Developing his ideas about a train of thought, Freud said that it might die out in the Preconscious system. But there was another pos-sibility. ". . . other directing ideas are lurking in the preconscious, which have their source in our unconscious and ever-active wishes." These "lurking" ideas may establish a connection with the train of thought thus bestowing on it the energy of the wishes. "We may say, then," Freud reported, "that the hitherto preconscious train of thought has been drawn into the unconscious."[30]

This question of what goes on in the Preconscious turns into an analysis of passageways and routes because Freud is visualizing a sort of geographical area. His topological thinking has become dominant. We shall look at these routes now, but we should keep in mind that more is involved than topological ingenuity. The essential problem concerns the fundamental forces in personality and their relations. Freud was trying to draw up a model depicting the balance of power as between the Conscious and the Unconscious.

He suggested that two kinds of trains of thought may exist in the Preconscious, (a) a neglected train, and (b) a suppressed train. Both of these trains may die out where they are unless they establish some kind of connection with the Unconscious. It appeared then that some trains of thought may be repressed before they have any contact with the Unconscious. Freud described a dynamic process here and not a maturation process and therefore the Meynert overlay cannot be used to explain it. It also appears that the repression must have taken place not because the "train of thought" was allied with the Unconscious but because it was unacceptable to the Conscious. We would conclude that the Conscious subsystem represses what it does not like at least so far as material in its own subsystem is concerned.

A further point to be noticed is that the Preconscious is emphatically catholic in its tastes. Neglected and repressed trains of thought may be there, also "other directing ideas" lurk there which are based on wishes from the Unconscious. These ideas may connect with the trains of thought thus gaining additional energy. These ideas are not the Un-conscious "wishes." They "have their source" in these wishes. But these ideas have some energy. They attach to the trains of thought— those that are pertinent—and thus revitalize them. So we are presented with a perplexing problem about the censor. The Unconscious "wish" could not get into the Preconscious. There must be a censor there. But ideas with sources in the Unconscious wishes could get by that censor. They could attach themselves to "thoughts" in the Preconscious, some of which might already have been suppressed. When such a connection was made Freud imagined a rather curious event. He said that the "hitherto preconscious train of thought has been drawn into the unconscious." We remember that the normal direction of Unconscious wishes is toward Consciousness. In this situation the Unconscious establishes a beachhead in the Preconscious and then voluntarily retreats into the Unconscious. This course is suggested by Freud in order to get the formation under repression where it can behave as Unconscious formations are supposed to behave. If Freud did not avail himself of this little conceit he would have the Unconscious formations becoming part of the Conscious and so upsetting his convictions about them. There was an alternative, which consisted of imagining two censors, one at the border between the Unconscious and the Preconscious, and another between the Preconscious and the Conscious subsystem. This hypothesis would make more complex the whole question of "resistance." But it would help us to see how Unconscious "ideas" could attach to Preconscious trains of thought and still be under repression. Furthermore, it would help us to make a distinction between the "lower part" of the Preconscious and the Unconscious. A censor was needed between these two areas. And the fact that repressed trains of thought could be higher up in the Preconscious lent color to the idea that there might be another censor somewhere between the upper Preconscious and the Conscious subsystem. Freud cautiously suggested the double censor. He said, of the Preconscious, that its excitations may be capable of reaching consciousness but ". . . perhaps not before they have *again* undergone censorship."[31] This hypothesis appeared satisfactory and he put it forth frankly in a later passage. "It is only on a dissection of hysterical mental processes that the manifold nature of the problem of consciousness becomes apparent. One then receives the impression that the transition from the preconscious to the conscious cathexis is associated with a censorship similar to that between the Ucs [Unconscious] and the Pcs [Preconscious]."[32]

The actions, relations, and locations of these censors are impossible to determine. Freud has not been able to construct an "ego" system that can be kept theoretically separate from the Unconscious and whose relations with the Unconscious are determinate. But he has tried to implement the insight that the major mental axis runs along the line: ego–repressed.

Chapter VI

PROBLEMS

OF THE

UNCONSCIOUS

LET US TURN our attention now to Freud's attempts to fashion some kind of workable model that would indicate the dynamic functioning of the Unconscious. Problems with this area that have long persisted show up clearly in Freud's analysis of certain categories of dreams.

We remember Freud's view that ". . . the child with all his impulses survives in the dream."[1] This is phrased somewhat differently and perhaps more accurately in the statement: ". . . in dreams . . . there is no lack of manifold relations to the impressions of . . . early childhood."[2] Why these early impressions should be so important was not an easy question to answer. Sexual excitation served as the basis for many if not all of them. But what if there was a modicum of these impressions—and the Meynert overlay suggested that there might be— that were not powered by sexual excitation?

We have pointed out that Freud proposed to ignore Unconscious infantile material lacking an erotic base. There were, however, at least two classes of such infantile material that had a role in dreams and could not be ignored. Freud suggested a kind of phylogenetic basis for these childhood impressions which was supposed to produce the necessary "excitation." "This age of childhood," said Freud, "in which the sense of shame is unknown, seems a paradise when we look back upon it later, and paradise itself is nothing but the mass-phantasy of the childhood of the individual. This is why in paradise men are naked and unashamed, until the moment arrives when shame and fear awaken; expulsion follows, and sexual life and cultural development begin. Into this paradise dreams can take us back every night; we have already ventured the conjecture that the impressions of our earliest childhood (from the prehistoric period until about the end of the third year) crave reproduction for their own sake . . . so their reproduction is a wish-fulfillment."[3] Freud tied that view in with the psychoneuroses. "From the theory of hysteria we borrow the proposition that such an abnormal psychic elaboration of a normal train of thought takes place only when the latter has been used for the transference of an unconscious wish which dates from the infantile life and is in a state of repression. Complying with this proposition, we have built up the theory of the dream on the assumption that the actuating dream-wish *invariably* originates in the unconscious . . ."[4] Having made assumptions validating the analysis Freud then proceeded to the analysis of certain childhood dreams that persisted into adulthood— death-wishes and dreams of nakedness.

He brought out that the death-wish in children is not as terrifying a phenomenon in the young as it would appear to adults. Death does not have the same meaning to the child as it does for the adult. "Perhaps," said Freud, "some readers will now object that inimical impulses of children toward their brothers and sisters may perhaps be admitted, but how does the childish character arrive at such heights of wickedness as to desire the death of a rival or a stronger playmate, as though all misdeeds could be atoned for only by death? Those who speak in this fashion forget that the child's idea of 'being dead' has little but the word in common with our own. The child knows nothing of the horrors of decay, of shivering in the cold grave, of the terror of the infinite. Nothing, the thought of which the adult, as all the myths of the hereafter testify, finds so intolerable. The fear of death is alien to the child; and so he plays with the horrid word, and threatens another child: 'If you do that again you will die, just like Francis died,' at which the poor mother shudders, unable perhaps to forget that the greater proportion of mortals do not survive beyond the years of childhood. Even at the age of eight, a child returning from a visit to a natural history museum may say to her mother: 'Mamma, I do love you so. If you ever die, I am going to have you stuffed and set up here in the room, so that I can always, always see you!' So different from our own is the childish conception of being dead."[5]

These infantile death-wishes, Freud said, remain in the Unconscious and should be distinguished from contemporary wishes. ". . . the wishes represented as fulfilled in dreams are not always current wishes. They may also be bygone, discarded, buried and repressed wishes, which we must nevertheless credit with a sort of continued existence, merely on account of their reappearance in a dream. . . . If anyone dreams that his father or mother, his brother or sister, has died, and his dream expresses grief, I should never adduce this as proof that he wishes any of them dead now. The theory of dreams does not go as far as to require this; it is satisfied with concluding that the dreamer has wished them dead at some time or other during his childhood."[6]

Let us examine some of the dreams which show the death-wish. "One day," Freud related, "I find a lady depressed and weeping. She says; 'I do not want to see my relatives any more; they must shudder at me.' Thereupon, almost without any transition, she tells me that she had remembered a dream whose significance of course she does not understand. She dreamed it when she was four years old, and it was this: 'A fox or lynx is walking about the roof; then something falls down, or she falls down, and after that, her mother is carried out of the house—dead; whereat the dreamer weeps bitterly.' I have no sooner informed her that this dream must signify a childish wish to see her mother dead, and that it is because of this dream that she thinks that her relatives must shudder at her, than she furnishes material in explanation of the dream. 'Lynx-eye' is an approbrious epithet which a street boy once bestowed on her when she was a very small child; and when she was three years old a brick or tile fell on her mother's head, so that she bled profusely."[7]

This example appears to be an ideal instance of the re-appearance in adulthood of an infantile death wish. The whole infantile dream was apparently re-dreamed. In childhood this dream gratified the "innocent" childhood desire to see the mother dead. But, in adulthood, it shocked the mature personality with its sophisticated idea of the meaning of death and so caused deep guilt feelings in the lady. We must keep in mind however that the reasons *why* this dream should appear in adulthood are not furnished. Perhaps Freud can "reduce" this infantile wish to "impressions of early childhood" in an attempt to invest it with *ad hoc* energy. In any event a dream, of this type, in Freud's view, should have nothing more than random relation with the events of the adult life. It should be a meaningless and recurrent intrusion into adult dream life. The dream of "lynx-eye" appears to be a dream of this type.

Let us consider another dream related to the death-wish. This relates to a girl who went through varied psychic states. She showed an aversion to her mother, abusing her and striking her. Then followed an apathetic period. At this stage Freud began analysing her dreams and reported that "An enormous number of these dealt, in a more or less veiled fashion, with the death of the girl's mother; now she was present at the funeral of an old woman, now she saw herself and her sister sitting at a table, dressed in mourning; the meaning of the dream could not be doubted."[8] These dreams took place after the dreamer has given every indication of present hostility toward the mother. They therefore present us with difficulties on two counts. In the first place they do not appear to have been transplanted from childhood. There are indications that the dreamer was mature in the dreams, that she was mature when present at the funeral of the old woman, and also when she was at the table dressed in mourning. A more serious difficulty attaches to the fact that the dreamer had an undoubted antipathy toward the mother at the time of the dreams so that the dreams actually expressed an adult attitude. Why should this happen if infantile death-wishes have their own built-in "repetition compulsion?"

A third case of infantile death-wishes has to do with a young man suffering from obsessional neurosis. The basis of his obsessive, murderous impulses was in his relations to his father. These impulses ". . . he had consciously expressed . . ." when he was seven years old, "but they had, of course, originated in a much earlier period of his childhood. After the painful illness and death of his father, when the young man was in his thirty-first year, the obsessive reproach made its appearance, which transferred itself to a stranger in the form of his phobia. Anyone capable of wishing to push his own father from a mountain-top into an abyss cannot be trusted to spare the lives of persons less closely related to him; he therefore does well to lock himself into his room."[9] Here Freud took a radically different view than in the earlier dreams. We do not find him arguing that the death-wish was innocuous because after all what were mountain peaks to a young child. This death-wish had been virulent from the beginning— although Freud implied that it was probably attached to an earlier wish of childhood—and was transformed into an obsessive reproach when the young man was thirty-one years of age. This death-wish, then, was far more than an idle reproduction. It was cram full of present threat, a threat to the stability of the man himself and to the safety of others. Where did the additional quantum of energy come from that was attached to this death-wish?

Freud overlooked the significant congeniality between some infantile death-wishes and an important aspect of the adult personality. One gets the impression that the death-wish has a contemporary function. This is evident in the following dream. Freud reported that ". . . another dream of a more gloomy character was offered me by a female patient in contradiction of my theory of the wish-dream. This patient, a young girl, began as follows: 'You remember that my sister has now only one boy, Charles. She lost the other one, Otto, while I was still living with her. I like the other little fellow, too, but, of course, not nearly as much as his dead brother. Now I dreamt last night that I saw Charles lying dead before me. He was lying in his little coffin, his hands folded; there were candles all about; and in short, it was just as it was at the time of little Otto's death, which gave me such a shock.' "[10] This young girl, the dreamer, had earlier fallen in love with a man of whom her sister had not approved. Her sister discouraged the relationship. Later, the girl saw the man clandestinely. In the dream this man had returned after a long absence and sat with her by the coffin of Otto. On the day following the dream she was planning to go to a certain concert where her lover would also be present. Freud gave the following interpretation of the dream: "Now if the other boy were to die, the same thing would happen again. You would spend all day with your sister; the Professor [her lover] would certainly come to offer his condolences, and you would see him once more under the same circumstances as before. The dream signifies nothing more than this wish of yours to see him again—a wish against which you are fighting inwardly. I know that you have the ticket for today's concert in your bag. . . . Your dream is a dream of impatience; it has anticipated by several hours the meeting which is to take place today."[11]

In the above dream the death-wish originated at the maturity of the dreamer. The child could not have harbored a wish for the death of Otto or Charles for they were not then born. As Freud said this was a dream of impatience. The dreaming girl employed a death-wish to bring her lover to her. So she not only anticipated the actual assignation but she also arranged it in her dream that she saw her lover under "proper" circumstances and avoided the guilt that might have attached to violating her sister's requests. We know that the girl consciously intended to see her lover and that she was consciously impatient. Therefore we cannot assume that upon going to sleep this impatience descended into the Unconscious. This mental formation would of course be in the Preconscious subsystem of the Conscious. And acting from this level it was able to conjure up a death-wish which would gratify its impatience and allay its feelings of guilt. We have no doubt that this is an adequate explanation of the dream, but it seems to us that the "young girl" was quite as vexatious as she intended to be. There was no primal death-wish here. What death-wish there was was an invention of the Conscious system. And if we admit (and anticipate an obvious objection) that the basic energy here was erotic it is nevertheless true that this erotic energy did not emerge from the Unconscious, but the Conscious.

The following dream gives full point to our criticisms. A lady saw her fifteen-year-old daughter lying dead before her in a box. Upon evidence which we do not need to present here Freud concluded that this box signified the mother's womb. And he stated, "At this stage of the explanation she no longer denied that the picture in the dream actually corresponded with a wish of hers. Like so many other young women, she was by no means happy on finding that she was pregnant, and she had confessed to me more than once the wish that her child might die before its birth; in a fit of anger, following a violent scene with her husband, she had even struck her abdomen with her fists, in order to injure the child within. The dead child was, therefore, really the fulfillment of a wish, but a wish that had been put aside for fifteen years, and it is not surprising that the fulfillment of the wish was no longer recognized after so long an interval."[12]

This lady did not want to have a child. This was a Conscious wish. She told her husband about it. She tried to injure the child. She wished the child dead. Fifteen years later this wish motivated a dream. Again we should notice that the death-wish was the wish of a mature person, not a child of three or younger, and it started not as libido-quantum in the Unconscious, but as a conscious design of the personality. A wish which originates after infancy, is conscious, and yet motivates a dream which occurs after an interval of fifteen years, is far from consistent with the Freudian theory of dreams. It is so far from consistent that Freud returned to the case and suggested a further explanation in a later section of *The Interpretation of Dreams.* Then, he said, "The dream of the dead child in the box . . . contained a wish that had been present fifteen years earlier, and which had at that time been frankly admitted as real. Further—and this, perhaps, is not unimportant from the standpoint of the theory of dreams—a recollection from the dreamer's earliest childhood was at the root of this wish also. When the dreamer was a little child—but exactly when cannot be definitely determined—she heard that her mother, during the pregnancy of which she was the outcome, had fallen into a profound emotional depression, and had passionately wished for the death of the child in her womb. Having herself grown up and become pregnant, she was only following the example set by her mother."[13] This seems to be an attempt to push a death-wish back into the infantile period. However, it is not successful on any count. In the first place we can speculate on the age of a little girl who could understand the fact that her mother had had a "profound emotional depression," and who comprehended well enough the mechanics of pregnancy. We also wonder who undertook to convey to a little girl of three that her mother "passionately wished" her dead! Obviously this must have taken place at a much later period. Leaving this point aside there was no death-wish involved here on the part of the child. The mother had a death-wish and we notice that it was a mature death-wish. It was conveyed to the child but there is no evidence that she had any kind of a wish at all. Later on, in the same circumstances as her mother, she had the same mature death-wish. The similarity of the design does not indicate an infantile death-wish on the part of the child. And if it did we would have to explain the death-wish of the mother. This could be done I suppose by repeating the pattern and assuming that the grandmother harbored a death-wish which was communicated to the mother.

If the reader re-examines the dreams analyzed here he will find they support the following views, (a) a death-wish may be an infantile or a mature death-wish, (b) the motivating wish in the dream may originate as a Conscious wish, (c) the motivating wish of the dreamer may employ the infantile death-wish to "express" itself. This is most clear in the dream having to do with the children, Otto and Charles. Here then we have further evidence that there are strong personality forces other than the forces stemming from the libido-quantum and impressions of early childhood.

More light will be thrown upon this question if we examine the relation of affect, emotion, to the dream. Some dreams involving death-wishes are highly charged with emotion, while others on the contrary are dry and drab. Freud suggested that we must distinguish between these types of dreams. He thought we could ignore the dreams in which the dreamer remains unmoved. ". . . they [such dreams] have no claim to be reckoned as typical. If they are analysed, it is found that they signify something that is not contained in them, that they are intended to mask another wish of some kind."[14] This other wish ". . . which is the real content of the dream, gives no cause for sorrow, and for that reason no sorrow is felt in the dream." From this we conclude that the affect in the dream is connected with the real source of the dream. ". . . the feeling contained in the dream does not belong to the manifest, but to the latent dream-content, and . . . the affective content has remained free from the distortion which has befallen the conceptual content."[15] In dreams where there is considerable emotional feeling, however, the death-wish is more sinister. "These [dreams] signify as their content tells us the wish that the person in question might die. . . ."[16]

Freud explained that infantile death-wishes are less highly charged with affect than we would expect, since the child does not understand the seriousness of death and therefore wishes people dead for relatively little reason. From this we would expect that these death-wish formations coming into our dreams from childhood would not be highly disturbing. Nor would they be highly significant. But it appears that they may get attached to quanta of energy or affect that were not originally so attached. The problem then is, how did this affect become attached to the death-wish and what is its source? In the dream about Otto and Charles the death-wish with reference to Charles meant only that the dreamer wanted to see her lover in some manner that would silence the objections of her sister. The affect attached to the dream was pleasurable. But there was profound affect attached to the dream of the man who proposed to push his father off a cliff. Freud considered that this dream meant that the dreamer might in fact perform acts of similar violence against someone.

It appears likely from the dreams we have considered that the significant affect attached to infantile death-wishes may arise in the Conscious system. When we consider that the Conscious can apparently conjure up a death wish that is not an infantile death wish and employ it in a dream, it would follow that the Conscious energy, investing an infantile death wish, could make it active in a dream. We could then discard the assumption that impressions of early childhood "crave reproduction for their own sake."

Freud preferred to cling to the hypothesis that death-wishes invariably originated in the Unconscious and emerged under their own power. In turn this brought him into trouble with the theory of the censor. If the death-wish and the affect connected with it came from the Unconscious then it should have been subjected to rigid censorship from the censor that Freud assumed to exist between the Preconscious subsystem and the Unconscious. But this did not happen. "These dreams show us the occurrence of a very unusual state of things;" said Freud. "They show us that the dream-thought created by the repressed wish completely escapes the censorship, and is transferred to the dream without alteration."[17] This actually confirms the expectation that these childhood death-wishes may not be repressed at all. Yet, there is some censorship in these dreams, although it is not applied to the death-wish as such. Freud, we remember, found it necessary to assume two censors. The first censor was assumed in order to keep the Unconscious intact with its store of libidinous energies and infantile impressions. In the case of the infantile death-wish we see that this censor does not act. On this evidence we would conclude that there is no censor between the Unconscious and the Preconscious, or, in other words, the Preconscious subsystem and the Unconscious cannot be usefully separated theoretically or empirically. In the class of dreams we have been considering it appears that the infantile death-wish may be unrepressed. It also appears, as in the dream where Otto and Charles were the principal characters, that the affect attached to the death-wish may be unrepressed. Since the dreamer's impatience in that case was basically erotic we would further conclude that there may be erotic currents, or libido-quantum existing unrepressed in the Conscious system. In addition, these unrepressed elements, the impatience and the death-wish, were able to form a very acceptable dream.

Freud's Unconscious does not stay put. The censor that is supposed to keep it in place does not work diligently. Yet there is censorship. So we think of Freud's second censor—the one that reviewed material for its appropriateness in the Conscious subsystem—and we can see that this censor is operating in some of these dreams so as to prevent the conjunction of affect with the infantile death-wish. This affect is a product of adult living, however, and so inconsistent with Freud's infantile bias and commitments that he passed it over as the essential dream-forming factor. Furthermore, it is this affect—the product of interpersonal experience long after childhood—that aroused the censor. The censor did not try to disguise the "innocent" infantile death-wish, but rather to disguise the significance of the quantum of affect that was suddenly attached to it. Again we see that while the arbitrary field of the Unconscious is not holding up, the dynamic field of the "repressed" appears more and more important.

Freud analysed another category of dreams, dreams of nakedness, The analysis is based on his usual assumptions about childhood. "Only in our childhood was there a time when we were seen by our relatives as well as by strange nurses, servants and visitors, in a state of insufficient clothing, and at that time we were not ashamed of our nakedness. In the case of many rather older children it may be observed that being undressed has an exciting effect upon them instead of making them feel ashamed. They laugh, they leap about, slap or thump their own bodies. . . ."[18] In adulthood we find recurrent nakedness-dreams. To explain them Freud refers back to and substantially repeats a previous passage which we also have quoted. ". . . we have already ventured the conjecture," he said, "that the impressions of earliest childhood (from the prehistoric period until about the end of the third year) crave reproduction for their own sake, perhaps without further reference to their content, so that repetition is a wish-fulfillment."[19] He also commented on the structure of adult nakedness-dreams. ". . . the dream of nakedness demands our attention only when shame and embarrassment are felt in it, when one wishes to escape or to hide, and when one feels the strange inhibition of being unable to stir from the spot, and of being utterly powerless to alter the painful situation. . . . The essential point is that one has a painful feeling of shame, and is anxious to hide one's nakedness, usually by means of locomotion, but is absolutely unable to do so. . . .

The persons before whom one is ashamed are almost always strangers, whose faces remain indeterminate. It never happens, in the typical dream, that one is reproved or even noticed on account of the lack of clothing which causes one such embarrassment. On the contrary the people in the dream appear to be quite indifferent; or, as I was able to note in one particularly vivid dream, they have stiff and solemn expressions."[20]

Again it is difficult to reconcile the dream-structure with a simple need for repetition. We may assume that these childhood dreams pass the censor quite as easily as the death-wishes. The *use* of the death-wishes indicated the interest of the secondary ego. Here, the re-shaping of the childhood scene indicates a similar interest. And, in turn, *the work of the secondary ego is censored.* As Freud pointed out: "The substitute for these persons offered by the dream, the 'number of strangers' who take no notice of the spectacle offered them, is precisely the counter-wish to that single intimately known person for whom the exposure was intended."[21] It is perhaps the realization of this fact that led Freud, in the development of his analysis, to disregard the childhood angle and re-emphasize the more "traditional" view that this dream was a routine libidinal one.

These dreams bring up anew the question of the relation between instinct or libido-quantum and object. We have seen that Freud has not assumed a "primal" relation between instinct and object. The Unconscious may be stocked with some primal symbols. But, in general, the aim of the libidinal impulse is tension reduction.

The Meynert model does get some more images into the Unconscious. For the psychic formations—of energy and images—in the primary ego can be held to descend into the Unconscious when the secondary ego develops. In the dreams that we have considered, however, the images are neither infantile nor primal and we must wonder how the energy and the images became associated.

Consider, for instance, how adult objects or images come into a cathectic relation with sexual instincts. For our data we can use the nakedness-dream described by Freud. He spoke of the "single intimately known person for whom the exposure is intended." If we accept his assumption of the boundaries between the Unconscious and the Conscious there is no way in which the libidinous current could cathect the intimately known person. However, if we accept the hypothesis we advanced with relation to death-wishes, then the intimately known person *could be presented to the libidinous current.* In the case of the death-wish we suggested that the affect or energy in the Conscious attached itself to a "free-floating" death wish from the infantile life. In the nakedness-dream the process seems to be similar. We do away with the first censor and again we find another censor which disguises the dream content. It looks more and more as though the essential dynamism is in the Conscious system, and that there is likely to be some kind of conflict there. Freud gave us an intimation of this point of view when he said, "In our dreams it [inhibition] represents to perfection a conflict of the will. . . ."[22] It appears from this analysis that dream dynamics is best seen as a conflict between two aspects of the Conscious system. The repressed sexual aspect of this conflict is seen by Freud as the Unconscious.

Freud tried to restructure the Unconscious to meet such objections as have been suggested. He added an element to his concept, "wish." Referring to the dream process as it is concerned with the wish Freud said, "An essential constituent of this experience is the appearance of a certain percept . . . the memory-image of which is henceforth associated with the memory trace of the excitation arising from the need. Thanks to the established connection, there results, at the next occurrence of this need, a psychic impulse which seeks to revive the memory-image of the former percept, and to re-evoke the former percept itself; that is, it actually seeks to re-establish the situation of the first satisfaction. Such an impulse is what we call a wish; the reappearances of the perception constitute the wish fulfillment, and the full cathexis of the perception, by the excitation springing from the need, constitutes the shortest path to the wish fulfillment."[23]

This introduces us to yet another of Freud's definitions of wishes. The first definition defined the wish as the "current in the apparatus." It was later paired with and contrasted with the ego-wish which was termed an incitement. The early wish was based on the pleasure-pain principle. It was essentially a libidinous wish and was closely related to sexual excitation and libido-quantum. The second kind of wish was one produced out of the Meynert cosmogony. It was a wish to reproduce the impressions of the organism from prehistory up to about the third year. The gratification involved here was in the mere reproduction of these impressions. The present definition of wish starts not with the wish but with the percept, the thing that is relevant to the wish. In most cases the percept would be a sexual percept. In the Hans case it would be Hans's mother. The percept arouses sexual excitation related to somatic need. When the object is no longer present there remains in the mind the remembrance of the object and of the sexual feeling that was associated with it. When the somatic excitation is produced again, when the need re-occurs, the "impulse in the apparatus" tends to call back the memory of the image and then to find the percept or thing that goes with that image so that gratification can be obtained. This movement related to the somatic situation is a "wish."

Freud, then, combined his two former definitions of wish. He retained the current in the apparatus from the first definition and he added the "memory-image" aspect which is derived from the Meynert view. But this definition avoids the limitations in the Meynert view. Freud escaped the constraint of infantilism. The impressions craving reproduction are no longer necessarily those up to the third year. They may be any impressions related to a "satisfaction." Furthermore, this view gives eyes, as it were, to the formerly blind "current in the apparatus." Once the experience of gratification has taken place, the memory of this remains in the mind and later impulses seek out the memory of this experience and also seek to bring about the gratification experience.

This definition probably strikes the reader as entirely reasonable. It was the way little Hans acted. It conforms to the testimony of common sense. *But it breaks down the dichotomy in the Freudian point of view.* This old dichotomy was based on sexualism, infantilism and the Unconscious. When Freud talks of the current joining up with the memory of an act he is giving it free access to what has been formerly confined in the Conscious system. Formerly, the current strived for the cathexis of the image, now the image is attached to the current. Or if it is not attached to the current, the current knows where it wants to go. It seeks to "revive the memory-image." When it seeks to go further than this and guide the organism to satisfaction of the excitation it is taking over the mechanisms of motility in the organism. This all indicates that Freud is not holding the line between the Conscious and the Unconscious. In this instance he is assuming that what were Conscious potentials are now to be attributed to the Unconscious. Formerly, it will be remembered, in his treatment of the Preconscious he placed some of the Unconscious potentials in the Conscious. All this, however, *does not dispose of the requirements for a sentient, experiential, initiating organism which produces the first cathexis between the "current" and the "percept."*

If the secondary ego, or the Conscious system, has the control of motility—and Freud has held that it has—then this area must have presented the object on the first occasion. It is then not at all necessary to assume that the libidinal force must perform all subsequent cathexes. There is no reason to assume that the secondary ego, or the Conscious system, would not maintain its initial interest and add its energy to that of the libidinal force. Freud's definitions of the Unconscious, the libidinal instinct and the Conscious system bound him to the view that object-presentation must first be undertaken by the Conscious system. We have pointed out some of the ways in which he sought to escape from his conclusion. In the meantime, evidence piles up which seems to confirm it. The Conscious system has a "power" that Freud has not reckoned with but which he cannot seem to explain away. We think of all the vicissitudes of the "resistance." And now we think of the interest of the Conscious system in death wishes and dreams of nakedness.

This power of the Conscious system could not be denied, however, so far as it applied to the control of motility. This led Freud to sketch a view that seems inappropriate, applied as it is to the "true psychic reality." He suggested that the wish impulse joined up with the memory image of the previous satisfaction and went no farther. "We may assume," he said, "a primitive state of the psychic apparatus in which this path is actually followed, i.e. in which the wish ends in hallucination. This first psychic activity, therefore, aims at an identity of perception; that is, at a repetition of that perception which is connected with the satisfaction of the need."[24] So the somatic excitation gives rise to an impulse which joins a memory-trace of a satisfaction and thus ends up in an hallucination of gratification. "The establishment of identity of perception by the short regressive path within the apparatus does not produce the same result in another respect as follows upon cathexis of the same perception coming from without. The satisfaction does not occur, and the need continues. . . . In order to attain to more appropriate use of the psychic energy, it becomes necessary to suspend the full regression. . . ."[25]

In this view the normal tendencies of the primitive apparatus, of the sexual impulse, have to be corrected—and by nothing less than the Conscious system. The resistance has a use after all. A sort of inhibition must take place that can guide the organism to satisfaction. "This inhibition," Freud concedes, "as well as the subsequent deflection of the excitation, becomes the task of a second system, which controls voluntary motility. . . ."[26]

By a sort of indirection Freud has advanced the cause of the Conscious system. He has made it the ally of somatic excitation. It is the eyes of the blind impulse. Freud finally stated that the wish-impulse requires the intervention of the Conscious for its satisfaction, ". . . a system whose activity first leads on to the use of motility for purposes remembered in advance."[27]

If the Conscious system is understood to produce an inhibition of hallucination and to guide the impulse to gratification, we can only conclude that the "wish" in the Unconscious is matched by an "incitement" in the Conscious system. In other words, the Conscious system matches the energy of the Unconscious with a supporting energy of its own. Since Freud's analysis of memory-images got him only into postulating normal regressions of the sexual apparatus it would be just as well to assign these memory-images to the Conscious system. It would appear that if this system is "incited" to present the libidinal object to the wish-impulse it also would be interested in presenting to it the libidinal memory-images.

The purport of this analysis, and the analysis of dreams of death wishes and nakedness, seems to be that the Conscious system is by no means to be seen as only a repressive system always trying to make life miserable for the libidinal wishes of the Unconscious. On the contrary, it seems to often be in league with them, sporting with them, and presenting to them suitable objects and images for cathexis. Energy is required for all this. So we have the picture of supporting energy sometimes emanating from the Conscious system and reenforcing the energy of the Unconscious system.

Perhaps this contributes to the solution of another probelm. Freud has repeatedly mentioned "gratifications" that do not actually involve somatic discharge. This was true in the Hans case. Such gratification must be meaningless as applied to the Unconscious wish impulse. But if the incitements of the Conscious system are sometimes added to the energy of the Unconscious wish impulses then *their* gratification could be of quite a different order from sexual somatic discharge.

The analysis in this chapter has demonstrated an amazing mutuality of relations between the Conscious system and the Unconscious system as Freud has defined them. Freud tried to maintain the integrity of the sexual dominance by, in a sense, absorbing part of the Conscious system (the Preconscious) into the Unconscious and by laying claim to some Conscious functions. These attempts, it seems to me, have only emphasized the multiple functions of the Conscious system. If there is to be a movement toward amalgamation it appears that the Conscious system should absorb the Unconscious system.

This would simply mean, of course, that the Unconscious is not a discrete category of process, but rather a type or types of psychic material such as sexual, primal or infantile material. The behavior of this material would include the strength and disposition of the energies associated with it. *But this material would not be theoretically isolated from other aspects of psychic process.* This would appear to be the lesson derived from the influx of all types of material into the Preconscious subsystem.

Freud proposed, however, to maintain the Unconscious process along the established lines even at the risk of positing defective primal mechanisms and arbitrary processes. "The dream," said Freud, "which fulfills its wishes by following the short regressive path, has thereby simply preserved for us a specimen of the primary method of operation of the psychic apparatus, which has been abandoned as inappropriate. What once prevailed in the waking state, when our psychic life was still young and inefficient, seems to have been banished into our nocturnal life. . . . Dreaming is a fragment of the superseded psychic life of the child."

This regressive character of the dream is not consistent with its tendency to attach itself to contemporary material, to the day's residues. To introduce the necessary compensating mechanism Freud assumed that the wish in the dream had a "need" for these residues. He pointed out the "surprising fact" that every dream seems to have a connection with waking impressions, and he concedes that so ". . . we have failed to understand the necessity for this addition to the dream mixture."[28] For the answer he dipped back into the theory of the neuroses. "We . . . then learn," he said, "that an unconscious idea, as such, is quite incapable of entering into the preconscious, and that it can exert influence there only by establishing touch with a harmless idea, already belonging to the preconscious, to which it transfers its intensity, and by which it allows itself to be screened. This is the fact of transference, which furnishes the explanation of so many surprising occurrences in the psychic life of neurotics. . . . If we assume that the same need for transference on the part of the repressed idea, of which we have become aware through the analysis of the neuroses, makes itself felt in dreams also, we can at once explain two of the problems of the dream: that every dream analysis reveals an interweaving of a recent impression, and that this recent element is often of the most indifferent character."[29]

At this time comes a clear light. It is at the end of the study of dreams where Freud seems to reach out for a new start. Referring to the Conscious system, Freud said that when material in the mind attracts the "attention of consciousness" it receives "hypercathexis."[30] The disposition of this energy indicated that it was a kind of mobile force. "A 'neglected' train of thought has received no such cathexis," and the ". . . cathexis has been withdrawn from one that was 'suppressed' or 'rejected.' " Such trains of thought have ". . . been left to their own excitations."[31]

Freud gave us a description of the cathectic powers of consciousness. He said that ". . . perception through our sense organs results in directing an attention-cathexis to the paths along which the incoming sensory excitation diffuses itself; the qualitative excitation of the Ps-system (Preconscious system) serves the mobile quantity in the psychic apparatus as a regulator of its discharge. We may claim the same function for the overlying sense organ of the Cs (Conscious) system. By perceiving new qualities, it furnishes a new contribution for the guidance and suitable distribution of the mobile cathexis-quantities.

By means of perception of pleasure and pain, it influences the course of the cathexes within the psychic apparatus, which otherwise operates unconsciously and by the displacement of quantities."[32] The Conscious system is seen to have even a greater influence than this. "It is probable that the pain-principle first of all regulates the displacement of cathexis automatically, but it is quite possible that consciousness contributes a second and more subtle regulation of these qualities, which may even oppose the first, and perfect the functional capacity of the apparatus, by placing it in a position contrary to its original design, subjecting even that which induces pain to cathexis and to elaboration."[33] This new model does not solve any of the dynamic problems that Freud has faced, but it presents a new framework within which to seek for their solution.

In our next chapter we shall sum up the stages of Freud's theory to the present point. After this, we shall observe the morphology of Freud's theory as he more resolutely attacked the Conscious system. (*The Interpretation of Dreams* has often been hailed as representing settled theory. We think that it represented an opportunity for Freud to test his psychoanalytic theory against the dynamism of the normal mind. This theory was found wanting and thus *The Interpretation of Dreams* served as a goad to drive Freud to more adequate models of personality process.)

Chapter VII

FREUD'S

EARLY THEORETIC

MODELS

FREUD'S DEFINITION of his concepts varied with time and place. A concept such as "libido" meant something quite different when it was "libido-quantum" or "ego-libido" from what it did later when Freud developed the view of the "libidinal cathexis of the ego." The student of Freud must accustom himself to the fact that concepts for Freud were static points erected over a moving flood of thought. The concepts gave him points of vantage and the basis for carefully selected simplifications. But the essential concern was this moving sea of thought. As time went on this fluid base changed in direction, contour, volume. In many, many instances the static vantage points remained fixed above the flood, but now they marked out something different from what they had before. The concept "libido" is perhaps our best example. As "libido-quantum" it was the direct representative of sexual, somatic energy. But the "libido" that cathects the ego is not the direct representative of sexual somatic energy. If we neglect to delimit the concept by the events on which it progressively bears we may think of "libido" as always "sexual." It is not. A further change, of course, take place in the hypothesis of the cathexis of the ego-ideal.

Freud was engaged from the beginning on the quest for a set of interrelated concepts that could be made to work together. This meant that the concepts had to be in some sense on the same level. They had to have relations to each other. It would be conceivable, for example,

99

that a person might try to "explain" the processes of personality by means of the central concept of "mana." Other concepts would then have to be related to this central concept. Freud took as his earliest key concept that of "somatic excitation." Here, especially in gross sexual manifestations in the male, was something scientifically tangible and observable. It appeared very early in Freud's work that many phenomena in the "mind" were related to these sexual manifestations. Freud was therefore encouraged to devise a series of organic concepts. These organic concepts would "explain" mental phenomena. At first it seemed that a simple set of such concepts would suffice. Or perhaps it would be more accurate to say that Freud purposely constructed a simplified system of concepts with the hope and expectation that more complicated concepts of the same general type could gradually be devised. An excellent example of these early analyses is Freud's views on hysteria and anxiety.

The difficulties that developed were probably rather different than Freud had expected. He had anticipated, perhaps, that he could explain more and more complicated mental events by the discovery of more and more complicated somatic events. An example of this attempt can be seen in the "thirteen cases of hysteria" where somatic sexual injury was thought to be the "cause" of that "resistance" that bulked so large in hysteria. That attempt ended in failure.

It became necessary then to construct concepts that had to do directly with mental proceedings. This course, as we have seen, involved a very slow emancipation from the idea of somatic causation as being sufficient causation. Our study of the Unconscious has shown that Freud laboriously struggled to create concepts that would identify mental proceedings with physical proceedings, and most of all, sexual proceedings. Yet, even while this struggle continued, Freud was minutely observing the complex operations of the mind. His study of dreams is a masterpiece of such observation. This study invited him to the formulation of more and more concepts. But there were not enough somatic manifestations to match the wealth of mental events. Yet to Freud it must have seemed that mental events would certainly be most illusory and elusive, unpredictable and unscientific, unless these mental events were tied to somatic events. Yet these somatic events were not, in any real sense, observable.

He pushed forward to the analysis, not only of the Unconscious, but of the Conscious. He did not, however, put somatic events out of his mind. He made two related assumptions about mental processes that gave an aspect of legitimacy to his work. In the first place he assumed that mental processes could be "reduced" to somatic processes and mainly sexual somatic processes. However, his interest was not in

precisely how this could be done. Freud devised a long string of concepts of organic relevance that carried with it the imputation of organic
reducibility. Ego "instincts" will serve as an example. These organic
concepts tended to obscure the fact that Freud was really trying to set
up a system of related concepts that would reflect mental events. In
the second place, Freud made *assumptions* about somatic conditions
that would fit with his observations of mental events. He felt compelled to retain his concepts of organic relevance. In some instances,
where the mental events did not have apparent "reducibility" he assumed somatic events that they could be reduced to. A good example of
this kind of assumption is in the concept of erotogenicity. We should
not fail to observe that something of major importance has happened
here. In his earlier thinking Freud accepted the somatic system as the
crucial system. His observations about it were to explain mental events.
In the case of erotogenicity he has done a complete turnabout. He has
taken the mental events as the crucial factors and on the basis of these
mental events he has assumed certain things about somatic events
that did not arise out of observation and experiment and which cannot
be confirmed by them.

These devices of reduction and somatic mechanism were not idly
employed by Freud. Without doubt the system of somatic or physical
causation was viewed by him as the most legitimate, as, in the last
analysis, the "real" system of causation. It was important then that
concepts about mental behavior be readily reducible. In some instances
it was important that assumptions of actual somatic events be made.
Even if these assumptions could not be confirmed they might be confirmed at some later date. However, it should be seen that assumptions
about reducibility and assumptions about somatic mechanisms became
post facto developments. The events observed were mental events and
the concepts devised had regard for these mental events.

These considerations point to the essential duality in Freudian
analysis. Mental events are "explained" by an evolving system of
"biological" concepts. Because of Freud's basic confidence in somatic
causation his biological concepts tend to impart a biological bias to
this thinking. We have seen examples of this in Freud's analysis of
dreams. The significance of this procedure is that Freud binds himself
to biological-type processes when, in fact, he has cast himself loose from
the true biological frame of reference. As a result Freud sketched
strange biological processes. We find "instincts" that seem to work
against the individual interest, and that are strangely complex and
devious. We find the assumption of primal instinctive processes that are
"defective." These tendencies slowed the progress of Freud's thought.
They not only slowed the progress of his thought but they also made it

difficult for him to recognize the importance of social experience in the personality development of the individual. We have already seen, in part, that when the importance of this kind of experience was seen it was subjected to reductionism and biologism just as were other mental events. It is precisely where the social experience of the individual most influences him that Freud is pressed into the assumption of extravagant processes. It was the genius of Freud to make major contributions to our understanding of the affect of social experience on personality. But for the most part these contributions have been hidden under the assumption of biological processes which imputed a biological frame of reference.

Let us review what our investigation has shown us to date.

PHASE 1.

The earliest form of Freud's thought assumed a simple relation between physical and mental events. Somatic excitation led directly to mental events which in turn led directly to action on the part of the organism. The emphasis was placed upon physical symptomology both at the level of cause and at the level of cure. Speech, as a physical exercise, was seen as a discharge agent for excitations. Mental events indicated physiological states, and were superseded by other (normal) mental events when the physiological system was properly treated through the abreactive process. There was little or no elaboration of somatic causation and cure or of mental dynamics. This phase of Freud's thought owed, of course, a great deal to Breuer. It is the frame of reference that Freud and Breuer tended to have in common.

PHASE 2.

This stage represents Freud's emphasis on sexual energy as the basic "force" in mental dynamics. It also represents, therefore, the time of his disagreement with Breuer. Somatic excitation is still the crucial element but now the sexual element in somatic excitation is isolated and termed libido-quantum. This libido-quantum has its representative in the mind in the form of ego-libido. This ego-libido, in turn, brings about discharge of the somatic excitation through "adequate action." Such a model as this strongly suggests sexual discharge as a cure for mental ills and Freud has been roundly condemned ever since for being the devil's advocate. This model did not stand up under rigorous testing and later models were not as open to criticism on this basis. But Freud's use of the term "libido" to cover a number of unrelated processes concealed from his critics and perhaps partially from himself the degree to which he later escaped from this old panacea of promiscuity.

This phase of Freudian thought also suggests close links between somatic process and mental process. The idea of a fortuitous parallel between these processes has been superseded by the concepts of "libido-quantum" and "ego-libido." These concepts support the view that there is a traceable relation between somatic excitation and mental events. There is a flow of energy from somatic excitation (libido-quantum), which is closely related to the flow of energy on the mental side (ego-libido). It is probable that Freud hoped to measure this flow on the somatic side, in the form of sexual excitation, and to calculate its results on the mental side. The process would have consisted of the correlation of mental events with somatic, sexual quantities. Perhaps, from this point of view, the introduction of libido dynamics later in Freud's thinking was an instance of "cultural lag." If the model outlined here had been sufficient a quantitative psychology would have been possible. By the time Freud had reached the stage of libido theory he had lost touch with somatic causation and was left with no quantities to measure. The first and perennial problem upsetting the quantitative approach was that of "resistance." The recognition of this factor brings us to the next stage of Freudian thought.

PHASE 3.

In this phase the "resistance of the subcortical conduction" introduces a major change. Libido-quantum is no longer translated directly into ego-libido. Some portion of it may be shunted off from the mind and expend itself as anxiety. On the other hand, libido-quantum might pass through the resistance and transform itself into ego-libido. This ego-libido might be properly discharged by the adequate action of the organism or it might lead to neurasthenia. Hysteria and compulsion neurosis were thought to be caused by some characteristic of the resistance itself.

This model of the psychosomatic process proved helpful in visualizing a possible way in which the neuroses might differ but it also raised questions. What really, for instance, was this "resistance of the subcortical conduction"? Freud seemed to see it as a physiological process, but what controls the variations in this process? And what now is the relation between libido-quantum and ego-libido? Before the introduction of the "resistance" the relationship was equivalence. This in itself was mysterious enough. But the relation promised to be stable when fully explained. And it was to be assumed, in the old models, that libido-quantum was the sole cause of ego-libido and therefore controlled its manifestations in the mind. This hopeful situation is quite destroyed by the innovation of resistance. Thus the baffling question—what is the source of ego-libido and what controls its dynamics?

PHASE 4.

If it should be possible to say in what precise manner the resistance acted upon libido-quantum it would also be possible to predict what quantities, under various circumstances, of libido-quantum would be available in the mind in the form of ego-libido. Simpler quantifying models had not worked but possibly this more complex model would work. Freud hypothesized that early sexual "injury" caused the later resistance to libido-quantum. This might furnish us a measure of the later resistance. Ego-libido would then be equivalent to sexual somatic excitation except as deflected by varying quantities of resistance. And the amount of this resistance would be determined by the amount of early sexual "injury."

This theoretical position was founded on certain empirical findings which proved in time to be unreliable. For a time Freud felt that this early sexual injury was enormously common. He flirted with the idea that this type of neurotic effect could be posited as a general principle of personality. This is not the last time that Freud suggested the universality of a neurotic or defective tendency in human behavior. But this one succumbed along with the findings in the "thirteen cases of hysteria."

PHASE 5.

We have seen that the introduction of the resistance destroyed the one-to-one relation between libido-quantum and ego-libido. Attempts to restore it failed. It was now clear that profound influences were exerted within the mind that could not be easily reduced to somatic process. Libido-quantum had outlived its usefulness.

At the same time Freud was convinced that somatic process, especially sexual process, had a profound effect on the mind. But it was necessary to have a more elastic concept than libido-quantum. And it was necessary to meet those perplexing mental events on their own ground, so to speak. Considerations such as these led Freud to the use of the concept, Unconscious. The Unconscious is a mental concept. But there is an osmosis-type interplay between somatic process and the Unconscious. And the resistance which formerly was seen as acting at the edge of the mind, so to speak, and fending off somatic threats, is now seen as acting within the mind between the Unconscious and the ego-libido. The formulation of the Unconscious is, of course, one of

Freud's great contributions to personality theory. The model—ego-libido, resistance, Unconscious—sets the style for all the models to follow.

PHASE 6.

In this phase Freud considered the nature of the resistance and the ego-libido. The Meynert theory of the primary and secondary ego comes in handy. The Unconscious is seen as basically the primary ego. The ego-libido and the resistance derive from the secondary ego.

This period of Freud's thought is significant. Many of the subsequent changes in his point of view are due to certain characteristics of this stage. Let us list some of the advantages and disadvantages of this model from Freud's point of view. First the advantages:

a) The secondary ego gives an organic explanation of the resistance and the ego-libido. It thus fits Freud's "frame of reference."

b) The secondary ego, being organic in nature, is relatively static and predictable. It therefore can be looked upon as a more or less universal "condition" in mental behavior. This again made possible the quantitative analysis that Freud sought to undertake. For if the secondary ego was a predictable maturation factor which acted as a universal obstacle course, then the sexual somatic excitation acting through the libido-quantum and the Unconscious became the significant variable.

c) The secondary ego, being a maturation factor, did not imply a superior "repressing" power in the secondary ego. This made it possible to hold to the position that the Unconscious possessed the dominant energy with reference to mobility and power.

The disadvantage:

The Meynert overlay turned the Unconscious into a heterogeneous area. It confined in the primary personality the whole childhood personality. It thus required Freud to accept a multitude of motivations in the Unconscious. Organic tensions, other than sexual tensions, fell into the Unconscious. Thus the "normal" fantasies of young children about taking trips or eating pie belonged in this area. This amounted to a serious watering of the sexualism of the Unconscious.

PHASE 7.

This phase represents a substantial elaboration of the earlier model. Freud's analysis of dreams led him gradually to furnish the Conscious-Preconscious system with something more than "morality" and "resistance." Up to now this "higher" system was static and bleak. Morality and resistance were organic developments but other organic developments and primal endowments were in the Unconscious where their admixture produced a kind of Tower of Babel. The dream process demonstrated, however, that the forces aligned against each other were not as unequal as this. A number of powers and functions existed in the Conscious-Preconscious system. Freud therefore filled out his two categories, the Conscious-Preconscious, and the Unconscious, in the manner indicated in Figure 1.

The elaboration affected energies, endowments and tendencies. There were two primal energies, egoism and sexualism, both in the Unconscious. Sexualism rose and fell with the quantity of sexual excitation which appeared to have close contact with the Unconscious. Egoism was not related to somatic process in this manner. Its possible quantitative fluctuations are not discussed. It appears to be pretty much of a primal constant. Endowments show a substantial increase. By endowments I am referring to universal mental elements that are assumed to perform specialized functions. In the Unconscious they consist of things like symbolism, judgment, fantasies, impressions craving reproduction, etc. The Conscious system is not quite so fortunate in its native endowments but it does have censorship, elaboration, and "incitements."

There are three dominant trends in the Unconscious. There is the trend associated with childhood impressions. They "crave" reproduction. Then there is a trend associated with Unconscious death-wishes. They flow into the Conscious-Preconscious system without encountering the censor. Lastly, there is the major trend of the Unconscious "wishes" toward cathecting ideas in the Conscious-Preconscious system and struggling to control the mechanisms of motility.

In the Conscious-Preconscious system a dominant trend is the censorship or repression and the elaboration and disguise of material entering the Conscious-Preconscious from the Unconscious. A second important trend is in the direction of "ideal masochism," the wish to create anxiety and feel pain. It should be noticed that the Conscious-Preconscious system has not been powered as has the Unconscious. The major energy sources are held to be in the Unconscious and yet large amounts of energy must be in the Conscious system also. Their sources are not indicated as yet. This problem has been left in abeyance since the failure of various attempts at explanation.

Figure 1 represents Freud's topology of personality at what we would term the end of his first period. He has now completed the inventory of the Unconscious and the Conscious. And he has also largely completed his analysis of the dynamics of the Unconscious. This first period has been devoted to an exploration of the possibilities of biological reductionism. The most compelling element has been sexualism. Attempts to theorize, consistently with the continual input of clinical data, have led Freud to more and more complicated models.

The end of the first major period in Freudian thought sees Freud picturing the Conscious as a static obstacle course for the dominant and dynamic Unconscious. (The suggestion of "hypercathexis" at the end of this period indicates a change in this view.) Biological conceptualization has really given way to psychological conceptualization but biological reduction remains a dominant interest. It should be kept in mind that the biological flavor of the Freudian concepts at this time are not dictated by the demands of the clinical evidence but by Freud's preference for "reduction." The functions of these concepts, however, the part they play in picturing personality process, are suggested by the requirements of the clinical data.

As we proceed to the second major period in Freud's development let us bear in mind the principal stresses in his thought. First and foremost is the problem of rigidity. In the Conscious-Preconscious he has endeavored to tie processes down to a narrow, mechanical specificity. The clinical evidence, particularly in dreams, has indicated that the Conscious-Preconscious is a fluent, changeable system, sometimes most catholic in its tastes, sometimes most exacting. It appears that Freud must recognize the energy potential and the integrated action of the Conscious-Preconscious, or secondary ego.

Next, we observe that Freud has no explanation which has proved satisfactory for the energy in the secondary ego. Until we know more about the energy of this system, its sources and uses, we cannot understand its relation to the Unconscious.

Finally, there is the momentous problem whether the Unconscious can survive at all as a significant and isolable category of mental process.

There are two basic hypotheses that are suggested by our study to this point. *Hypothesis 1.* A major element in the formation of the Conscious-Preconscious system is the effect of interpersonal relations upon the individual personality. There are obvious corollaries that attach to this. If we assume the hypothesis to be true then a major field for investigation is *the structure of the social situation in which the individual lives,* for this social situation must be an important causative factor in the content of the Conscious system. *Hypothesis 2.* If we are to make a distinction between the Conscious and the Unconscious along the lines that Freud has done we must allocate the dominant energy to the Conscious system rather than to the Unconscious system. This hypothesis is suggested from the obstacles Freud has found in assuming the opposite position, and from the nature of the clinical data itself. *We can reconcile some of Freud's theory and at the same time conform more adequately to his own data by this assumption.* This suggestion was made in the Hans case, and it seemed to us to be a theoretical necessity in the explanation of dream-process. Yet this reversal of a classical position cannot be lightly conceded. In the next section we will implement this view from Freud's theory and his clinical data.

Part Two

THE STRUCTURE
OF THE MIND

Chapter VIII

ORIGINS OF

LIBIDO THEORY

FREUD HAD LONG considered that "ego" forces were theoretically less significant than they appeared at first glance. It would be Quixotic to tilt with them, he thought. But in "Instincts and Their Vicissitudes" (1915), and "On Narcissism" (1914), we find Freud suggesting the existence of "ego-instincts." This is a startling turn of events for a person who, but a few short years before, considered that the ego, the resistance, was the result of damage to the sexual apparatus. We know that the concept "instinct" has not been applied by Freud to minor processes in personality. The concept "ego-instincts" therefore gives us an indication that at long last Freud is prepared to grant the devil his due. The ego has usurped too much power to escape recognition and analysis. At the same time we shall find this early analysis by Freud eminently unsatisfactory. We shall be struck by the tenacity with which he lumped together theoretically distinctive variables in the interest of "libido theory." We shall marvel at his dedication to most any kind of reductionism, and to phylogenetic mechanisms that are conjured up in the interest of theoretical consistency. The machinery of thought creaks indeed. Yet behind this machinery we can sense that Freud's attention is being directed to important data and processes. Later, these data and processes may generate more adequate concepts.

We can see from the use of the term "ego-instincts" that Freud is prepared to "reduce" the ego to somatic processes just as he reduced the Unconscious. This is the period in which he pushed libido theory to its furthest extent. The first step is to pick up the help that is available

111

from Meynert. The effects of "shame and loathing" were observable as for instance in the Hans case. Their existence must be forthrightly recognized. "The sexual instinct," said Freud, "has to struggle against certain psychic forces, resistances, among which shame and loathing are most prominent. We may presume that these forces are employed to restrict the instinct to the accepted normal limits, and as they have developed in the individual before the sexual instinct has attained its full strength, it is really they which have directed its course of development."[1] There must, however, be some kind of organic base for these forces. Freud was of the opinion that ". . . the restricting forces of sexual evolution—disgust, shame, morality—must . . . be looked upon as historical precipitates of the outer inhibitions which the sexual instinct experienced in the psychogenesis of humanity. One can observe that they appear during the development of the individual as if they were spontaneously at the call of education and other influences."[2]

If Freud has not been able to explain these developments by the experiences of contemporary children, it is doubtful if he can be more successful by attaching the explanation to long gone generations of children whose experiences are assumed to have become phylogenetically decisive. Freud stressed the organic basis of the "moral" tendencies at latency. "It is during this period of total or at least partial latency that the psychic forces develop which later act as inhibitions on the sexual life and narrow its direction like dams. These psychic forces are loathing, shame, and moral and aesthetic ideal demands. We may gain the impression that the erection of these dams in the civilized child is the work of education; and surely education contributes to it. In reality, however, this development is organically determined and can occasionally be produced without the help of education. Indeed, education remains properly within its assigned domain if it strictly follows the path laid out by the organic, and only imprints it somewhat cleaner and deeper."[3]

If we are to have a full-blown "libidinal" theory of the ego we must go considerably farther than this. There is one important consideration that stands in the way of Freud's further progress. In his "Three Contributions to a Theory of Sexuality" (1905), Freud stated that libido is distinguished ". . . from the energy which is at the basis of the psychic processes in general so far as their special origin is concerned, and we thus attribute to it also a qualitative character. In separating libidinal from other psychic energy, we give expression to the assumption that the sexual processes of the organism are differentiated from the nutritional processes through a special chemism."[4] But when Freud came to the study of the ego-instincts he reversed this view of libido. "Are we to suppose," he stated, "that the different instincts which operate upon the mind but of which the origin is somatic are also distinguished by different qualities and act in the mental life in a manner qualitatively different? This supposition does not seem to be justified; we are much more likely to find the simpler assumption sufficient— namely, that the instincts are all qualitatively alike and owe the effect they produce only to the quantities of excitation accompanying them or perhaps further to certain functions of this quantity. The difference in the mental effects produced by the different instincts may be traced to their sources."[5]

Remembering the willingness that Freud has shown to invent concepts and multiply processes, we must wonder at this pious strain for simplicity in this case. There was no such strain when Freud talked of the "primal regression" and later the "need for transference" in dream processes. These earlier complexities were used to support a stubbornly held view and the same is true of this sudden simplicity. Freud proposed to "libidinize" the ego. He was attaching a kind of libido to "shame and loathing" by deriving them from "primordial" sexual inhibition. But clearly the energy attached to these moral reactions was far removed from libido-quantum. Confident of his "sources" and hoping to prove his "effects" Freud was faced with the alternative of recognizing different qualitative aspects of libidinal energy or of reversing an earlier position and maintaining that there was no qualitative difference between psychic energies after all. The first alternative would require Freud to identify energies by these qualities and *in the ego* this would be impossible. The second alternative not only freed Freud from this embarrassment but made it possible to assign energy quanta and types to ego processes without empirical confirmation. Ego energy was now completely at the beck and call of theory—or perhaps it would be better to say of assumption. Its libidinal source was in a primal past and its "quality" was the same as other energy qualities. How then will Freud be able to identify and allocate this energy?

Freud assumed that there was a "primary cathexis of the ego" by libido and this of course "libidinized" the ego. Was this libidinal rite sufficient? ". . . if we concede to the ego," he said, "a primary cathexis of libido, why is there any necessity for further distinguishing a sexual libido from a nonsexual energy pertaining to the ego-instincts? Would not the assumption of a uniform mental energy save us all the difficulties of differentiating the energy of the ego-instincts from ego-libido, and ego-libido from object-libido?" This is a candid question. But it would have been more candid if Freud had frankly stated that any assumption of sexualism at all was based purely on unsupported conjecture, and that he had been compelled to give up earlier ideas about libido in order to put forth even these conjectures, tenuous as they were. Freud's answer was curious, ". . . it is impossible to suppose that a unity comparable to the ego can exist in the individual from the very start; the ego has to develop. But the auto-erotic instincts are primordial; so there must be something added to auto-eroticism—some new operation in the mind—in order that narcissism may come into being."[6] The auto-erotic instinct, which we assume is old-fashioned libido-quantum, cathected the ego and produced narcissism. This is a curious "sexual" object for libido-quantum and shows that "egoism" had a strong counter-influence on the "auto-erotic" instincts. Even the time sequence appears doubtful. Freud and Meynert considered egoism about as primal as you can get. However, in narcissism, Freud was transplanting Meynert's egoism—which was in the *primary* ego—from the Unconscious into the ego.

These assumptions, then, are fanciful at best. But they are of immense practical value to Freud. He has, in this manner, prepared the stage for his own grand entrance. By libidinizing the ego through assumption and conjecture he has "legitimized" the area for further study. And the nebulous quality of these assumptions has a certain advantage. It is clear in advance that Freud can use them to explain nearly any kind of process that he finds in the ego. Thus, in a very important way, his hands are freed for a careful analysis of ego processes.

Freud assumed not only that the sexual instincts were prior to the ego—to cathect it—but also subsequent to the ego—to lean upon it." At their first appearance," said Freud, "the sexual instincts . . . support themselves upon the instincts of self-preservation." From this support the sexual instincts ". . . only gradually detach themselves. . . ." In their life cycle the sexual instincts are much influenced by the ego-instincts. ". . . in their choice of object also they [the sexual instincts] follow paths indicated by the ego-instincts. Some of them remain throughout life associated with these latter and furnish them with libidinal components, which with normal functioning easily escape notice and are clearly recognizable only when disease is present. They have this distinctive characteristic—that they have in a high degree the capacity to act vicariously—and that they can readily change their objects. In consequence of the last-mentioned properties they are capable of activities widely removed from their original modes of attaining their aims (sublimation)."[7]

Here we find "sexual instincts" which have no certain somatic base, no qualitative difference in energy and no characteristic aims. If we assumed merely a general ego-energy we could grant to it as a "normal" aim the power to act vicariously. But since Freud assumed a libidinal energy he must perforce "correct" the "normal" purport of this energy by noting that it acts differently from the usual sexual energy. Sublimation, in this aspect, is the assignment of "defective" action to sexual energy.

Freud made clear that this model was based largely on his convictions about biological processes and their effects on the mind and in so doing he confirmed an approach that he had used from the beginning. He said, "Just because I try in general to keep apart from psychology everything that is not strictly within its scope, even biological thought, I wish at this point expressly to admit that the hypothesis of separate ego-instincts and sexual instincts (that is to say, the libido-theory) rests scarcely at all upon a psychological basis, but is essentially supported upon the facts of biology. It may be, then that—when we penetrate deepest and furthest—sexual energy, the libido, will be found to be only the product of a differentiation in the energy at work generally in the mind."[8]

Freud then tested this model in a dynamic context. He started by the consideration of physical pain. ". . . a person suffering organic pain and discomfort relinquishes his interest in the things of the outside world, in so far as they do not concern his suffering. Closer observation teaches us that at the same time he withdraws libidinal interest from his love-objects; so long as he suffers he ceases to love. . . . We should then say: the sick man withdraws his libidinal cathexes back upon his own ego, and sends them forth again when he recovers. . . ."

A somewhat different description of this process could be made in terms of concepts suggested by Freud before he libidinized the ego by fiat. In his earlier discussion of energies in the ego he distinguished between Unconscious energy, energy of sensation, energy of psychic formations and energy of the ego. Pain would be a sensation equipped with its own energy. A large amount of this energy would attract the "attention" (Freud has granted theoretical importance to this "faculty" of Consciousness) of the ego resulting in a redistribution of psychic energy. We would expect a person in these circumstances to relinquish interest "in the things of the outside world" as a result of this redistribution of energy. The withdrawal of interest in "love-objects" would be a part of this larger event. We can see how the commitment resulting from the "facts of biology" has narrowed the range of events in which Freud has a lively interest.

Freud's use of the word "libido," without indicating the type of libido, has permitted him to join narcissistic libido with sexual libido as though they drew from the same fund of energy. But, even under Freud's model, this can hardly be assumed. Narcissism, which invests the ego, is related to a primal cathexis of the ego and presumably this fact in some manner produces the energy of narcissism and the ego-instincts. In the present discussion, however, the libidinal component of the self-preservative instincts is in question. This component comes from the sexual instincts themselves and would appear to be a discrete and self-contained fund of energy, also. In addition, we might point out at this time that "shame and loathing" also have their private libidinal "cause" in the primal inhibition of the sexual instincts. Freud does not indicate that these typologies are interdependent and indeed it is quite impossible to see how they could be interdependent. It does not appear to be admissible, then, for Freud to borrow energy from sexual object-cathexes to satisfy the increased need for ego-cathexes. This re-deployment of sexual energy requires a great deal of that "vicarious" behavior that Freud has attributed to the sexual instincts.

Freud turned to the consideration of the hypochondriac. The hypochondriac exhibited variations in the distribution of libido. Yet the "distressing sensations" in hypochondria were not based on demonstrable organic changes. But these organic changes must be present. A painful stimulation of the body produces a redistribution of libido. Perhaps this redistribution was automatic on the application of the organic stimulus. Something similar might happen in hypochondria. Perhaps there was something resembling somatic pain at the root of hypochondria. Perhaps somatic pain produced libido.

Freud had already found the sexual instinct to be sufficiently perverse to warrant it being considered even more so. We can see in the following passage how, by considering the sexual somatic process a little more perverse and a little more "vicarious" Freud was able to provide a strong and continuous somatic base for ego-cathexis. "Now the familiar prototype," said Freud, "of an organ sensitive to pain, in some way changed, and yet not diseased in the ordinary sense, is that of the genital organ in a state of excitation. It becomes congested with blood, swollen, moist, and is the seat of manifold sensations. If we apply to that activity of a given bodily area which consists in conveying sexually exciting stimuli to the mind the term erotogenicity, and if we reflect that the conclusions of our theory of sexuality have long accustomed us to the notion that certain other areas of the body—the erotogenic zones—may act as substitutes for the genitals, and behave analagously to them, we then have only one step further to venture here. We can make up our minds to regard erotogenicity as a property common to all organs and are then justified in speaking of an increase or decrease in the degree of it in any given part of the body. It is possible that for every such change in the erotogenicity of the organs there is a parallel change in the libidinal cathexis of the ego."[9]

We are indeed back on old ground. Freud's sophistication has increased remarkably, even if the model has changed hardly at all. He no longer talks of "resistance" or the growth of morality. He talks rather of the distribution of energies and cathexes. As usual he finds that the secret of ego process is hidden in sexual, somatic process.

But libido theory is in truly bad shape. It has come loose at both ends. The time was when Freud had an observable somatic process, sexual excitation. He then tried to trace its effect on the mind. This did not work out. Freud shifted from a primary emphasis on somatic processes to a primary emphasis on mental processes and he tried to work backward. He tried to trace mental events backward to somatic events and primarily to sexual excitation. When time was available he worked on the Meynert overlay. Things went rather poorly in the Unconscious.

But they have not gone at all well with the ego. Freud discerned the significantly different processes of the ego. He "reduced" these to significantly different somatic events, ontogenetic, phylogenetic, and organic. Perhaps it was the very rigid nature of these assumptions that led him to try a different solution. So he was led to the concept of erotogenicity which has the amazing properties of being able to produce theoretically different types of libido for the ego and to produce these types in precisely the "right" amounts. Both of these functions are possible because the libido theory has come loose at the somatic end and refers to practically no observable events. The amount and type of libido produced is determined entirely by Freud's ideas about what the ego requires at any moment.

But libido theory has come loose at the other end too. Formerly Freud felt that he could identify libidinal energy in the mind by its aim, or by the objects toward which the energy was directed. But now it appears we may find libido that is sublimated, or for no obvious reason its aims may become vicarious.

Libido theory has also come loose in the middle. Formerly there was a qualitative aspect to libidinal energy and a special chemism. It could be identified in this manner. But no more. In neither of these respects can it be distinguished from other energies operating in the ego.

Considering the variables that exist in the ego how is it going to be possible to work from erotogenicity to the operation of these variables? How can somatic dominance be established such that the ego variables function in a reasonable manner with reference to each other? Freud produced a kind of pseudo-hydraulic theory. Somehow quantities at the somatic level must produce qualitatively different behaviors at the ego level. A succession of erotogenetic stimulations will increase the amount of libido. How does this effect ego processes? We may think of the ego as something in the nature of a pot or vessel of given "li-bidinal" capacity. Because of erotogenicity the physical organs produce libido which flows into this vessel which we call the ego. When the pressure is sufficient and the quantity great enough the libido will be forced over the top of this vessel, the ego, and will then flow on the outside of it into another one which is large enough to contain the first and which we can call object-cathexes. So, when the ego is filled with libido (resulting from the production of the organs) the surplus will overflow into the other vessel which we have called objects. In this manner sexually stimulating impulses may control the distribution of libido. But the process can only be in one direction and of one type. The ego must first be "filled" with libido. Then the libido can "overflow" and attach itself to objects. In the first process we have ego-cathexis. In the second process we have object-cathexis. Freud had a model of this type in mind. He said, ". . . whence does that necessity arise that urges our mental life to pass on beyond the limits of narcissism and to attach the libido to objects? The answer which could follow from our line of thought would once more be that we are so impelled when the cathexis of the ego with libido exceeds a certain degree. A strong egoism is a protection against diseases, but in the last resort we must begin to love in order that we may not fall ill, and must fall ill if, in consequence of frustration, we cannot love."[10]

The process which Freud developed above repeats the theme of "sexual injury" on the mental side. Here is a picture of somatically caused sexual energy attaching itself first to the ego. At a certain level it overflows onto objects and we "love." If for any reason we do not love when the intensity of the libido reaches a certain degree (a certain quantum really) we shall "fall ill." We are reminded of the "sub-cortical expenditure" of libido-quantum, or the "inadequate action" associated with neurasthenia.

This explanation is hardly convincing and Freud looked for a further reason for the outflow of libido from the ego to objects. He suggested that somehow the quantity of libido in the mind might be transformed into "pain." "Of course," he said, "curiosity will here suggest the question why such a damming-up of libido in the ego should be experienced as 'painful.' There I shall content myself with the answer that 'pain' is in general the expression of increased tension, and thus a quantity of the material event is, here as elsewhere, transformed into the quality of 'pain' in the mind; nevertheless, it may be not the absolute amount of the physical process which is decisive for the development of pain, but rather a certain function of this absolute amount."[11] What is this function of the absolute amount of tension which may be decisive for "pain"? We do not have to alter this picture very much to show how similar it is to another. In earlier thinking Freud remarked that culture and breeding might determine what the sexual constitution accepted as injury. In the present case the implication is that some other factor than pure quantity of libido may be decisive for "pain" in the mind. This other factor will presently reduce to "culture and breeding."

Freud was now ready to embark upon a sophisticated analysis of proceedings in the ego. His three guideposts are, erotogenicity, ego-cathexis and object-cathexis. His quantitative index is libido. The amount of this index is determined by the energy value of a somatic event. The energy value of any somatic event is sexual. The disposition of this energy, libido, consists of a preference for attaching itself to the ego. Upon reaching a certain quantity or pressure point it "overflows" and attaches to objects. If it reaches this pressure point and does not attach to objects for some reason the organism is likely to "fall ill." This is due in part to the raw quantity of libido, and in part to a "certain function" of this quantity.

When the libido attaches to the ego we have the phenomenon that Freud called "narcissism." How are we to understand this process? Freud's clinical work inclined him to the feeling that ". . . a disposition of the libido which must be described as narcissistic might have to be reckoned with . . ." and that ". . . it might claim a place in the regular sexual development of human beings."[12] We would expect sexual energy to be expended in sexual gratification but this universal development convinced Freud that narcissism cannot be considered a perversion, but may be considered ". . . the libidinal complement of the egoism of the instincts of self-preservation, a measure of which may justifiably be attributed to every living creature."[13] At the stage of his thinking that Freud had then reached the "ego" as an organized element in mental process had not taken clear shape. In this passage it seems to us that Freud's attention was directed to the variable, egoism, and that he saw egoism largely through the eyes of Meynert. He was aware that egoism is an independent variable; and he became aware that it should be attached somewhere in the Conscious system. The reader will remember that Meynert attached egoism to the primary ego as a result of which, in Freud's thought, it would fall into the Unconscious. Freud transplanted egoism to the Conscious system and fastened it on to the instincts of self-preservation which he also established in the Conscious system. When he then attached a libidinal component to egoism he was not merely repeating other assertions about the libidinal energy supporting itself on the self-preservative instincts but was putting motive power into egoism, itself.

Freud went on to consider the varieties of object-choice. First, he spoke of the "anaclitic type." This is a "libidinal" type that leans on the self-preservative instincts. Thus a child may take the person who is feeding, caring for and protecting him as a sexual object. Freud called attention to another type. He said that side by side with the anaclitic type we may find ". . . a second type, the existence of which we had not suspected. . . . We have found, especially in persons whose libidinal development has suffered some disturbance, as in perverts and homosexuals, that in the choice of their love-object, they have taken as their model not the mother but their own selves. They are plainly seeking themselves as a love-object and their type of object-choice may be termed narcissistic."[14]

Freud felt that there were fundamental differences between the sexes in respect of types of object-choice. Anaclitic object-love, i.e. libidinal interest based on the instinct of self-preservation, is characteristic of the man. "It displays the marked sexual over-estimation which is doubtless derived from the original narcissism of the child, now transferred to the sexual object."[15] In the beginning, then, there was narcissism. This was related to egoism which in turn was related to the instincts of self-preservation. Later the sexual instinct "grew" and supported itself on the self-preservative instinct. There then developed a sexual object-cathexis, an erotic interest in some person who was caring for or protecting the individual. The early egoism and narcissism were still observable in the high valuation of this person.

The situation with women was somewhat different. "With the development of puberty," said Freud, "the maturing of the female sexual organs, which up till then have been in a condition of latency, seems to bring about an intensification of the original narcissism, and this is unfavorable to the development of a true object-love with its accompanying sexual over-estimation. Strictly speaking such women love only themselves with an intensity comparable to that of the man's love for them. Nor does their need lie in the direction of loving, but of being loved."[16] Freud has often been accused of not doing justice to the ladies and there is certainly some basis for this criticism. The sexual processes of men were his primary concern, although the majority of his patients were certainly women. In the present instance he obviously favored the balance between narcissism and "sexualism" that he believed existed in men. The implication is that women are a bit on the side of "defective" process. They are over-stocked with narcissism. Freud pointed out that perverts and homosexuals are also over-stocked with narcissism and he said that this indicated "some disturbance" in their libidinal development. Freud referred to the development of women as "stunted."

There are some indications here, however, that the hydraulic view of libido dynamics is not working very well. The first qualification in this view is clearly that between men and women. We must assume that the female ego can stand a much higher degree of cathexis than can the male ego. There is a more serious difficulty. Freud pointed out that anaclitic object-cathexes may carry with them some of the narcissism of the child. If this is true anaclitic relations do not necessarily use only surplus libido (after the ego is surfeited) but may actually draw off some of the libido from the ego-cathexis itself. At this point the hydraulic theory breaks down.

In view of the clinical evidence Freud considered that this "draw-off" from the ego was quite possible. He pointed out that if women tend to specialize in narcissism, men may suffer from excessive "draw-off." Men inclined to sexual over-estimation, a state ". . . suggestive of a neurotic compulsion, which is thus traceable to an impoverishment of the ego in respect of libido in favor of the love-object."[17] So the men have their troubles, too.

The "hydraulic" view is a naïve point of view, considering the theoretical sophistication that Freud had gained since his first attempt to trace libido-quantum directly into the mind through the concept of ego-libido. In the present attempt Freud assumed an exceedingly variable organic base and thus could produce untold quantities of libido. And he set up a two-step process in the mind, hoping that the activation of these steps could be related to quantities of libido. It turned out to be far from satisfactory. We must go back, sooner or later, to that other hypothesis that maybe a certain "function" of the quantity holds the secret of ego dynamics.

Freud has lumped together a number of libidinal "qualities" in this discussion and I would like to sort them out for the reader's consideration. The first libidinal quality is the familiar sexual type. A person may sexually cathect any desirable object and it appears from Freud's discussion that protectors are often convenient for this purpose. A second libidinal quality consists of gratefulness or esteem for those who protect us and cater to our needs. This libidinal quality is often attached to protectors also and is related to the fact that the protector reduces the tension of our "self-preservative instincts." The third and fourth libidinal qualities are lumped together by Freud as narcissism. They are self-concern and self-love. Through the cathexis of the ego Freud assumed that these libidinal qualities merged. Analytically these four variables could attach to either "egoism" or the "self-preservative instincts" and then in turn invest objects. Freud selected certain types or combinations for elaboration.

Freud's distinction between narcissistic object-choice and anaclitic object-choice led him to a classification of types of outside interests individuals could have. As he put it, narcissistically a person may love (a) what he is himself, (b) what he once was, (c) what he would like to be, (d) someone who was once part of himself. Anaclitically, a man may love the woman who tends, and the woman may love the man who protects.[18]

Freud cleared the Unconscious of the Meynert primary ego which lingered there for so long. Egoism and the self-preservative instincts are securely lodged in the Conscious system where libidinal applications give them propulsion. In fact, we can see that the libidinal touches to egoism and the self-preservative instincts make possible a dynamism that was lacking in the Meynert view.

With egoism as the base concept it is quite impossible to arrange a world of candid object-cathexes. Egoism only throws the individual back upon himself. His world is the self. Objects are extensions of the self. There can be no *outgoingness*. Yet this very outgoingness is a vital element in personality behavior. The problem is to transform the essential egoism into an outgoing force. In this connection the sexual impulse offers real help. This impulse is "egoistic" to be sure in that it strives to reduce its own tension, not the tension of another. But it is object-oriented in that it strives to discover in the outside world the means of its gratification. And the outside means can be effective (in the case of the usual heterosexual impulse) only if the object is preserved *as itself,* as *other,* and not transformed into an extension of the ego. (This problem of outgoingness, of mastery, remains a problem and Freud returns to consideration of it again and again.) Freud therefore got some much needed help when he applied the sexual impulse to events in the ego to "explain" the object-cathexes that constitute a large part of individual behavior.

Libido was compounded with egoism through the cathexis of the ego. The self-preservative instincts maintained their identity. But, since the early studies, Freud had become aware that protectors might seduce children and that children were likely to have fantasies and "wishes" about seduction by protectors. It appeared that the sexual instincts often made use of self-preservative instincts and behaviors to gratify themselves. It was for this reason, perhaps, that Freud suggested that at the beginning the sexual instincts supported themselves on the self-preservative instincts. While libido theory was a failure as a method of quantitative analysis, it made a marked contribution to the dynamism of Freud's thinking.

Chapter IX

FAILURE OF

LIBIDO THEORY

THE TIME HAD COME for Freud to deal once more with the problem of "culture and breeding." Libido theory opened up to him the possibility of handling this matter without too much of a departure from established points of view. Freud outlined the basic problem as follows, "We have learnt that libidinal impulses are fated to undergo pathogenic repression if they come into conflict with the subject's cultural and ethical ideas. But this we do not ever mean: if the individual in question has a merely intellectual knowledge of the existence of these ideas; we always mean: if he recognizes them as constituting a standard for himself and acknowledges the claims they make upon him."[1] Repression, then, proceeds from the ego, or from the "self-respect of the ego." The source of this self-respect is held to be the subject's cultural and ethical ideas. The interpersonal experiences of the individual contained the potentialities for the mechanism known as repression. These experiences contained "standards" of conduct. As long as they existed outside of the individual they were not directly concerned with repression, but when they were absorbed by the individual, recognized as binding on himself, they did form the basis of repression.

This complex of standards Freud termed the "ego-ideal" and, he said, this ". . . ideal would be the condition of repression."[2] What happened to the distribution of libido? "The narcissism," said Freud, "seems to be now displaced on to this new ideal ego, which, like the infantile ego, deems itself the possessor of all perfections." If, as an individual develops, ". . . he is disturbed by the admonitions of others and his own critical judgment is awakened, he seeks to recover the early perfection, thus wrested from him, in the new form of an ego-ideal. That which he projects ahead of him as his ideal is merely his substitute for the lost narcissism of his childhood—the time when he was his own ideal."[3]

Thus, with considerable grace and ingenuousness, Freud introduced a new factor into his analysis under cover of the libido theory. We have moved of a sudden, from an automatic ego to a selective ego, from an organic ego to a "social" ego. In the concepts, primary cathexis, self-preservative instincts, narcissism, anaclitic and narcissistic object-cathexes, we have been concerned with universal and automatic facets of personality. There was no volition involved in the original ego-cathexis. A person did not elect to establish an anaclitic object-cathexis. These processes were deemed to be the "natural workings" of the ego machine. The ego-ideal, however, is not primordial. It grows out of the social experience of the individual. Individuals can have different ego-ideals. And the nature of this ideal depends in part upon the volitional attitude of the person. He accepts or rejects standards. Presumably, if he were never exposed to social customs he would never develop an ego-ideal. And the kind of ego-ideal he does develop will depend on the complex of customs with which he is in contact. This leads us to the point that this ego-ideal is not only a volitional process, in part, it is also a social process. The ideal is drawn from the standards of society. It had no relation to self-preservative instincts. *It is custom within.*

The effect of the ego-ideal on mental events cannot be described as a mechanical or "hydraulic" process. It differs with the "structure" of the ego-ideal, and the structure of the ego-ideal differs from person to person depending on the total of his "culture and breeding."

All of this constitutes a serious obstacle for libido theory. So long as energy distribution in the mind was looked upon as automatic we would think of the energy, the libido, as the dominant factor. But now the significant factor is the structure of the ego-ideal. We have to think of the energy being distributed *by the ego-ideal.* To speak therefore of energy disposition is meaningless. Since this disposition is no longer automatic, or referable to somatic excitation or phylogenetic mechanisms it becomes vital to discover the factors that *are* causally related to variations in energy dispositions. The inference in the quoted passage is that these variations are related to characteristics of the ego-ideal.

Freud has mentioned the "displacement" of the libido onto the ego-ideal. I think there is a greater theoretical displacement here. I have already referred to two fundamental changes or displacements in Freudian theory. One took place when Freud introduced libido-quantum directly into the mind, thus indicating that the focus of his attention was going to be no longer somatic events but mental events. The second major shift was the "cathexis of the ego." This signalled Freud's determination to recognize the ego or the Conscious as a theoretically significant area of analysis. The cathexis of the ego was merely a device for transporting his theoretical tools directly into the ego. Once he got there, as we have seen, the cathexis of the ego seemed much less important and he began to emphasize the importance of erotogenicity. And here I think is a third major shift. Organic "causes" of ego events have proved inadequate. "Pressure" theories stemming from erotogenicity and flowing through established lines in the ego have likewise proved unsatisfactory. It has become necessary to introduce a whole new theoretical category, the ego-ideal, which can take into account the effects of interpersonal experience on psychic events. Some such concept is long overdue.

But again Freud must carry his tools with him. The genius of Freud is in the degree to which his periodic insights outstripped his "plodding" theory and concepts. One of the problems in the "routinization" of the present insight is to subsume it under the orthodox libido theory. Freud suggested that there is perhaps ". . . a special institution in the mind which performs the task of seeing that narcissistic gratification is secured from the ego-ideal, and that, with this end in view, it constantly watches the real ego and measures it by that ideal."[4] This institution Freud called the conscience. "Large quantities of libido," he said, "which is essentially homosexual are in this way drawn into the formation of the narcissistic ego ideal and find outlet and gratification in maintaining it. . . ."[5] In seeking to assimilate the ego-ideal Freud invented a new libidinal energy, homosexual libido, and assumed that this energy amuses itself in the formation of ego-ideals by means of which it receives its gratification.

How is this component of libido related to the other components? By definition it is not sexual libido in the usual sense. If it is a perverse type of sexual libido as the term suggests, it has no appropriate aim in investing the ego-ideal. Is it perhaps sublimated sexual libido? It does not seem so, for Freud said that "A man who has exchanged his narcissism for the worship of a high ego-ideal has not necessarily on that account succeeded in sublimating his libidinal instincts."[6] On the other hand, this energy cannot be assigned to the type that cathected the ego for this was an egoistic type not given to finding gratifications in objects different from the ego itself. We would conclude that Freud is referring here to a new qualitative type of libido to go with the new theoretical category that he has established.

Freud attempted to assimilate this new type of homosexual libido within the general body of sexual libido. In this way he hoped to bring the ego-ideal itself within the field of libido analysis. The ego-ideal is concerned with "perfection" and the movement of the homosexual libido indicates that it seeks to gratify itself on visions of perfection. Is it possible that, after all, this is nothing very new? The ego has always been centered on itself. It has always been characterized by "self-regard." Is it not merely another aspect of self-regard when a quantum of libido cathects the ego ideal? This is perhaps the way Freud looked at it, but he does not explain how this quantum of energy becomes interested in forming a mental structure *different from the ego* and in gratifying itself upon it.

This was a difficult point. Freud kept hoping that in some manner it could be shown that this homosexual libido was not too much unlike the ordinary type of libido. He suggested that ". . . where the erotic life is concerned, not being loved lowers the self-regarding feelings, while being loved raises them."[7] Freud was trying vainly to tie "self-regard" into a nexus with egoism and sexualism. He was making libido as heterogeneous a concept as the Unconscious. The new element involved in the ego-ideal is self-evaluation. Egoism and narcissism involve self-love and self-concern. But the very suggestion of the term, ego-ideal, indicates that a new principle of behavior has been introduced into the mind which has the function of judgment. And this judgment, this system of self-evaluation, is directed *against* the ego. Is it perhaps because something "abnormal" has happened here, something contrary to established process, that Freud employed the phrase, "homosexual libido"?

Freud's attempts to "reduce" this new quality to former quantities only succeeded in emphasizing the interpersonal aspect of the new idea. ". . . it is easy to observe," he said, "that libidinal object-cathexis does not raise the self-regard. The effect of the dependence upon the loved object is to lower that feeling; the lover is humble. He who loves has, so to speak, forfeited a part of his narcissism, which can only be replaced by his being loved."[8] Freud was trying to master this new quality by the use of an old model. Object-cathexes were frequently made at the cost of ego-cathexis. Therefore, since self-regard was merely an aspect of self-concern, self-regard obviously would decline as a result of libidinal object-cathexis. Freud avoided the question of self-evaluation. He was closer to the problem in the earlier passage where he intimated that not being loved could lower one's evaluation of the self. For this suggested that the ego-ideal is a social product and that therefore the state of self-evaluation is significantly related to the ideas of others about us. Self-evaluation is derived from "other" evaluation and importantly dependent on it.

Freud sought to encompass this whole dynamic situation in terms of libido theory. "The development of the ego," he said, "consists in a departure from the primary narcissism and results in a vigorous attempt to recover it. This departure is brought about by means of the displacement of libido to an ego-ideal *imposed from without* (Italics ours.), while gratification is derived from the attainment of this ideal. At the same time the ego has put forth its libidinal object-cathexes. It becomes impoverished in consequence of these cathexes and of the formation of the ego-ideal, and it enriches itself again both by gratification of its object-love and by fulfilling its ideal."[9] The ego-ideal is established as an object which can be cathected like other objects. It is "imposed from without"—in other words, produced by interpersonal experience. Here is the new theoretical category. It required a complete shift in the dynamics of cathexis. We are familiar with the ego putting forth object-cathexes and depleting itself and then withdrawing these cathexes and acquiring stability again. We quoted two passages having to do with love-objects. In the first passage Freud recognized the new element involved in the ego-ideal and suggested that being loved raised the "self-regarding feelings." In the next passage, however, he was trying to emphasize the old libido theory and he came to the conclusion that "libidinal object-cathexis" lowered the self-regarding feelings. In the passage above he has apparently settled upon a radical amendment to the older libido theory. Object-cathexes do not necessarily lower the self-regarding feelings, *if there is gratification.*

The gratification in the case of the ego-ideal is obviously a measuring up to the evaluation standards of the ego-ideal. And why is gratification now an enriching process in relation to object-love? From Freud's remarks about the lover "being humble" and the effects of not being loved, it is clear that Freud has his eye on the same self-evaluation element here also. The lover is gratified by the love experience which satisfies his standards of self-evaluation. In libido terms, homosexual libido is concerned with the self-evaluation of the ego resulting from the development of a criticizing system known as the ego-ideal. Narcissism and egoism are now not enough. The stability of the ego depends on the "gratification" of this homosexual libido or the satisfaction of the evaluation standards of the ego-ideal. A new and dominant principle of motivation has been introduced into the ego. Furthermore, this same element of self-evaluation has also invested love-objects. In terms of libido theory, then, we would say that homosexual libido also invests some love-objects. And the deprivation that the ego suffers by the withdrawal of ego-cathexes in the service of object-cathexes is more than made up by the gratification of satisfying the homosexual libidinal component, i.e. by receiving favorable treatment from the love-object in terms of one's self-evaluation standards.

Freud described the importance of the ego-ideal. "The ego-ideal is of great importance for the understanding of group psychology. Besides its individual side, this ideal has a social side; it is also the common ideal of a family, a class, or a nation."[10] Here is a concrete extension of that "culture and breeding," that "shame and loathing," which has recurred so often. And it appears that the ego-ideal has shaken itself loose from a primal past and organic limitations. Freud transposed the process into libido terms. "It [the ideal] not only binds the narcissistic libido, but also a considerable amount of the person's homosexual libido, which in this way becomes turned back into the ego."[11] This, I would assume, is intended to point out that when there is satisfaction of the "ideal demands" of the ego-ideal the ego is in a state of equilibrium with regard to self-concern, self-love and self-evaluation.

But what happens when the homosexual libido is not gratified? What happens when the self-evaluation standards of the individual are not fulfilled? Here, in order to keep libido analysis in operation, Freud returned to an earlier view, that of the "subcortical expenditure of libido-quantum." "The dissatisfaction due to the non-fulfillment of this ideal liberates homosexual libido, which is transformed into a sense of guilt (dread of the community). Originally this was a fear of punishment by the parents, or, more correctly, the dread of losing their love; later the parents are replaced by an indefinite number of fellow-men."[12] The libido theory is turning into a white elephant but Freud tried hard to make it work. This is not the first time that Freud has suggested an epiphenomenal approach to ego events. He is suggesting here that the liberation of the homosexual libido is the essential fact and the dread of the community is its attendant epiphenomenon. Thus the whole development of the ego-ideal and the consequent self-judgment associated with it turns into an epiphenomenal process and the fluctuations of libido become the "true" cause. The dissatisfaction with the ego-ideal brings about an automatic kind of mental injury.

If we do not take the view that the events of daily life are a snare and a delusion we must come to the conclusion that Freud's view masks the actual lines of causation. The ego ideal has, at least in part, come from the community and the failure to "live up" to this ideal therefore violates not only the self-evaluation requirements of the individual, but it is likely to violate the expectations and standards of the community. Thus the dread comes from a realistic appraisal of the social environment. Although Freud has erected a barrier between libido theory and the dynamics of social relations the barrier is now thin. As osmosis took place between the Unconscious and somatic processes, *so here it is taking place between the ego and the social environment.* The compulsion to look to the social environment (with reference to the ego-ideal) is all the more inevitable in view of the changes Freud has made in his ideas of energy. Since he has no measureable somatic sources, and since he has no way of distinguishing energies by quality or chemism, *the only observable reference field for the ego-ideal is the social experience of the individual.* It is quite immaterial—in fact, a matter of philosophic taste—whether we look look upon such data as epiphenomenal or not.

We have mentioned the qualities into which libido theory breaks down. We have to add another quality now, that of self-evaluation. Among these variables—erotism, esteem (for others), self-concern, self-love and now self-evaluation—there is only one that has been established as a truly *sexual* quality. However the other variables are obviously active in ego processes; so they must be equipped with varying amounts of energy and their interrelations must be studied.

Freud's analysis of the ego-ideal indicates a further difficulty with libido analysis. In earlier instances of quantitative analysis (as in the case of libido-quantum) Freud felt that the source of the energy, or the quantity, was in somatic processes. Libido-quantum was believed to be a direct reflection of sexual somatic excitation. In the present instance, Freud employs the same model but the control of the energy is no longer in somatic process. The control of the energy is in the ego-ideal. Conscience and the dread of the community proceeds *from the ego-ideal.* When Freud said that homosexual energy, when not gratified by the ego-ideal, turned into dread of the community he was really indicating that the ego-ideal could take punitive action against the ego and that therefore it was capable of mobilizing energy. If we think of the libido as an electric current, the ego-ideal, in this instance, controls the switch. But Freud tried to explain the switchman by the variations in the current. In addition, Freud imagined the current as proceeding in the wrong direction—as proceeding toward the switchman instead of from him. This might be termed an instance of "theory lag." Originally, libido was imagined to issue from sexual somatic excitation and this furnished the clue to the direction of the current. In later thinking the current proceeded in the same direction but it stopped off to invest the ego and it attached itself to the self-preservative instincts. Then, finally, as homosexual libido, it proceeded *to* the investment of the ego-ideal. But in this case it is the ego-ideal that is producing the energy, so the direction of the current should be reversed.

But, no matter how we reverse currents, and no matter how we distinguish various qualities of libido and relate them to the fundamental ego forces and the fundamental self-preservative instincts, Freud has lost the base for libido dynamics. He cannot get at energy sources. Thus libido analysis falls a long way behind his insights. In fact, his insights must be twisted and malformed in order to conform to the formalities of libido analysis. Thus the input into this type of analysis is intuitive and not systematic.

But Freud has outlined three dynamic areas which should be kept in mind. He has pointed out that gross sexual activation is important in mental processes. He has pointed out various events in the mind— egoism, narcissism, cathexis—that indicate important intra-psychic behaviors. And he has indicated the importance for mental adjustment of certain interpersonal experiences that have been absorbed by the individual or internalized. These exterior social events are much easier to observe than the varieties of energy arising from erotogenicity. But to Freud they appear outside his frame of reference. He does not propose to initiate "libidinal" currents *from* them. He will continue the old system. In the following section we shall see how this system worked out upon application to a concrete situation. (We shall see that in a later stage of his thought Freud did "libidinize" the external social situation and derive his "electrical current" from there.)

AN EMPIRICAL TEST
OF LIBIDO THEORY

In "Mourning and Melancholia," published in 1917, Freud analysed these two mental states using libido concepts. I will indicate the course of Freud's analysis and point out how his concepts did not permit him to exploit to the full that basic quality that he termed the "self-respect of the ego." (No expertness in mental illness is claimed here or elsewhere. It is the effectiveness of Freud's theory in terms of the facts he presents that is being considered here.)

"Mourning," said Freud, "is regularly the reaction to the loss of a loved person, or to the loss of some abstraction which has taken the place of one, such as fatherland, liberty, an ideal, and so on. As an effect of the same influence, melancholia instead of a state of grief develops in some people, whom we consequently suspect of a morbid pathological disposition."[13] There are certain distinguishing mental features of melancholia such as painful dejection, loss of interest in the outside world, loss of ability to love . . . and a lowering of the self-regarding feelings to a degree that finds utterance in self-reproaches and self-revilings and culminates in a delusional expectation of punishment."[14] Freud pointed out that the same traits are found in grief except for the fall in self-esteem.

In mourning, Freud said, the testing of reality shows that the loved one no longer exists, therefore all the libido attached formerly to this object has to be withdrawn. "The task is now carried through bit by bit, under great pressure of time and cathectic energy, while all the time the existence of the lost object is continued in the mind. . . . Why this process of carrying out the behest of reality bit by bit . . . should be so extraordinarily painful is not at all easy to explain in terms of mental economics. . . . The fact is, however, that when the work of mourning is completed the ego becomes free and uninhibited again."[15]

We have mentioned earlier that the outgoingness of personality is most difficult to account for in Freud's present view. The more significant this outgoingness is the more perplexing it becomes. Freud was able to take account of some object-cathexes by attaching "sexuality" to egoism and the self-preservative instincts. But emotional fixations that are not reduceable to these factors are enigmas. Furthermore, Freud's "economic" assumptions indicate that the ego is "replenished" when object-cathexes are withdrawn. This reluctance to withdraw object-cathexes even after the death of a person reverses the predicted result under libido theory. (See the later development of Eros. Eros corrected this problem.)

Freud explained that in melancholia the symptoms may be traceable to the loss of an object of love but the patient may not be aware of this. "This would suggest," said Freud, "that melancholia is in some way related to an unconscious loss of a love-object, in contradistinction to mourning, in which there is nothing unconscious about the loss."[16] The melancholiac displays a quality that is lacking in grief, ". . . an extraordinary fall in his self-esteem, an impoverishment of his ego on a grand scale. . . . The patient represents his ego to us as worthless, incapable of any effort and morally despicable; he reproaches himself, vilifies himself and expects to be cast out and chastised. He abases himself before everyone and commiserates his own relatives for being connected with someone so unworthy."[17] This delusional belittling is "predominantly moral." Sometimes this self-criticism is justified. The patient may have come "very near self-knowledge." However, on the whole ". . . a good capable, conscientious woman . . . is more likely to fall ill of the disease" than ". . . a worthless one."[18] The melancholiac's behavior, however, is not just the same as that of one attacked by remorse. "Shame before others, which would characterize this condition above everything, is lacking in him, or at least there is little sign of it. One would almost say that the opposite trait of insistent talking about himself and pleasure in the consequent exposure of himself predominates in the melancholiac."[19] The melancholiac has, then "lost his self-respect" but this presents Freud with a difficulty. From the analogy with grief we should conclude that the loss in the melancholiac is of some object, but, ". . . according to what he says the loss is one in himself."[20]

Freud's insight has struck fire in this comparison between grief and melancholia. In each case an "object" is lost. But while the object is a physical person in the case of grief it must be a certain aspect of a person in the case of melancholia. Since melancholia is intimately related to self-respect it must be this aspect of the object that is important. So the object must have had an important supporting role with reference to the ego-ideal. The object loss in melancholia, then, would be the loss not of the individual as such but of the individual *in this supporting role*. It is apparent that in melancholia this supporting role must be extremely important in sustaining the ego-ideal, for upon the loss of the "object" the ego-ideal turns upon the ego and produces a significant decrease in self-respect. Here then is an "external ego-ideal" that, in the case of melancholia, bears an important relation to the internal ego-ideal. We remember that the ego-ideal is "imposed" from without.

Freud pointed out that these self-accusations of the melancholiac often do not really apply to the patient, but rather to someone else, some person, "whom the patient loves, has loved or ought to love."[21] Often unconsciously, then, the melancholiac accuses the external ego-ideal. This accusation has a realistic basis in the fact that the external ego-ideal did not die but voluntarily withdrew its supporting role from the patient and thereby presented a new dimension for adjustment to the melancholiac that did not apply to grief. The melancholiac must adjust to the adverse judgment implied in the withdrawal of support by the external ego-ideal. This is especially difficult, for the melancholiac has apparently relied on the supportive behavior of the external ego-ideal to maintain his own personality stability.

Freud transposed this into interesting libido terms. First, there was an object-choice. Then the libido was withdrawn to the ego when the object relationship was undermined. "The result was not the normal one of withdrawal of the libido from this object and transference of it to a new one, but something different for which various conditions seem to be necessary. The object-cathexis proved to have little power of resistance, and was abandoned; but the free libido was withdrawn into the ego and not directed to another object. It did not find application there, however, in any one of several possible ways, but served simply to establish an identification of the ego with the abandoned object. Thus the shadow of the object fell upon the ego, so that the latter could henceforth be criticized by a special mental faculty like an object, like the forsaken object. In this way the loss of the object became transformed into a cleavage between the criticising faculty of the ego and the ego altered by the identification."[22] This description furnishes a brilliant example of Freudian exposition. However, the identification must have existed before the "break." For apparently the melancholiac has accepted the external ego-ideal to some degree in place of his own. It is the problem of energy distribution that drives Freud to the contrary view. When the energy is withdrawn from the object there is energy in the ego that must be accounted for under the libido theory. In prior cases energy has expended itself "subcortically" and in "inadequate action" and in giving rise to the "dread of the community." Here it expends itself by forming an identification.

Freud brings out the fact that even in grief there may be a self-evaluation dimension. "The loss of a love-object," he said, "constitutes an excellent opportunity for the ambivalence in love relationships to make itself felt and come to the fore. Consequently where there is a disposition to obsessional neurosis the conflict of ambivalence casts a pathological shade on the grief, forcing it to express itself in the form of self-reproaches, to the effect that the mourner himself is to blame for the loss of the loved one, i.e. desired it." The "pathological" element here implies that the employment of energy in this way is "abnormal" when actually it is reasonably related to the facts of social relationships. Freud sensed that all of that which did not conform to the basic assumptions about energy disposition and allocation was abnormal. In the following passage we see that he has quite left the external situation and buried himself in energy allocations *as though* they were qualitatively distinct and quantitatively measureable. In melancholia, he noted, the occasions for ambivalence extend beyond the case of a loss by death and include situations ". . . of being wounded, hurt, neglected, out of favor, or disappointed, which can import opposite feelings of love and hate into the relationship or reinforce an already existing ambivalence."[23] Then the melancholiac's "erotic cathexis" of the object undergoes a twofold fate, ". . . a part of it regresses to identification, but the other part, under the influence of the conflict of ambivalence, is reduced to the stage of sadism, which is nearer to the conflict."[24] Thus melancholia turns into a rigid disposition of energies. It becomes frozen in pathology. Being so frozen and so assigned to the Unconscious the whole series of ego events and social events that have given the basis for this libido description are viewed as epiphenomenal. The real conflict which is in the Unconscious takes on a different form in the Conscious and ". . . *appears* (a) as a conflict between one part of the ego and its self-criticizing faculty."

Working with this newly "closed" system and cutting himself off from the relevant data Freud finds himself unable to explain "mania." "By analogy with various other situations," said Freud, "we expected to discover in the ambivalence prevailing in melancholia the economic condition for the appearance of mania when the melancholia has run it course. But there is one fact to which our expectations must bow. Of the three conditioning factors in melancholia—loss of the object, ambivalence, and regression of libido into the ego—the first two are found also in the obsessional reproaches arising after the death of loved persons. In these it is indubitably the ambivalence that motivates the conflict, and observations show that after it has run its course nothing in the nature of a triumph or a manic state of mind is left. We are thus directed to the third factor as the only one that can have this effect. That accumulation of cathexis which is first of all 'bound' and then, after termination of the work of melancholia, becomes free and makes mania possible, must be connected with the regression of the libido into narcissism. The conflict in the ego which in melancholia is substituted for the struggle surging around the object, must act like a painful wound which calls out unusually strong anti-cathexes."[25] Previously Freud had told us that the libido that was withdrawn from the "love object" in melancholia regressed into identification. Now he thinks it regresses into narcissism. In any event there is no solution to mania here. A "wound" exists as much in the case of grief as in the case of melancholia. Freud explored the matter further and suggested that the mania associated with melancholia might be economically conditioned like such mental states as joy. It will be noticed that to make this suggestion intelligible Freud resorts to a social situation. "First," he said, "there is always a long-sustained condition of great mental expenditure . . . upon which at last some influence supervenes making it superfluous, so that a volume of energy becomes available or manifold possible applications and ways of discharge—for instance, when some poor devil, by winning a large sum of money, is suddenly relieved from perpetual anxiety about his daily bread. . . ."[26] What is this influence that supervenes? ". . . the ego must have surmounted the loss of the object . . . whereupon the whole amount of anti-cathexis which the painful suffering of melancholia drew from the ego and 'bound' has become available. Besides this, the maniac plainly shows us that he has become free from the object by whom his suffering was caused, for he runs after new object-cathexes like a starving man after bread."[27] This does not tell us much about what happened to "sadism" and "identification." And it does not suggest a tenable distinction between mourning and melancholia. As Freud admitted, ". . . it is easy to say and to write that 'the unconscious (thing-) presentation of the object has been abandoned by the libido.' In reality, however, this presentation is made up of innumerable single impressions (unconscious traces of them), so that this withdrawal of libido is not a process that can be accomplished in a moment, but must certainly be, like grief, one in which progress is slow and gradual. The character of withdrawing the libido bit by bit is therefore to be ascribed alike to mourning and to melancholia; it is probably sustained by the same economic arrangements and serves the same purposes in both."[28]

This is as good an example as any of how Freud cannot make a closed system of libido analysis work. His various descriptions of libido dynamics—and we have mentioned a number of them—are all more or less appropriate to the concrete context but they do not furnish generalizations about the workings of libido. The concrete description of melancholia broke down when the question of mania came up and Freud resorted to earlier ideas of energy allocation which were no more satisfactory. Libido theory requires nourishment from the facts of interpersonal relations and the qualitative distinctions to which they give rise. The "setting" for the libidinal currents is determined by this reference.

Freud, then, has not been able to organize the ego by his libido theory. An energy theory of the ego is doubtless valuable. But Freud assumed an energy that pulsated according to assumed variations of organic input and which in its protean forms produced or was attended by certain psychic manifestations. A satisfactory energy theory of the mind must assume a variety of energy sources such as the body, the ego, the ego-ideal and the "community." Qualities and quantities must be referred to these "sources."

Chapter X

REFORMULATIONS

OF THE

UNCONSCIOUS

WE HAVE POINTED out why we think Freud's "libido theory" did not work. At the same time we hope we have made clear that Freud's insights were at their strongest in his isolation of significant ego variables. Freud, as we know, never really discredited concepts or theories. He may in fact return to them from time to time for limited purposes. In this chapter we will see that Freud, in his development of the dynamics of cathexis, has moved beyond libido theory. And the varieties of ego behavior have suggested the need for further alterations in the Unconscious. We shall be concerned here with Freud's following works: "A Note on the Unconscious in Psychoanalysis" (1912), "On Narcissism: An Introduction" (1914), "Repression" (1915), "The Unconscious" (1915), "Metapsychological Supplement to the Theory of Dreams" (1916).

Freud's work on the Conscious system required a reconsideration of the Unconscious system. The introduction of libido into the ego required an explanation of the differences between the energy in the Unconscious and the energy in the ego (or Conscious system). In addition, the problem of repression again came to the fore. Must the famous triad, infantilism, sexualism and the Unconscious face further limitation?

REPRESSION AND THE INDEX VALUE
OF THE UNCONSCIOUS

Clinical experience with the neuroses and evidence to be gathered from hypnosis pointed to the necessity for assuming the existence of Unconscious ideas that are active in the mind. "The mind of the hysterical patient," says Freud, "is full of active yet unconscious ideas; all her symptoms proceed from such ideas. It is in fact the most striking character of the hysterical mind to be ruled by them. If the hysterical woman vomits, she may do so from the idea of being pregnant. She has, however, no knowledge of this idea, although it can be easily detected in her mind, and made conscious to her, by one of the technical procedures of psychoanalysis. If she is executing the jerks and movements constituting her 'fit,' she does not even consciously represent to herself the intended actions, and she may perceive these actions with the detached feelings of an onlooker. Nevertheless analysis will show that she was acting her part in the dramatic reproduction of some incident in her life, and the memory of this was unconsciously active during the attack."[1]

As we know, Freud drew a pretty hard and fast line between the two types of ideas: the type that could and the type that could not enter consciousness. The Unconscious system, then, contained ideas with a certain dynamic character. They were ideas ". . . keeping apart from consciousness in spite of their intensity and activity."[2]

Do these ideas "keep apart" from consciousness because of the compulsion of an exterior force or because of their own nature? Freud called attention to the repulsion which must be overcome when the psychoanalyst tries to bring unconscious ideas into the conscious mind of the patient. "We learn," he said, "that unconscious ideas are excluded from consciousness by living forces which oppose themselves to its reception, while they do not object to other ideas, the preconscious ones."[3]

What of these Unconscious ideas? Are they homogeneous or heterogeneous and, whether they be one or the other, does their quality spring from the nature of the Unconscious or the nature of the forces of repression? Freud has held to the view that there were uniformities in Unconscious ideas that were due to the nature of the Unconscious and not the repressing agent. This view he now affirms. "Unconsciou~ seemed to us at first only an enigmatical characteristic of ? mental act. Now it means more for us. It is a sign that thi~ of the nature of a certain mental category known to ~ more important features, and that it belongs to a activity which is deserving of our fullest attention. The index-value of the unconscious has far outgrown its importance as a property."[4]

This expresses a high point of satisfaction with the Unconscious. Yet already the concept of repression as Freud has developed it has cast a serious shadow on this view. This shadow is lengthened by the concept of the ego-ideal and its influence on repression. This ideal is variable and Freud indicated as much. Furthermore, he indicated that it ". . . would be the condition of repression." It followed as a matter of simple deduction that on these premises the unconscious material would vary in quality from individual to individual. What then is left of the "index-value of the unconscious"?

To understand Freud's "answer" to this problem we must reverse our point of view. We must assume that the index-value of the Unconscious is a valid proposition and that the mechanism of repression is also a valid proposition. It is then necessary to discover mechanisms which explain repression and yet leave the primary initiative in the Unconscious. Freud's mechanism of primal repression serves this purpose. "Now we have reason for assuming a primal repression, a first phase of repression, which consists in a denial of entry into consciousness to the mental (ideational) presentation of the instinct. This is accompanied by a fixation; the ideational presentation in question persists unaltered from then onwards and the instinct remains attached to it."[5] It is not explained to us how the instinct became equipped with ideational content without ever having access to the Conscious-Preconscious system. Overlooking this difficulty we see that Freud has avoided propositions about the amorphous influence of interpersonal experience on the ego-ideal by postulating a rigid process imbedded in the organism as such. In the device "homosexual investment of the ego-ideal" there is a marked difference of structure. But all of these devices are useful in that they make it possible for Freud to fit new data into an existing body of theory.

Devices such as this tend to be *ad hoc*. As such, they may answer the immediate problem fairly well. But they are likely to come into violent collision with other important ideas not presently in the center of attention. The present idea of primal repression restores automatism to the Conscious-Preconscious system. But it flies directly in the face of all the evidence with reference to the undifferentiated structure of the infant mind.

Freud pressed this assumption however. Striving for homogeneity and precedence in the Unconscious it became necessary for him to exclude even that influence that would be wielded by the ego-ideal. It is necessary to supplement the primal repression with a second device that will preserve the homogeneity of the Unconscious. Freud furnished this second device in the following passage. "The second phase of repression, repression proper, concerns mental derivatives of the repressed instinct-presentation, or such trains of thought as, originating elsewhere, have come into associative connection with it. On account of this association, these ideas experience the same fate as that which underwent primal repression. Repression proper, therefore, is actually an after-expulsion. Moreover, it is a mistake to emphasize only the rejection which operates from the side of consciousness upon what is to be repressed. We have to consider just as much the attraction exercised by what was originally repressed upon everything with which it can establish a connection. Probably the tendency to repression would fail of its purpose if these forces did not co-operate, if there were not something previously repressed ready to assimilate that which is rejected from consciousness."[6]

By means of these assumptions it is brought about that the content of the Unconscious is composed solely of instinctual material or its derivatives. In the Unconscious this material prospers. ". . . repression does not hinder the instinct-presentation from continuing to exist in the unconscious and from organizing itself further, putting forth derivatives and instituting connections. Really, repression interferes only with the relation of the instinct-presentation to one system of the mind, namely to consciousness."[7]

When Freud turned from structure to dynamics he quite forgot the mechanical rigidity of the system he had constructed. We learn to our surprise that there may be unrepressed derivatives of the Unconscious and the fate of these ideas is frequently decided by the degree of their activity or cathexis. ". . . it is an everyday occurrence," said Freud, "that such a derivative can remain unrepressed so long as it represents only a small amount of energy, although its content is of such a nature as to give rise to a conflict with conscious control. . . . the quantitative factor is manifestly decisive for this conflict; as soon as an idea which is fundamentally offensive exceeds a certain degree of strength, the conflict takes on actuality, and it is precisely the activation of the idea that leads to its repression."[8]

This view of the importance of cathexis restores the dynamic-quantitative view but it is inconsistent with the implications of the primal repression and the subsequent after-expulsion. We are seeing that the systems Unconscious and Conscious-Preconscious serve to sort psychic material. But they do not seem able to sort it well enough to lay claim to any great theoretical usefulness. The systems mingle in the Preconscious. The more Freud worked to establish the autonomy of the Unconscious the more it seemed to send its energies and currents exploring into the Preconscious. The more Freud sought to validate the index-value of the Unconscious the stronger the implication that the crucial factors might lie elsewhere . . . in the ego-ideal, or in the mechanisms of primal repression and after-expulsion. Even sex, which formerly was held within the boundaries of the Unconscious has now extended itself through the length and breadth of the mind by means of the concept of erotogenicity and the extension of libido to the ego.

CONSIDERATION OF CERTAIN OBSERVABLE
MENTAL PHENOMENA.
IDEAS AND AFFECTS

As we know Freud first stressed biological concepts and later mental concepts. There are always intervening variables which articulate either with the biological concepts or with the mental concepts. Where possible Freud tried to keep the path of biological reduction open. The early development of ego-libido is an illustration of an intervening variable articulated with a biological concept, sexual somatic excitation. Later developments of libido theory show that this variable gradually changes to articulate with mental events and that it no longer *articulates with,* but *reduces to,* biological events. We should give some attention now to the observable mental events that Freud proposed to explain. Let us observe first however that Freud signaled the change in his theoretical interest by a withdrawal of "instinct" as a central concept. "I am . . . of the opinion," he said, "that the antithesis of conscious and unconscious does not hold for instincts. An instinct can never be an object of consciousness—only the idea that represents the instinct. Even in the unconscious, moreover, it can only be represented by the idea. If the instinct did not attach itself to an idea or manifest itself as an affective state, we could know nothing about it. Though we do speak of an unconscious or a repressed instinctual impulse, this is a looseness of phraseology which is quite harmless. We can only mean an instinctual impulse the ideational presentation of which is unconscious, for nothing else comes into consideration."[9] In effect, this withdraws "instinct" as a useful concept in the organization of mental phenomena. Perhaps this is a belated withdrawal. The "current in the apparatus" which was associated with instinct has proved of limited theoretical importance. It is clear that there is a current in the apparatus, a derivative of sexual somatic energy, and it is clear that it has energic value. Freud's clinical work and his analysis of dreams established this beyond peradventure. But this orientation has not been broadly useful in handling mental phenomena. The attempt to add use-

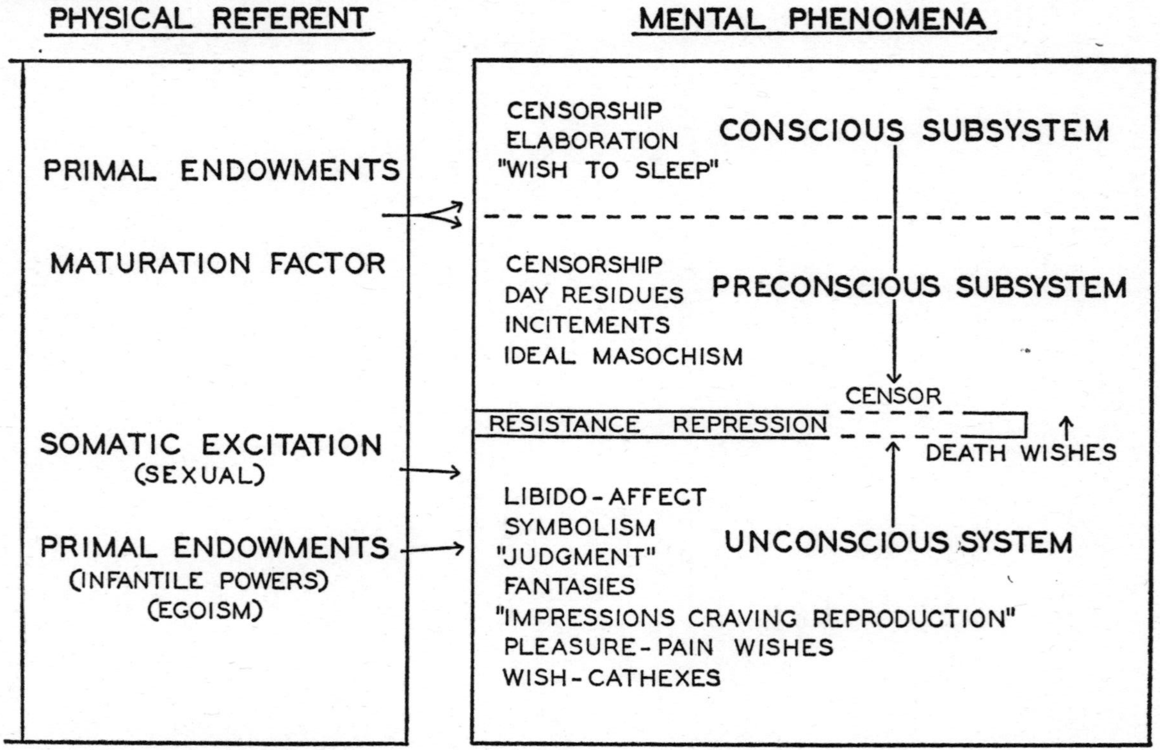

PHYSICAL REFERENT

PRIMAL ENDOWMENTS

MATURATION FACTOR

SOMATIC EXCITATION
(SEXUAL)

PRIMAL ENDOWMENTS
(INFANTILE POWERS)
(EGOISM)

MENTAL PHENOMENA

CONSCIOUS SUBSYSTEM

CENSORSHIP
ELABORATION
"WISH TO SLEEP"

PRECONSCIOUS SUBSYSTEM

CENSORSHIP
DAY RESIDUES
INCITEMENTS
IDEAL MASOCHISM

RESISTANCE REPRESSION

CENSOR

DEATH WISHES

UNCONSCIOUS SYSTEM

LIBIDO - AFFECT
SYMBOLISM
"JUDGMENT"
FANTASIES
"IMPRESSIONS CRAVING REPRODUCTION"
PLEASURE - PAIN WISHES
WISH - CATHEXES

Fig. I

fulness to the instinct concept by multiplying instincts, as in the case of the "ego-instincts," only complicated the theoretical picture. The shift to libido theory was, as we have seen, not really a shift from the instinct to its energy representative but a shift to an intervening variable, libido, which is articulated not with somatic quantities but with mental qualities and, especially, with an aspect of the social input in personalities. The above statement, then, recognized an accomplished fact. It is significant that it is stated, however, for we can believe that Freud must be set upon a new approach to his problems.

We shall see that this is so. Having established his intervening variable, libido, and having in fact quite given up the idea of combining it with somatic states in forming a system of concepts, he proceeded to suggest those observable mental events with which he proposed to correlate it. The observable (subjectively observable) events which now rise to importance are ideas and affects. These phenomena are reduced to instinct, but it is now their dynamics and not their origin which is at the center of Freud's interest. Doubtless this new advance is rendered possible largely by the assumption of primal repression. It permits Freud to rest assured that certain ideas in the mind are as surely reducible to sexual excitation as libido itself.

However, is it any more meaningful to speak of unconscious affect, or emotion, than of unconscious energy? Is it not part of the definition of an emotion that it is perceived? Freud felt that it was. "It is surely the essence of an emotion," he said, "that we should feel it, i.e. that it should enter consciousness. So for emotions, feelings, and affects to be unconscious would be quite out of the question."[10] But if we make this assumption what do we mean by such phrases as "unconscious affect" or "unconscious anxiety"? Freud solved this by making a distinction between unconscious affect, as such, and the misinterpretation of the idea proper to the affect. This misinterpretation in the conscious mind may consist of assigning the wrong idea to the affect or in separating the affect from any idea at all. The affect is unconscious in the sense that its correct ideational connection is not known to consciousness. This situation is likely to develop where the proper ideational connection has been repressed. Freud indicated that "If we restore the true connection, we call the original affect 'unconscious', although the affect was never unconscious but its ideational presentation had undergone repression."[11]

Conscious affect seemed to imply that this affect is a product of the Conscious-Preconscious system. Affect has energy value. It would follow that large increments of energy are generated in the Conscious-Preconscious system. Freud avoided this by the assumption of what he calls "affect-formations," or formations having the potentiality of producing affect in the Conscious-Preconscious system although they are themselves in the Unconscious. Thus the cause of conscious affect is not contained in the system where it manifests itself but is assumed to be in the Unconscious. However, ". . . the system Cs (Conscious) normally controls affectivity as well as access to motility."[12] The idea of resistance operating between the Conscious-Preconscious and the Unconscious is now supplanted by or supplemented with an additional conflict between affectivity in the Conscious-Preconscious which is caused by affect-formations in the Unconscious and whatever energy results in the "control" of this affectivity in the Conscious system. As long as the Conscious system successfully controls affectivity and motility the mental condition of an individual is "normal." However, "Whereas the control of the system Cs (Conscious) over voluntary motility is firmly rooted, regularly withstands the onslaught of neurosis and only breaks down in psychosis, the control of the Cs over affective development is less firmly established. Even in normal life we can recognize that a constant struggle for primacy over affectivity goes on between the two systems Cs and Pcs, that certain spheres of influence are marked off one from another and that the forces at work tend to mingle."[13] The problem that confronts us with reference to feelings, affect, emotions, does not apply to ideas. The unconscious idea ". . . continues, after repression, as an actual formation in the system Ucs. . . ."[14]

The concept "affect-formation" is another concept attributing priority to the Unconscious. It assigns cause to the Unconscious but it does not appear to be an energy concept since affect is itself an energy concept. It is a most feeble attempt to activate the Unconscious system.

It remains for us to indicate how Freud brought the concept, "cathexis," to bear on this new, dynamic approach. On the basis of primal repression, following Freud's reasoning, we know that certain ideas are repressed constituting part of the Unconscious system. Those shadowy progenitors, affect-formations, occupy the same area. In the Preconscious are the affects and ideas. Some ideas are "proper" to the area. They may be associated with affects. Other ideas, presumably, are not "proper" to the area. They are subject to repression at any moment. They too may be joined with affects. Then there are affects which are associated with no ideas and affects which are associated with wrong ideas. We would assume that all these formations in the Preconscious are energy formations. It is clear that this enrichment of the Preconscious has taken place at the expense of the Unconscious. Since the Conscious system tries to control these formations we must assume that there is energy in the Conscious system which is directed against the Unconscious formations.

Freud was indeed right when he said that ". . . the forces at work tend to mingle." The concept of cathexis grew out of the concept libido, just as the concept libido grew out of the concepts ego-libido and libido-quantum. Cathexis expresses the affinity of energy for ideas or objects. It may apply to energy in general or it may apply to the energy value of any given association of energy and idea in the Preconscious. The specific advantage of cathexis over libido is that cathexis is a more versatile concept insofar as it refers to mental formations. Further-more, cathexis tends to place the emphasis on where energy is going rather than where it came from. In this sense it is more sensitive than libido to the dynamics of mental events, and a radical departure from "libido theory."

What is the relation of the two systems Preconscious-Conscious and Unconscious in terms of cathexis? Freud said, "Let us take the case of repression proper (after-expulsion) as it affects an idea which is pre-conscious or even has already entered consciousness. Repression can consist here only in the withdrawal from the idea of the preconscious cathexis which belongs to the system Pcs. The idea then remains with-out cathexis, or receives cathexis from the Ucs, or retains the uncon-scious cathexis which it previously had."[15]

There is no automatic after-expulsion. The cathected idea wanders in the Preconscious. The boundary between the Unconscious and the Preconscious, so stoutly maintained in the study of dreams, has been all but given up. And the strategic element in the repression is the *withdrawal of preconscious cathexis*. This preconscious cathexis can refer only to a fund of energy which belongs to the Preconscious-Conscious system. It appears then, that there is a fund of energy in the mind which must be distinguished from purely sexual energy. It also appears that, at least in some cases, the idea with unconscious cathexis cannot get into the Conscious-Preconscious system without Precon-scious cathexis, i.e. energy bestowed upon it from the Preconscious. This view permits these inferences. (1) Repression is not so much repression as Preconscious *disinterest*. (2) The original emergence of an idea from the Unconscious depends upon the degree of Precon-scious interest, i.e. the amount of Preconscious energy the mind is will-ing to grant to the idea.

For the moment at least, Freud has robbed his Unconscious system of much of its content in order to furnish the Preconscious. Consid-erable Unconscious energy must be taken from the Unconscious and given to the Preconscious. This would permit us to discard the concept of affect-formations. Then we would have, mingling in the Precon-scious, (1) energy of sexual derivation and (2) energy of Precon-scious-Conscious derivation, (3) energy formations cathected by "sexual" energy and/or Preconscious-Conscious energy. That Conscious-Preconscious energy and sexual energy may supplement each other is a noval attitude in Freud but it is implied in his view of repression. Furthermore, the explanation of repression mentioned above discounts the familiar Freudian view that sexual energy is dominant in the mind.

We will remember that previously Freud suggested that the mind might properly be divided into the ego and the repressed. He did not implement the idea then. The passage we have quoted, however, clearly reinstates that view although it now tends to substitute Preconscious for ego. The passage also supplements the earlier view for it makes definite suggestions about energy distributions in this system.

Freud considered cathexis, the affinity value of mental energy, reducible to sexual somatic excitation and therefore attracted to suitable ideas and objects. Insofar as Preconscious energy supports and reinforces what we might term raw libidinal energy it is considered as hyper-cathexis. Difficulties with the theory of repression as it relates to the assumption of primal repression required the further concept of anti-cathexis. These difficulties concerned the process of primal repression. It was clear that primal repression could not have taken place in the same manner as after-expulsion since there could not have been any prior Preconscious hyper-cathexis which could be withdrawn. Perhaps then there is another factor in repression in addition to those already considered. "What we are looking for," said Freud, ". . . is another process which maintains the repression in the first case and, in the second, insures its being established and continued; and this other process we can only find in the assumption of an anti-cathexis, by means of which the system Pcs guards itself against the intrusion of the unconscious idea."[16] He continued, "The anti-cathexis is the sole mechanism of primal repression; in the case of repression proper (after-expulsion) there is in addition withdrawal of the preconscious cathexis."[17]

THE DYNAMICS OF CATHEXIS

A further consideration of affects, ideas, and cathexis will convince us that the Unconscious has not been able to repair its fortunes. *Le roi est mort. Vive le roi!* The old king had his kingdom in the Unconscious. The new king has his in the "repressed." The old king had a monopoly on libidinal energy and made every attempt to employ it exclusively. The new king has no such monopoly. But, on the other hand, he has access to a number of functionally distinctive energies so that he can engage in all manner of undertakings.

It is true that Freud kept stocking his Unconscious with enduring content. "The *kernel* of the system Ucs," he said, "consists of instinct presentations whose aim is to discharge their cathexis. . . . These instinctual impulses are co-ordinate with one another, exist independently side by side, and are exempt from mutual contradiction."[18] And it is a bee hive of industry. In the Unconscious ". . . intensity of cathexis is mobile in a far greater degree than in the other systems. By the process of displacement one idea may surrender to another the whole value of its cathexis; by that of condensation it may appropriate the whole cathexis of several other ideas."[19] But the Unconscious, unfortunately for theory, cannot keep away from the Preconscious. The Unconscious ". . . maintains a number of . . . relations to the Pcs, amongst them that of co-operation."[20] And a study of the "derivatives of the Ucs" shows that they are in no sense homogeneous. We know that these derivatives can get out of the Ucs into the Pcs. But, even when they are to be found in the Unconscious they may combine in themselves opposite features. Freud pointed this out: "On the one hand, they are highly organized, exempt from self-contradictoriness, have made use of every acquisition of the system Cs, and would hardly be distinguished by our ordinary judgment from the formations of that system. On the other hand, they are unconscious and are incapable of becoming conscious. Thus they belong according to their qualities in the system Pcs, but in actual fact to the Ucs. . . . We may then compare them with those human half-breeds who, taken all round, resemble white men, but betray their coloured descent by some striking feature or other, on account of which they are excluded from society and enjoy none of the privileges of white people."[21]

The following sentiment of Freud seems inevitable: "Study of the derivatives of the Ucs will altogether disappoint our expectations of a schematically clear division of the one mental system from the other. This circumstance will certainly give rise to dissatisfaction with our results and will probably be used to cast doubts upon the value of our way of distinguishing the two groups of mental processes."[22]

The Unconscious has come to have two major characteristics. In the first place it refers to energy of organic origin. In the second place it refers to mental formations in the state of unconsciousness as the result of repression. The first characteristic emphasizes the importance of distinguishing between types of energy but this energy is no longer isolated in the Unconscious. The second point assumes that there is something theoretically important about distinguishing all repressed material from all unrepressed material. This repressed material may be heterogeneous with respect to the energies that are attached to it. It is convenient to think of repressed material as occupying a psychic region, as being contiguous, because of the displacements and condensations that take place between material in a repressed state.

The concept of primal repression was directed toward a problem that seems to fade out of the picture now. In trying to maintain the Unconscious Freud fought a long battle to maintain it against the resistance, to give it a monopoly of energy and to give "eyes" (ideas, images) to the blind current in the system. Primal repression was an aid in setting up the Unconscious and a very great aid in getting images into the Unconscious that otherwise could result only from the Meynert primary ego. This in turn permitted the dynamics of cathexis that Freud has examined.

But the study of this dynamic broke down the barrier between the Preconscious and the Unconscious—and it is this barrier that primal repression was intended to preserve.

Freud experimented with a pseudo-Unconscious composed of the Unconscious and the Preconscious. "Consciousness," he said, "regards the whole sum of mental processes as belonging to the realm of the preconscious. A very great part of this preconscious material originates in the unconscious, has the characteristics of derivatives of the unconscious, and is subject to a censorship before it can pass into consciousness. Another part of the Pcs can become conscious without any censorship. Here we light upon a contradiction of an earlier assumption; from the point of view of repression we were obliged to place the censorship which is decisive for consciousness between the Pcs and the Cs. But we shall do well not to regard this complication as a difficulty, but to assume that to every transition from one system to that immediately above it (that is, every advance to a higher stage of mental organization) there corresponds a new censorship."[23] By the introduction of a censor between the Cs and the Pcs Freud was able to insist on the importance of different mental energies. The censor between the Pcs and the Ucs no longer served this purpose.

The conclusions that suggest themselves are either that the regional distinction is not theoretically useful, or that the index of differentiation is not what Freud thought it was. This index of differentiation was energy differentiation. From the beginning, where we do not find regional differentiation we have found energy differentiation. The two have usually been bound together. As the regional view has grown less useful the energy distinction has become more important, although numerous considerations have pointed to the fact that energies, theoretically distinct, may be combined in mental formations. We have never learned what both of these opposing energies were. One has been the mental representative of sexual somatic energy. The other has been various things, all of which were supposed in some manner to reduce to sexual somatic energy. But the dynamics of this energy has been significantly different from the dynamics of energy directly traced to organic tension. Libido theory is largely an attempt to combine energy analysis with regional assumptions. The movement toward analysis, in terms of cathexis, concentrated more upon the mental formations and thus tended to be a three-way method of analysis involving energies, mental formations and regions. The regional dimension was the most unsatisfactory element and has become even more unsatisfactory. The emphasis upon the Conscious and the Preconscious system is an attempt to make it more workable.

The resulting picture of mental dynamics was unwieldy as we see in the following passage: "We see that derivatives of the Pcs enter consciousness as substitute-formations and as symptoms, generally after undergoing great distortion, in contrast to the Ucs, although often many characteristics inviting repression have been retained. We find that many preconscious formations remain unconscious, though, to judge by their nature, we should suppose that they might very well become conscious. We are led to look for the more important differences, not between the conscious and the preconscious, but between the preconscious and the unconscious. On the border of the Pcs the censorship thrusts back the Ucs, but its derivatives can circumvent this censorship, achieve a high degree of organization and in the Pcs reach a certain intensity of cathexis: when, however, this is exceeded and they try to force themselves into consciousness, they are recognized as derivatives of the Pcs and are repressed afresh at the new frontier by the censorship between the Cs and the Pcs. Thus the former censorship is exercised against the Ucs itself, and the latter against its preconscious derivatives. We might suppose that in the course of individual development the censorship has been advanced a step."[24]

As we look back over the vicissitudes of the Unconscious we see that it has always *theoretically* represented integral process and isolated energy. Empirically both the process and the isolation of the energy have broken down repeatedly. The energy and the process were closely bound together. If they existed elsewhere in the psyche, or if they were compromised by different processes or energies in the Unconscious, then the Unconscious failed as a workable, theoretical category. It has failed now.

Does this mean there is but one energy in the mind? We will remember that Freud himself said that this might turn out to be true. His "libido theory" seemed at least in part an attempt to reduce all psychic behavior to one energy. This attempt could not disguise the fact that energies of the mind must be distinguished by their functions. Our previous analysis of Freud's thought shows that this is the *only way*

left to talk intelligibly about energy quantities. Among the energies of
the mind (judged by the criterion of function) there is, doubtless, the
classical libidinal energy. Other energies, however, must be assigned to
the ego variables that Freud isolated. I refer to the "self-preservative
instincts," "narcissism," "egoism," and the "ego ideal."

Freud also suggested, as we have pointed out, that in the long run
the most workable process differentiation might be between the ego
and the repressed. The dynamic analysis that Freud has undertaken in
the studies we have discussed is more consistent with such a distinction
than that between the Unconscious, the Preconscious and the Conscious. The category of the repressed can free us from a slavish fidelity
to one energy. It can open up for study the dynamics of *energy mix-
tures* in mental formations. This in turn can point to clearer relations
between the ego and the repressed than existed between the secondary
ego and the Unconscious.

NEW TRENDS IN THE THEORY
OF DREAMS

We find at least the beginning of an answer to the questions we have
raised in Freud's reconsideration of his earlier analysis of dreams. In
his "Metapsychological Supplement to the Theory of Dreams," published in 1916, he rediscovered the discarded concept, ego-libido, and
used it interchangeably with the concept, ego-interest. This is perhaps a
cue to the fact that Freud has recognized the implications of his impoverishment of the Unconscious and his consequent enrichment of the
Preconscious. This view is confirmed by Freud's statement that the
dream-wish is in the Preconscious. It will be remembered that in *Traumdeutung* he took the position that the ". . . motive power needed by
the dream had to be contributed by a wish . . ." and this wish, ". . .
whatever the nature of the waking thoughts . . . ," is ". . . invariably" and "indisputably" a wish ". . . from the unconscious."[25] In his
"Metapsychological Supplement to the Theory of Dreams," however,
he found that the ". . . preconscious dream-wish is formed, which expresses the unconscious impulse in the material of the preconscious
day's residues."[26] The unconscious impulse, itself, hast lost its habitat
in the Unconscious. In early dream theory this impulse remained in the
Unconscious until sleep let down the barriers between the Unconscious
and the Preconscious. But now the impulse may get into the Preconscious material during the day. The *location* of these impulses no
longer seems important. They are ". . . perhaps, but by no means

necessarily, to be found amongst the preconscious (latent) dream thoughts."[27]

The new view with reference to cathectic changes in sleep is a marked departure from the former view. The nature of this departure very possibly marks a crucial change in the whole system of personality dynamics. It will be remembered that earlier Freud held that the libido was in the system Ucs and that it strove to break into the Preconscious system, and when it succeeded, it formed the motive power for dreams. Thus the libido was "feared by the ego and combatted by repression." In *Traumdeutung,* Freud said of sleep, "I cannot say what change is produced in the Pcs system by the state of sleep, but there is no doubt that the psychological characteristics of sleep are to be sought mainly in the cathectic changes occurring just in this system. . . . On the other hand, I have found nothing in the psychology of dreams to warrant the assumption that sleep produces any but secondary changes in the condition of the Ucs system."[28] This view made possible the hypothesis that, in sleep, the Preconscious system became weaker and was no longer able to guard successfully the border between the Preconscious and the Unconscious. As a result the Unconscious penetrated into the Preconscious and commandeered the resources there for the purpose of dream-formation.

This view cannot now be maintained by Freud in view of the theoretical breakdown of the boundary between the Unconscious and the Preconscious. The logical conclusion would seem to be that if the state of sleep influences the Preconscious it must influence the instinctive impulse which may be there. Freud felt his way in this direction. "The narcissism of sleep does signify," he said, "the withdrawal of cathexis from all ideas of objects, both from the unconscious and the preconscious parts of them."[29] This admission destroys the basis for the type of dream analysis employed in Freud's earlier work. Freud recognized this. "If the narcissistic state of sleep has resulted in withdrawal of all cathexes belonging to the systems Ucs and Pcs, then there can no longer be any possibility of the preconscious day's residues being reinforced by unconscious instinctual impulses, which have themselves surrendered their cathexes to the ego. Here the theory of dream formation ends in a contradiction unless we can rescue it by modifying our assumption of the narcissism of sleep."[30]

Freud proposed to solve this dilemma by certain assumptions about the nature of repressed material. ". . . that part of the system Ucs which is under repression," he said, "does not comply with the ego's desire for sleep, but retains its cathexes in whole or in part, and in general has acquired in consequence of repression, a certain measure of independence of the ego."[31] What is the strategic factor that grants this resistance to repressed material? ". . . the desire for sleep endeavours to call in all the cathexes *put forth by the ego* (Italics ours.) and to establish an absolute narcissism. This can only partly succeed, for the repressed material in the system Ucs does not yield to the desire for sleep."[32]

It is clear here that repressed material has now become the important factor. The attempt by the ego to call in cathexes and its subsequent failure seems to me to indicate the probability that the ego, itself, or some section of it, has become implicated in the repressed material. We remember that Freud pointed out that some formations under repression could hardly be distinguished from the formations of the Conscious system. This statement together with the difficulty encountered by the ego in withdrawing cathexes suggests that an important aspect of repression is the tendency *on the part of the ego* to support the claims of the repressed material.

I think the hypothesis that ego energy has cathected the repressed material in some measure furnishes a satisfactory solution to the problem of repression. It seems inevitable in view of Freud's analyses indicating that both Unconscious motivations and Conscious motivations are tolerated in both systems. Freud mentioned that anti-cathexis was employed by the ego to hold down the repressed material. I would infer that it is hyper-cathexis of the repressed material by ego energy which contributes to the difficulty of controlling it and which makes it difficult for "sleep" to withdraw all ego cathexes from the psyche.

But if ego-cathexis, or ego-interest characterizes repressed material, and if repressed material is the source of the dream process, then it follows that there must be some degree of ego procurement in the dream process. In some manner the ego must be seeking "gratification." Yet it follows equally clearly that, if there be anticathexis, the ego is also interested in preventing this gratification. Our hypotheses suggest that the essential dichotomy in mental process is in the ego itself.

THE DREAM PROCESS

"What actually happens in dream-formation," said Freud, "constitutes a very remarkable and quite unforeseen solution. The process begun in the Pcs and reinforced by the Ucs pursues a retrogressive course, through the Ucs, to perception, which forces itself upon consciousness."[33] The dream process then is regressive and reverses the normal order. Furthermore, ". . . the dream-wish is converted into an hallucination, and as such, commands belief in the reality of its fulfillment. It is just round this concluding piece of dream-formation that the gravest uncertainties centre, to explain which we have set out to compare with dreams the pathological states allied to them."[34] Through the mechanism of hallucination "hidden or repressed wishes" are brought into consciousness ". . . and that in such a way as to command entire belief."[35]

Dream process, then, is another example of the pathological or defective functioning of the mind. Freud thought that the reasons for the existence of the hallucinations are to be found in the structure of the Cs system. It appeared ". . . that hallucination consists in a cathexis of the system Cs (Pcpt) (the perceptual function in the Conscious) which, however, does not proceed—as normally—from without, but from within, the condition being that regression shall be carried far enough to reach this system itself and thus to pass beyond the testing of reality."[36] The function of orientating the individual ". . . by discrimination between inner and outer must . . . be ascribed to the system Cs (Pcpt) alone."[37] But the ego does not always employ this "great institution." The testing of reality may be abolished or put out of action. For instance, "Amentia is the reaction to a loss which reality affirms, but which the ego tries to deny, since it finds it insupportable. Thereupon the ego breaks off its relation to reality. . . ."[38] Something of the same nature may therefore happen in dreams. There is a voluntary renunciation. "Sleep desires to know nothing of the outer world, nor is it interested in reality. . . . Hence sleep withdraws cathexes from the system Cs as well as from the other systems, Pcs and Ucs, in so far as the libido-positions contained in them obey the sleep-wish. When the system Cs is thus devoid of cathexis, the possibility of a testing of reality is abandoned; and those excitations which have, independently of the state of sleep, entered on the path of regression will find it clear as far as the system Cs, where they will count as undisputed reality."[39]

On this view we see that the dream is a random rattling of the psychic apparatus, and a rattling in reverse. As Freud says, dreams ". . . are remnants of mental activity made possible by the imperfect extent to which the narcissistic state of sleep has been achieved."[40]

This confession of purposelessness makes us wonder how so much that was affirmatively valuable was derived by Freud from his earlier study of dreams. We pointed out at that time that the dream left something to be desired if it was interpreted as a gratification system for sexual excitations. On the other hand the dream gave every evidence of "meaning." It expressed intents and purposes and feelings of the dreamers. Most of the time these "wishes" had a sexual base. But these sexual interests were expressed not in terms of primal images but in terms of contemporary reality. How did the sexual impulse become associated with contemporary images? Freud tried various devices to furnish the instinct with images but these images could not be other than primal images. We suggested that in some manner we would have to think of the ego as presenting the image to the instinct.

In view of our hypotheses it is not sufficient to say that there is no libidinal gratification in the dream. The further question must be asked, is there any function in the dream for the ego-interest? Although the instinctual impulse must be considered in terms of its "gratification" or discharge, the ego-interest may be considered in terms of its fulfill-ment. If we consider the ego-interest the vital element in the repression, it would appear to be the vital element in the dream process. If we think of sexual discharge only, then the dream ends up in mere hallu-cination, a sort of random dead end. But if we think of ego-interest this hallucination may be fulfillment and we again establish the dream as a meaningful psychic process.

A new view of the dream-work is suggested by this line of reasoning. Since only repressed matter is involved in dream process it follows that merely unconscious matter is unimportant. *Sexually cathected ma-terial is not then important in dream-formation unless it is repressed.* But repression involves both ego-cathexis and ego anti-cathexis. On this view what is the dream-work? *It is a mediator between two quali-tatively different aspects of the ego.* These aspects are represented by the two forces: cathexis and anti-cathexis.

This view, it should be noted, does not negate the value of "instinc-tive" energy. It merely recognizes what must be learned from Freud's repeated failures to organize instinctive energy as a separate and domi-nant element in personality, namely, that instinctive energy *usually* fails of that liminal value necessary to coerce action in the psyche. The strategic formation is the increment of ego energy. Added to the instinc-tive energy it appears to have high value for action. This is particularly visible in the case of repression.

Freud's point of view selected the case where the ego-interest cathected the instinctual impulse and added its energy to that of the impulse. By thus piling Ossa on Pelion an active formation was ob-tained. It follows logically that under certain conditions ego-interest, by itself, or organic impulse by itself might generate a quantum of energy sufficient for definite mental activity. Freud's attention has been directed to a special case but a very usual one. His failure to organize the mind around the concept of instinctual energy indicates that only in rare limiting cases does the instinctual impulse become dominant. It appeared dominant for so long because the attachment of the strategic ego-cathexis was not perceived.

Freud, at various times, endeavoured to extricate himself from the criticism that his psychic solutions always involved sexual release. He was not entirely successful in doing this. But when ego-cathexis becomes the strategic concept, even if it is added to organic tension, then mental instability may be theoretically corrected without somatic discharge.

THE ROLE OF THE DREAM

We have, in our inferences, gone beyond any explicit statement by Freud. We think that our suggestions follow precisely from Freud's own assumptions. Our aim has been to explore the consequences of these assumptions. We think that they are consistent with the new emphasis upon the Conscious-Preconscious system and that they suggest a consistent picture of repression and of the dream process without the resort to primal mechanisms or defective or regressive structures. We propose for the moment to look a little more closely at these consequences, particularly the relation between cathexis and anti-cathexis.

We have suggested that repressed material has ego-cathexis and that repressed material is vital in the formations of dreams. This as we have pointed out isolates ego-cathexis as a strategic element in dream-formation. But this ego-cathexis has undergone repression. It has proved inferior in its energy value to the force of anti-cathexis. If the contrary were true then presumably no repression would have been possible unless it were a reverse repression. (It seems likely that something like this may be quite possible.) In terms of ego dynamics, then, the ego energy that has cathected the formation is weaker than the repressing energy. But the repressing energy is also ego energy. So we not only have two orders of ego energy arrayed against each other but we have unequal quanta of ego energy. There is then dominant and servient ego energy. The dominant energy is represented by the anti-cathexis. The servient energy is confined in the repressed formation. *However, both species of energy represent psychic needs.* The problem of the dream is how to grant some measure of satisfaction to both kinds of needs. Somatic discharge may be involved in some cases.

At this point it will help us to proceed by analogy and to move from the psychic level to that of the social system. A functional view of a social system sees this system as tending to meet or satisfy certain requirements that are vital to the continuance of any social system. Analysis of the parts of a social system may consist of describing their contributions to these requirements. However, these parts may generate pressures within the social system and other structures may develop that relieve these pressures. Thus in the United States we find the periodic growth of political parties of protest. These parties may not succeed in gaining power but they give their members an opportunity to gain the public ear, to blow off steam.

Thus we find in a social system certain behaviors which may be viewed not as contributing to generalized "needs," but as relieving "pressures." Let us call these latter patterns servient patterns. They are servient in that they are not germane to the core functioning of the system, and they are servient in that they represent isolated interests. These servient structures are important however in that they tend to discharge pressures not otherwise discharged within the main core of the social system. We might carry over to this context the words that Freud finds useful in analyzing personality process. We could call the core system, the "bound" social system, and we could call the servient system, the "unbound" social system. (We use the words "dominant" and "bound," and "servient" and "unbound" interchangeably.) The bound system, not being perfect, tends to generate pressures within the system which require "gratification." The unbound system grows around these pressures tending to furnish a limited "gratification."

Carrying our analogy over to personality process we suggest that an important function of the dream is to grant satisfaction to the "unbound" structures of the mind. Since this satisfaction is not in accordance with the policy of the organized ego it is essential that the dream process should not command the means of motility. Furthermore, since the servient interest may not be and probably will not be integrated with the objectives of the "bound" ego it becomes essential that certain limitations be attached to the dream. In the first place, as Freud has pointed out, the ego may put an end to the dream by waking. Thus the dream-work becomes essential, and the type of mediation that operates under the concept, censor. In the dream process the servient ego must at least feign to operate under the general values of the bound ego just as, in a social system, protest movements must protest their allegiance to the general values of the society if they expect to be listened to.

By the denial of access to the powers of motility, and by the abrogation of reality-testing, the stage is set for *functional* employment of dream hallucinations. Except in cases of somatic discharge this hallucinatory process cannot be considered as gratification for the sexual "current." It operates generally as satisfaction of ego-interests.

When we consider the dream process in this light we observe that there is more than one obstacle to the gratification of ego-interests. We have mentioned the opposition of the "bound" ego. But the "bound" ego is also limited in its goal by the "reality" situation. So dream hallucinations can serve a purpose for the "bound" ego, too—

by granting a "satisfaction" that cannot or may not be obtained in fact. From this point of view hallucination is not the result of the failure of the psychic system but an example of its striving for stability. This view of the dream functions seems quite consistent with the dream processes that Freud analysed in *The Interpretation of Dreams.*

Dreams involving fear and the desire for punishment fit easily into this view. The "ego-ideal" obviously has a strong influence on the ego. Learned ideas about the propitiatory and expiatory nature of "punishment" may give birth to "incitements" for self-punishing behavior. "Ideal masochism" need not then be reduced to some aberration in the sexual constitution.

The existence of anxiety-deams and punishment-dreams requires us to assume that the liminal intensity required for dream formation may be achieved by the ego. This, as we remember, is quite consistent with a view expressed by Freud earlier but discarded by him on the ground of theoretical commitments developed from the psychoneuroses.

It is clear why Freud has not been able to establish his "censor" in any one or two positions. The "censor" was designed to separate ego activity from formations containing libidinal energy. The interchange of energy that actually existed made the concept unworkable.

The view we have suggested simplifies the analysis of the variables—images, ideas, and affects. It was more than difficult for Freud to explain the conjunction of contemporary images with libidinal energy. This function—of presenting the image to the energy—would now fall to the ego.

Chapter XI

THE THINKER

AND HIS

THEORETICAL SYSTEM

THE SYSTEM

THREE BASIC CHANGES have taken place in the Freudian system. First, mental energy has been divided into three parts which can be referred to as sexualism, moralism and egoism. Secondly, the "topographical" approach has given way to the "metapsychological" approach. Thirdly, the strategic "areas" of the mind are now "bound" or "unbound" areas, and repressed or unrepressed areas. Of course, it is hardly correct to refer to areas at all. But the terms "bound" and "unbound," "repressed" and "unrepressed," point to common characteristics of of classes of mental material.

Libido theory was an energy theory of mental action that sought its major referent in sexual somatic conditions. We have seen how these conditions failed to throw sufficient light on mental processes. But libido analysis disclosed three important processes; sexual processes, egoistic processes, and moral processes.

A lasting aspect of libido theory was, however, the emphasis on energy. There is mobility in mental events. And these mobility trends are consistent with their prime "causes": sexualism, egoism or moral-

157

ism. Their impact on mental events and their interdependence is one great dimension of personality process.

These three categories are intimately associated with organic process. Egoism and sexualism are biological concepts but they are quite differently structured. Sexualism refers to a concrete biological "force." Sexual representation in the mind is viewed as related to the somatic tension in erogenous areas. Egoism has two aspects. It refers to the biological tensions that are related to self-preservation. These are the "self-preservative instincts." In the other aspect egoism refers to the self-regard, self-assertion and self-love of the ego. This form of egoism Freud isolated as "narcissism."

The "ego-ideal" has developed from the socialization of the individual, from the internalization of norms, affects, ideas and images. Any change on the part of the organism from the satisfaction of organic urges as they become manifest to the ego raises a suspicion that the ego-ideal has influenced the ego. Libido theory teaches us that the ego-ideal, or the "social self" is, in an important sense, a "body" ideal. It gives forth energy currents that crave reduction. Just as the libidinal forces, in dreams, may seek to fight their way through to motility, so the ego-ideal seeks to appropriate the "institutions" of the mind, to coerce action. The self-evaluation trend in psychic process can only be related to the ego-ideal.

The ego sorts mental material, binds mental material, represses mental material. The ego is energized to act for the gratification of "primal" organic tensions or for the gratification of tensions produced by the cognitive-affective aspects of the ego-ideal.

Freud first tied the organism to sexualism. Later he tied the "secondary process" to egoism, then to egoism and sexualism. The tendency is to give the ego some independent initiative. This separation of the "self" from the major categories influencing it makes possible useful theorizing about repression. It also makes possible useful thinking about socialization and the re-alignment of energy in the ego. Freud's addiction to somatic reduction as an ideal state endowed him with an enduring pessimism about imposed forces that might interfere with it.

Although the ego-ideal has emerged as a clear category of analysis, libido theory hangs round its neck like an albatross. Important things to know about the ego-ideal are: how it was developed out of the social environment, how it makes it peace with other factors in the psyche, and what final position and influence it gains in the structure of the self. Freud's libido theory is of minimum usefulness here. "Homosexual libido" does not lead us to the new frontiers that are waiting to be examined.

Freud's early thinking looked for a convenient tidiness in mental events. This is the reason his earlier "topographical" approach is often preferred for empirical application. But the "metapsychological" approach showed that mental events were not tidy. They had little regard for logical distinctions in energy. Mental material bunched itself into "formations" that took on the appearance of molecules and were composed of ideas, affects, cathexes, and images. These images attracted and repelled each other. They acted as "boundary maintaining" units. It is reasonable to suppose that these formations may range in composition from the simplicity of the atom to the complexity of the protein molecule. It seems clear that they may adhere to each other. Perhaps the bound area of the ego is a combination of such adhering formations. (The "formation" may relate to the concepts, "temperament," "trait," "attitude.")

To recapitulate, here are three categories of mental innervation: sexual, egoistic, and normative. There are a number of structural characteristics of mind such as cognition, perception and volition. The assumption that these faculties are exercised *on* mental material requires us to assume a directing faculty. Freud refers to this directing faculty as the ego. He also refers to the general dynamic process attached to mental events (above the repressed) as *in* the ego. We shall not resolve this terminological problem at this time. Libido or energy furnishes the principle of movement in the mind. There are three basic processes in the mind, (a) "formation" dynamics, (b) ego dynamics, (c) "repressed" dynamics. The formation, as I have said, seems to be the elemental unit in mental activity. It exists both in the ego and in the repressed. A bound organization of formations exists *in* the ego which constitutes the bound or organized ego. Other formations, relatively independent of the organized ego but not under repression constitute the unbound or unorganized ego. The bound ego tends to act as an holistic process. For instance, it exercises censorship in dreams and furnishes the energy for repression. The repressed represents that body of material that is unacceptable to the bound ego. The fact of repression seems to produce an organization of the repressed and a dynamic tension between the bound ego and the repressed. The distribution throughout these processes of the innervations we have mentioned above must be determined empirically.

We think that these suggestions issue logically from the substance of Freud's analyses during the "metapsychological" period.

THE THINKER

Freud did not clearly mark out the difference between a conceptual system and an empirical process. At the very beginning he saw a process and a concept mixed together in the fact of sexual, somatic excita-tion. His gradual turn to the theoretical ordering of mental events took place by way of the Unconscious which seemed to be placed halfway between fact and theory. The assumptions of mechanisms and topolo-gies has demonstrated again and again the closeness Freud saw between empirical events and his theory about them.

Freudian concepts live a sort of biological life. They grow, mature and die, or at least retreat into a logical limbo. They may endure long and prosper, or they may wither soon and pine away. No concept seems to become extinct. At any time it may be revived to satisfy the needs of the moment. It is one of the characteristics of the Freudian system that many of the concepts are *ad hoc* solutions to temporary, localized clinical problems. Freud moved from spot to spot advancing the line of these concepts and moving in that way toward general theory. Freud's empirical integrity makes possible a study of this nature. As he moved from one trouble spot to another he mixed new insights with patent contradictions, and covered up conceptual inadequacy with new concepts which as likely as not involved new contradictions. The genius of Freud is not only in his clinical insight but in the fact that the body of his theory did move toward a general view of per-sonality process. We have tried to show this tendency toward conver-gence.

Freud developed two convictions that strongly influenced his think-ing. They are particularly important in the third and last period of his thought so I would like to consider them here. The first conviction was that some kind of defective process attached to the sex life of homo sapiens; and the second was that "love" and "esteem" could be held to overlap clinically in such a manner that they could be handled by the same concepts.

SEX AS DEFECTIVE PROCESS

The devious and self-contradictory ways that sexual excitation seemed to find expression in the mind led Freud to estimate it as some kind of defective, regressive or primal process. He found that "cultural education" involved a general lowering of the sexual object, and he added that, ". . . on the other hand, unrestrained sexual liberty from the beginning leads to no better result." This curious dilemma is brought about by the fact that ". . . the value the mind sets on the erotic needs instantly sinks as soon as satisfaction becomes readily ob-tainable. Some obstacles are necessary to swell the tide of the libido to its height; and in all the periods of history, wherever natural barriers in the way of satisfaction have not sufficed, mankind has erected conventional ones in order to be able to enjoy love."[1] This is indeed a remarkable point of view in one who considered that the aim of the personality was to resist the overwhelming force of "love." It seems that societies have devoted themselves to the contruction of obstacles to eroticism in order to vex their members with overweening libido.

Freud's researches did not indicate that much "enjoyment" comes out of this. He carried his point further. "In times during which no obstacles to sexual satisfaction existed," he said, "such as, may be, during the decline of the civilizations of antiquity, love became worthless, life became empty, and strong reaction-formations were necessary before the indispensable emotional value of love could be recovered. In this context it may be stated that the ascetic tendency of Christianity had the effect of raising the psychical value of love in a way that heathen antiquity could never achieve; it developed greatest significance in the lives of the ascetic monks, which were almost entirely occupied against libidinous temptation. . . ."[2] This is indeed an anomaly. We must deny love to enjoy it. Then when we have built it up sufficiently to enjoy it we find ourselves continuing to resist it.

Searching for an answer Freud turned to the structure of the instincts or drives themselves. "One's first inclination," he said, "is to see in this difficulty a universal characteristic of our organic instincts." But further consideration showed this was not so. "Is it not a fact that wine always affords the drinker the same toxic satisfaction—one that in poetry has so often been likened to the erotic. . . ? Do we ever find a drinker impelled to go to another country where the wine is dearer or where alcohol is prohibited, in order to stimulate his dwindling pleasure in it by these obstacles?"[3] Since the sexual instinct does not operate like thirst, something must distinguish the sexual instinct from other instincts. ". . . I think the possibility must be considered that something in the nature of the sexual instinct itself is unfavourable to the achievement of absolute gratification."[4] First there is the possibility that the intervention of the incest tabu brings about a situation in which the ego can never present to the instinct the original object of desire but only a substitute for it. This of course refers to the Oedipus fixation. Freud suggested another explanation. ". . . the coprophilic elements in the instinct have proved incompatible with our aesthetic ideas, probably since the time when man developed an upright posture, and so removed the organ of smell from the ground."[5] This paints a dismal picture indeed for the sex life of homo sapiens. Freud added that, "The fundamental processes which promote erotic excitation remain always the same. Excremental things are all too intimately and inseparably bound up with sexual things; the position of the genital organs—*inter urinas et faeces*—remains the decisive and unchangeable factor. One might say, modifying a well-known saying of the great Napoleon's 'Anatomy is destiny.' The genitals themselves have not undergone the development of the rest of the human form in the direction of beauty; they have retained their animal cast; and so even today love, too, is in essence as animal as it ever was."[6]

The sexual instinct then is of importance only when it is not gratified for a period of time. However, evolutionary changes have brought it about that man tends to be repelled by his own sexual instinct. Thus after he has erected barriers to enjoy love, man is unable to consummate that enjoyment. The anatomic "destiny" is therefore most discouraging. And Freud voiced the following melancholy thought. "So, perhaps we must make up our minds to the idea that altogether it is not possible for the claims of the sexual instinct to be reconciled with the demands of culture, that in consequence of his cultural development renunciation and suffering, as well as the danger of his extinction at some far future time, are not to be eluded by the race of man."[7]

If Freud had been more acutely aware of the cultural factors bearing on this problem he might have seen a solution in a program of social change. But he came to relate the ego-ideal to the Oedipus complex, and the Oedipus complex was considered a biological mechanism. So sex has not evolved with man. It was not capable of complete satisfaction.

These views about sex, impressed ever deeper by Freud's clinical experience, constituted a basic assumption about human life.

THE MERGER OF LOVE AND ESTEEM

The ego-ideal has its roots back in the 'resistance' to Unconscious impulses which Freud observed at the beginning of his career. An interpretation of this "resistance" was required and such an interpretation grew out of the study, "On Narcissism," and was applied to specific processes in "Mourning and Melancholia." It is at least worth considering that this early interpretation of the phenomenon of self-evaluation did some disservice to Freud's development. In "Mourning and Melancholia" 'love' became highly ambiguous. It referred to sexual satisfaction as such. It also referred to the regard that one felt for those that had shielded and protected one in infancy. In this respect the sexual instinct was, then, "supported on" the self-preservative instincts. A third factor was hardly considered by Freud. He saw that the ego-ideal criticized the ego but he did not stress the possibility that third persons have an influence on the form of the ego-ideal. What

might therefore have been a very essential factor in the difference between mourning and melancholia was omitted. Nevertheless, Freud's
analysis of the struggle between the ego-ideal and the ego indicated
that there was a "self-regarding faculty" at work. The ego was subject
to criticism for noncompliance with the ego-ideal.

This self-criticism, as a dimension of personality process, was rather
summarily disposed of in part because Freud was intent on libido
dynamics. It was the unfortunate lot of the ego-ideal to be energized
with a dose of homosexual libido. And this early assimilation of "value"
theory to libido theory persisted. "Love," not only to Freud, but to
his followers, seemed to be a monolithic substance. Even the theoretical difference between libidinal love and anaclitic love was frequently
forgotten. But little or no consideration was given to that love which
was shown for people who were not major sexual interests and who
had not given support and protection in childhood. We are referring,
of course, to the "love for" the "external" ego-ideal. This esteem can
be duly libidinized. It can be traced back to "anaclitic" love on the
ground that "ego-ideal" love is related to *social* rather than *organic*
security. But no amount of simplification can reduce this third type of
love, dynamically, to one of the other two. It has three components.
First, there is an internalized system of normative orientations. Second, there is the tendency to judge external reality in terms of these
internalized norms. And in the third place there is the tendency to
judge the self, the ego, in terms of these same normative orientations.

The combination of the two convictions we have mentioned can be
seen in Freud's analysis of the phenomenon of transference. The physician's task is to help the neurotic ". . . make that advance from the
pleasure-principle to the reality-principle by which the mature human
being is distinguished from the child."[8] The physician achieves this
goal in the following manner. "In this educative process," said Freud,
"the clearer insight of the physician plays but an insignificant part; as
a rule he can say to his patient only what the latter's own reason can
say to him. . . . Let us say that the physician in his educative work
makes use of one of the components of love. . . . By the side of the
necessities of existence, love is the great teacher; and it is by his love
for those nearest him that the incomplete human being is induced to
respect the decrees of necessity and to spare himself the punishment
attendant on any infringement of it."[9] Freud appears to rely here on
his theory of anaclitic love but it is only by analogy that he can reduce
the psychoanalyst's influence to the self-preservative instincts. Freud
painted the clinical picture of "transference." "We observe . . ." he
said, "that the patient . . . begins to develop a particular interest
in the person of the physician. Everything connected with this person

seems to him more important than his own affairs and to distract him from his illness."[10] Ultimately, however, a "very powerful resistance" arises in the patient. The cause is in ". . . certain intense feelings of affection which the patient has transferred to the physician, not accounted for by the latter's behavior nor by the relationship involved by the treatment."[11] In this process there is a factor that ". . . alters the whole problem and puts our scientific calculations to shame." Transference may express itself as erotic love between a young female patient and a young psychoanalyst. On the other hand, it still exists ". . . even in circumstances of a positively grotesque incongruity—in elderly women, in relation to gray-bearded men, even on occasions when our judgment assures us that no temptations exist. Then we are compelled to give up the idea of a disturbing accident and to admit that we have to deal with a phenomenon in itself essentially bound up with the nature of the disease."[12] We then, ". . . no longer have to do with the previous illness, but with a newly created and transformed neurosis which has replaced the earlier one. . . . All the patient's symptoms have abandoned their original significance and have adapted themselves to a new meaning, which is contained in their relationships to the transference. . . . The conquest of this new artificially acquired neurosis coincides with the removal of the illness which existed prior to the treatment, that is, with accomplishing the therapeutic task."[13]

Does the role of the psychoanalyst involve any tampering with the norms of patients? Freud said, ". . . so far as possible we refrain from playing the part of mentor; we want nothing better than that the patient should find his own solutions for himself. . . . You must not be led away by my eagerness to defend myself against the accusation that in analytic treatment neurotics are encouraged to 'live a free life' and conclude from it that we influence them in favor of conventional morality. . . . We are not reformers, it is true, we are merely observers; *but we cannot avoid observing with critical eyes, and we have found it impossible to give our support to conventional sexual morality or to approve highly of the means by which society attempts to arrange the practical problems of sexuality in life. We can demonstrate with ease that what the world calls its code of morals demands more sacrifices than it is worth, and that its behavior is neither dictated by honesty nor instituted with wisdom. We do not absolve our patients from listening to these criticisms; we accustom them to an unprejudiced consideration of sexual matters like all other matters; and if after they have become independent by the affect of the treatment they choose some intermediate course between unrestrained sexual license and unconditional asceticism, our conscience is not burdened whatever the outcome.*"[14] (Italics ours.)

Is there any relation between the "transference" that Freud discovered and the "philosophy" that he feels so intensely? This philosophy could have the effect of changing the traditional point of view of a patient. If the traditional point of view was causally related to the neurosis then the change in it might well result in an improvement in the neurotic conditions.

This hypothesis is suggested by the Hans case. The reader will remember that in that case I suggested that the mother's principles had become unsupportable to little Hans. It was not of course just the principle but the principle to which the affect was attached. We have examined the possibility that Hans got along by a strong attack on this new element in his developing "ego-ideal." Hans's father was able to give him the support and strength he needed to overcome that disturbing introjected element that had come from Hans's mother.

We note from the passages above that Freud, with reference to neurotic tensions that were sexually based, could give the same help to his patients that Hans's father could give to Hans. Freud could relieve them from the intolerable requirements of their ego-ideals. This in turn would render the physician the probable object of libidinal cathexis.

In support of this view I should like to point out that psychoanalysis, according to Freud, was not effective in all mental disturbances. In fact, it was only effective in those disturbances where there was a certain type of libidinal involvement. Freud brought this out in the following: "There are other forms of illness . . . which our therapeutic treatment never is successful in treating, in spite of the similarity of conditions. In them also there was originally a conflict between ego and libido, leading to repression—although this conflict may be characterized by topographical differences from the conflict of the transference neuroses; in them too it is possible to trace out the point in the patient's life at which the repressions occurred; we apply the same method, are ready with the same assurances, offer the same assistance by telling the patient what to look out for; and here also the interval in time between the present and the point at which the repressions were established is all in favour of a better outcome of the conflict. And yet we cannot succeed in overcoming one resistance or in removing one of the repressions. These patients, paranoiacs, melancholics, and those suffering from dementia praecox, remain on the whole unaffected, proof against psychoanalytic treatment."[15]

The above discussion indicates to us that a libidinal element in "transference" is quite understandable. But it also indicates that a good deal of psychoanalytic work was done on the "ego-ideal" as I suggested in the Hans case and which now seems clear from Freud's statement.

However, it seems likely that another element entered into the transference which was lost sight of because of Freud's oversimplification of "love" behavior. It is no easy task to make changes in ego-ideals. An ego-ideal consists, in part, of a set of rules for conduct. No matter how onerous these rules may be they are binding on the ego until a new set of principles appears *that the ego is justified in accepting.*

Freud has stated that the ego-ideal is "imposed from without." Other people have imposed their expectations upon the ego. The society, in this sense, has imposed on the ego. *It follows that only the society can withdraw this imposition.*

In the Hans case the father was a great help to Hans. He had sufficient prestige with Hans to make possible an alteration in the ego-ideal. Parents may have this kind of prestige with reference to their children. But adults must look elsewhere. The psychoanalyst, i.e. the physician, holds the necessary position. The patient is not going to be punished for telling the "truth" to the physician. His non-conforming behavior is tolerated. His grievances against his ego-ideal may be "abreacted" without any "dread of the community." Thus, in the case of the neurotic, the patient lives in a temporary world of *moral* security in which the temporary, relaxed requirements of the physician free him both from the real dangers of social sanction and the equally real dangers of chastisement by his ego-ideal. The emotional satisfactions associated with this should normally invest the physician and be part of the transference Freud described.

It appears, also, that like Hans's father, Freud did work on the ego-ideal by trying to put it in a better permanent condition. Until this remolding of the ego-ideal was complete the patient could not hope to endure apart from the physician. This would tend to produce malingering and shock at parting from the physician.

By libidinizing the ego-ideal Freud over-simplified the elements concerned with it. This I think led to an incomplete explanation of transference and even of the role of the psychoanalyst in therapy.

The two convictions we have mentioned are something more than hypotheses as they work in Freud's mind. Reenforced by the biological frame of reference they stop, at the empirical level, consideration of these moments of personality process that must be referred to social learning and to normative orientation.

But insights have emerged. We think the conceptual suggestions we made in this and the last chapter are consistent with these insights and demanded by them. They continue to emerge in the next period of Freud's thought. We shall find the development of what we interpret as imposing "social" categories.

Part Three

THE SOCIAL
STRUCTURE
IN THE MIND

Chapter XII

REPETITION-COMPULSION

THE KEY TO Freud's "third period" lies in four concepts: the pleasure-principle, the reality-principle, repetition-compulsion, and the death-instinct. These concepts tell us of the new direction taken by his thought and they give us a clear indication of the kind of framework in which he proposes to work. We are, then, not surprised that the pleasure-principle becomes the newest expression of somatic reduction. The addition of the reality-principle, which supplements and limits the pleasure-principle, is something distinctly new although there are intimations of it earlier in Freud's thought. The reality-principle is another attempt to inject a satisfactory amount of initiative into the Conscious-Preconscious system without at the same time vitiating the importance of the Unconscious. The attempt to make this view hold requires the invention of further concepts. We end up with a "ring" of concepts that in their function are similar to earlier concepts such as primal repression.

THE PLEASURE-PRINCIPLE

"We have decided," said Freud, "to consider pleasure and 'pain' in relation to the quantity of excitation present in the psychic life—and not confined in any way—along such lines that 'pain' corresponds with an increase and pleasure with a decrease in this quantity."[1] This seems to be like the libido theory with the addition of the assumption that mental representations of pleasure and pain attend the diminution and the increase of the libido. Difficulties with earlier libido analysis make Freud cautious, however, "We do not thereby commit ourselves to a simple relationship between the strength of the feelings and the changes corresponding with them, least of all, judging from psycho-physiological experiences, to any view of a direct proportion existing between them. . . ."[2]

Freud mentioned Fechner's conception of pleasure and pain as related to conditions of stability and instability. However, Freud's conclusions did not tally with Fechner's. Fechner held that "every psycho-physical movement rising above the threshold of consciousness is charged with pleasure in proportion as it approximates—beyond a certain limit—to complete equilibrium, and with 'pain' in proportion as it departs from it beyond a certain limit; while between the two limits which may be described as the qualitative thresholds of 'pain' or pleasure, there is a certain area of aesthetic indifference."[3] Freud felt that ". . . there is an attempt on the part of the psychic apparatus to keep the quantity of excitation present as low as possible or at least constant." As between these possibilities of keeping the tension low or in keeping it constant Freud settles finally on the view that the organism tends to keep it low. This of course was a radical departure from the Fechner viewpoint.[4]

Indeed, if the pleasure-principle as Freud expresses it were to operate alone the end result would appear to be the rapid self-destruction of organisms since the state of death is the state of minimum tension. Fechner's view does not require a further principle to explain the tendency of organisms to live rather than to die. Freud's enunciation of his version of the pleasure-principle does require a supplementary principle to deal with the survival tendencies in organisms. The reader will note that Freud's pleasure-principle is in fact a death-principle and therefore involves the elements later incorporated in the death-instinct. It also is apparent that the pleasure-principle as developed by Freud is not really complemented by the reality-principle. The reality-principle in broad perspective permits the organism to guide itself to its death *safely*. If the organism does not appear to act in accordance with these principles we require some kind of principle of survival. This is finally furnished by the life instinct.

Freud recognized the baleful intimations in the pleasure-principle. He said this principle is ". . . useless and indeed extremely dangerous for the preservation of the organism amid the difficulties of the external world."[5] Something else is needed, then, if the organism is to survive and this is provided by the reality-principle. Under the influence of the instinct of the ego for self-preservation the pleasure-principle ". . . is replaced by the 'reality-principle,' which without giving up the intention of ultimately attaining pleasure yet demands and enforces the post-ponement of the satisfaction, and the renunciation of manifold possibilities of it, and the temporary endurance of 'pain' on the long and circuitous road to pleasure."[6]

According to this view the denial of instinct gratification because of the restraining hand of the reality-principle will be experienced as pain. However, pain may also be experienced *when there is tension reduction*. Freud stated that pain results when instincts fight ". . . their way through—along circuitous routes—to a direct or a substitutive gratification."[7] When this happens, ". . . this success, which might otherwise have brought pleasure is experienced by the ego as 'pain.' "[8] The reason, said Freud, that this gratification results in pain rather than pleasure is that the instincts expressing themselves have been under repression. "The details of the process by which repression changes a possibility of pleasure into a source of 'pain' are not yet fully understood, or are not yet capable of clear presentation, but it is certain that all neurotic 'pain' is of this kind, is pleasure which cannot be experienced as such."[9]

Freud suggested that the pain may be associated with the "danger signal" which indicates to the ego that instinct satisfaction cannot be safely permitted. Thus the pain does not ". . . impugn the supremacy of the pleasure-principle." Most of the pain experienced in the ego ". . . is of a perceptual order, perception either of the urge of unsatisfied instincts or of something in the external world which may be painful in itself or may arouse painful anticipations in the psychic apparatus and is recognized by it as 'danger.' The reaction to these claims of impulse and these threats of danger, a reaction in which the real activity of the psychic apparatus is manifested, may be guided correctly by the pleasure-principle or by the reality-principle which modifies this."[10]

The pleasure-principle suggests the libido theory in many respects. But as Freud has pointed out there is no necessary correlation between the degree of somatic excitation and the intensity of the feelings of pleasure or pain. This view opens up the possibility of a new examination of mental events. At the same time the possibilities of the reduction of the pleasure-principle to somatic excitation remain undoubted. On the ego side of the equation the reality-principle acts as a supplementary power to the repressive action of the ego. The reality-principle distinguishes the perceptual function of the ego and assumes that the ego has considerable initiative in its ability to guide behavior of the organism between the Scylla of organic excitation and the Charybdis of reality dangers.

Freud treated pleasure as the attendant to tension reduction. One type of pain is associated with increase of somatic tension. The other kind of pain is experienced by the ego, and results from perceptions of things in the external world.

An unsolved problem is that instinct satisfaction by "direct" gratification may be experienced by the ego as "pain." It remains for Freud to demonstrate how this experience of pain can be explained in terms of the reality-principle.

This general view, as would be expected, hinges upon the assumption that somatic tension reduction constitutes the sole object of action. The reality-principle in the ego discovers the most judicious paths to this tension reduction. It seems rather as though Freud has returned temporarily to the logical simplicity of earlier models. But, although he does seem to be going pretty far back he has also introduced important new factors. Will the theoretical changes involved in the pleasure-principle and the reality-principle lend themselves to more satisfactory system-making?

REPETITION-COMPULSION

Freud gave us a vivid account of the clinical evidence which required him to assume a psychic mechanism to supplement the pleasure-principle. The data were drawn from the behavior of a small boy. "The child," Freud reported, "was in no respect forward in his intellectual development; at eighteen months he spoke only a few intelligible words, making besides sundry significant sounds which were understood by those about him. . . . He did not disturb his parents at night; he scrupulously obeyed orders about not touching various objects and not going into certain rooms; and above all he never cried when his mother went out and left him for hours together, although the tie to his mother was a very close one; she had not only nourished him herself, but had cared for him and brought him up without any outside help. Occasionally, however, this well-behaved child evinced the troublesome habit of flinging into the corner of the room or under the bed all the little things he could lay his hands on, so that to gather up his toys was often no light task. He accompanied this by an expression of interest and gratification, emitting a loud long-drawn out 'o-o-o-oh' which in the judgment of the mother (one that coincided with my own) was not an interjection but meant 'go away' (fort). I saw at last that this was a game, and that the child used all his toys only to play 'being gone' with them. One day I made an observation that confirmed my view. The child had a wooden reel with a piece of string wound round it. It never occurred to him, for example, to drag this after him on the floor and so play horse and cart with it, but he kept throwing it with considerable skill, held by the string, over the side of his little draped cot, so that the reel disappeared into it, then said his significant 'o-o-o-oh' and drew the reel by the string out of the cot again, greeting its reappearance with a joyful 'Da' (there). This was therefore the complete game, disappearance and return, the first act being the one generally observed by the onlookers, and the one untiringly repeated by the child as a game for its own sake, although the greater pleasure unquestionably attached to the second act."[11] Freud's interpretation was confirmed by a further observation. "One day when the mother had been out for some hours she was greeted on her return by the information 'Baby o-o-o-oh' which at first remained unintelligible. It soon proved that during his long lonely hours he had found a method of bringing about his own disappearance. He had discovered his reflection in the long mirror which nearly reached to the ground and had then crouched down in front of it, so that the reflection was 'fort.' "[12]

Freud's view was that the child was dramatizing the departure of his mother. However, since the departure could not have been a source of pleasure to the child it did not seem consistent with the pleasure-principle that the child should repeat this experiment over and over as a game. Perhaps the departure was only the prelude to the joyful return. "As against this, however, there is the observation that the first act, the going away, was played by itself, as a game, and far more frequently than the whole drama with its joyful conclusion."[13]

Why then did the child, in play, reproduce a "painful" experience? Freud offered a novel explanation. "This effort might be ascribed to the impulse to obtain the mastery of a situation (the 'power' instinct) which remains independent of any question of whether the recollection was a pleasant one or not."[14] And he added, "We see that children repeat in their play everything that has made a great impression on them in actual life, that they thereby abreact the strength of the impression and so to speak make themselves masters of the situation. But on the other hand it is clear enough that all their play is influenced by the dominant wish of their time of life: viz. to be grown-up and to be able to do what grown-up people do. It is also observable that the unpleasing character of the experience does not always prevent its being utilized as a game."[15] Generalizing in a later passage, Freud stated that "In the play of children we seem to arrive at the conclusion that the child repeats even the unpleasant experiences because through his own activity he gains a far more thorough mastery of the strong impression than was possible by mere passive experience. Every fresh repetition seems to strengthen this mastery for which the child strives; even with pleasurable experiences the child cannot do enough in the way of repetition and will inexorably insist on the identity of the impression. The child . . . never gets tired of demanding from a grown-up the repetition of a game he has played with him before or has shown him, till at last the grown-up refuses, utterly worn out; similarly if he has been told a pretty story, he wants always to hear the same story instead of a new one, insists inexorably on exact repetition and corrects each deviation which the narrator lets slip by mistake, which perhaps he even thought to gain new merit by inserting. Here there is no contradiction of the pleasure-principle."[16]

Freud found that such situations terminate in a final pleasure gain and that ". . . for our purposes they are of no help since they presuppose the existence and supremacy of the pleasure-principle and bear no witness to the operation of tendencies beyond the pleasure-principle."[17] This tendency to mastery closely resembles, in its assumptions, the relief gained from the expression of tension through speech as explained by Freud in one of his early papers.[18] Freud, in the present case, recognized the similarity himself when he said that children repeat in their play those things that have made an impression on them in actual life, and that ". . . they thereby *abreact* (italics ours) the strength of the impression and so to speak make themselves masters of the situation."[19] In 1894, date of the publication of "The Defense Neuro-Psychoses," Freud had developed the idea of ". . . the discharge of excitement through speech."

Now he has suggested the idea of discharge of excitement through action. The difference is perhaps in the fact that in the old cathartic method there appeared to be an actual discharge of emotional tension. In the present case, however, this is not so evident. Therefore, since empirically there *is* pleasure it is necessary to assume some other kind of tension-reduction. The drive for mastery furnishes the possibility. Freud assumed that it was exercised in play and might be applied not only to pleasant situations but also to painful ones. The tendency to play the game again and again with the same tension-producing situation presumably would produce a balance of pleasure through the "satisfaction" or "gratification" of the drive for mastery.

Perhaps this was no violation of the pleasure principle but it certainly looks like a new kind of pleasure. Either Freud must assimilate this type of behavior to his larger theory or he must account for it in a different way.

Freud took the later course and proceeded to his formulation of the process, repetition-compulsion.

He mentioned the difficulties of therapy encountered by psychoanalysis and reported that interpreting the unconscious to the patient was not enough. It was necessary to compel the patient to confirm the interpretation through his own memory. Great resistances appeared in the patient and it was important to call the patient's attention to these resistances and ". . . by human influence—here came in suggestion acting as transference—teaching him to abandon the resistances."[20] However, it was not possible to bring the unconscious into consciousness by this method either. Instead of recollecting the patient would tend to ". . . repeat as a current experience what is repressed."[21] This repetition ". . . is played regularly in the sphere of transference, i.e. the relationship to the physician."[22]

What does this repetition mean? Evidently the patient does not undo the repression but instead incorporates the physician into the neurotic system. Thus a new neurosis replaces the old one. "The physician makes it his concern to limit the scope of this transference-neurosis as much as he can, to force into memory as much as possible, and to leave as little as possible to repetition."[23] To effect a cure the physician ". . . must let him (the patient) live through a certain fragment of his forgotten life, and has to see to it that some measure of ascendency remains, in the light of which the apparent reality is always recognized as a reflection of a forgotten past. If this is successfully accomplished then conviction on the part of the patient is attained and with it, the therapeutic result that depends on it."[24] It appears then that the repetition-compulsion may be terminated when the patient can be brought to recognize its existence.

Freud found it rather difficult to incorporate this repetition mechanism into his general theory. The Ucs, as he pointed out, ". . . has no other aim than to force its way through the pressure weighing on it, either to consciousness or to discharge by means of some real action."[25] So the repetition mechanism does not appear to belong to the Ucs. Furthermore, the repetition does not operate syntonically with the Ucs. On the contrary, "The resistance in the treatment proceeds from the same higher levels and systems in the psychic life that in their time brought about the repression."[26] Nevertheless, the resistance or the repetition is unconscious. Freud has discovered that the ego seems to have its own private Ucs. This consideration leads him again to suggest a redefinition of his topographical system. The reader will perceive that it is the *same* redefinition that he suggested back in *The Interpretation of Dreams* when he was perplexed by some of the clinical data concerned with dreams. "We escape ambiguity," he suggested, "if we contrast not the conscious and the unconscious but the coherent ego and the repressed. Much in the ego is certainly unconscious itself, just what may be called the kernel of the ego; only a part of it comes under the category of preconscious."[27] This assumption makes it possible to say ". . . that the resistance on the part of the analysed person proceeds from his ego, and then we at once see that the repetition-compulsion must be ascribed to the repressed element in the unconscious."[28]

Difficulties with "repetition-compulsion" have given rise to an improved version of the ego. The "kernel" of the ego is seen as unconscious and part of this kernel is repressed. Thus ego conflicts can proceed below the level of consciousness. But when we remember the conscious play involved in the child's game reported above we wonder how the repetition-compulsion can be assigned to the repressed area of the ego. And how can it be deprived of its function—as appeared there—of giving some stability to the ego in the face of the reality situation?

Can the theory of the child's game be extended to transference and to repetition-compulsion as it is found in analysis? That depends on whether there is a "reality situation" here and whether the "kernel of the ego" has an interest in such a distribution of cathexes as will conform to reality requirements.

We have pointed out that the physician is in a unique position with reference to the patient and that many factors make it sensible for the patient to wish to continue this relationship. And the relationship can only be continued by a *repetition of the symptoms,* or by such behavior as indicates that the patient is still "sick." The patient, in other words, has the benefit of a temporary social relationship which is subjectively valuable to him. We have indicated that this relationship removes the "dread of the community." The social relationship of physician and patient also encourages the expression of those tensions and object-cathexes which were formerly held under restraint. Thus the patient has many "reality" reasons for continuing the symptoms and "expressing" transference. We would adopt Freud's suggestion that this process takes place in the ego but below the level of consciousness. On this view we are not compelled to the conclusion that the "repetition-compulsion" is a mechanical process but that it is merely one of the adjustive mechanisms of the ego.

Is there still another reality situation here that requires consideration? Freud gave us more reminders of the child's game in the following passage. "The bonds of tenderness linking the child more especially to the parent of the opposite sex succumbed to disappointment, to the vain expectation of satisfaction, and to the jealousy aroused by the birth of a new child, unmistakable proof as it is of the faithlessness of the loved parent. . . . All these undesired happenings and painful affective situations are repeated by neurotics in the 'transference' stage and re-animated with much ingenuity. They struggle to break off the unfinished treatment, they know how to re-create the feelings of being disdained, how to force the physician to adopt brusque speech and a

chilling manner towards them, they find suitable objects for their
jealousy, they substitute for the ardently desired child of early days
the promise of some great gift which becomes as real as that was. Nothing of all this could ever have afforded any pleasure; one would suppose
it ought to bring about somewhat less 'pain' if revealed as memory
rather than if lived through as a new experience. It is a question
naturally of the action of impulses that should lead to satisfaction,
but the experience that instead of this they even then brought 'pain' has
borne no result. The act is repeated in spite of everything: a powerful
compulsion insists on it."[29]

The description here is so similar to the situation in the child's
game that we can hardly resist applying the same hypothesis to it that
Freud applied in the earlier case. The patient is endeavouring to obtain
a mastery of the "painful" material in some manner similar to the
mastery obtained by the child. Here, however, the "play" element is
not uppermost. This suggests that play may be only one of the tech-
niques for the mastery of mental tension-situations, perhaps the conscious one. In the case of the child there was a redistribution of ego-
cathexes as a result of the game situation. Is it not likely that some kind
of redistribution of cathexes is also the aim in this repetition of ancient
tensions?

If this view is explored we must wonder what cathexes can be re-
distributed by the ego. Freud disregarded the potentialities of hyper-
cathexis and anti-cathexis in developing the mechanism of repetition-
compulsion. He bypassed the initiative of the ego, as he has done so
many times before, by assuming an automatic ego mechanism that
would account for this apparent initiative. But the hypothesis seems
sound that the ego by the repetition is seeking to obtain a redistribution
of "mobile quantities" (anti-cathexis and hyper-cathexis) to reduce
the tension of the psychic formations.

If we entertain this hypothesis we see another reality orientation of
the "kernel of the ego." It not only adjusts to the potentialities of the
social situation but it also adjusts to the realities of psychic formations
by "appropriate action." An empirical extension of this theory is immediately obvious. Is not the dream process precisely the same kind of
process? Do we not then find in repetition-compulsion, transference
and the dream-process examples of the reality orientation of the "*coherent ego*" as it tries to re-distribute cathexes with the aim of self-
therapy?

It seems to us that Freud's suggestion about the "kernel of the ego"
indicates *that ego process itself is largely and perhaps most importantly
an unconscious process.* And it well may be that one aspect of the
"external world" and the "reality situation" to the coherent ego *is the*

conscious element itself. It appears that to some extent the state of consciousness may be controlled by the coherent ego. Yet, of course, the control of motility and of the perceptual faculties are in large part within the conscious system. The resistance of repetition-compulsion appears to be one faculty at the disposal of the coherent ego in the mutuality of its relations with the Conscious. It is clear also that the Conscious may deny entry to Consciousness of material from the coherent ego. *Thus the censorship is a two-way system.*

The meaning we have found in "repetition-compulsion" has led us to establish it in the coherent ego with the recognition that a great deal of the process in the coherent ego is unconscious. Here is perhaps that "true psychic reality" that Freud once located in the Unconscious. Freud, on the other hand, found no meaning in repetition-compulsion in spite of his first tendency to connect it with a "mastery" principle. We suggest that it acts as an extension of the reality-principle.

Chapter XIII

THE DEATH INSTINCT

REPETITION-COMPULSION led Freud into at least a temporary alteration in his "topological" outlook. The Unconscious remains pretty much the way it was, although it is losing a good deal of its effectiveness. The "secondary process," however, is now seen to possess two types of unconscious material. First, the innocuous preconscious material, and second, the far from innocuous repressed material. Repressed material is not only in a state of repression; it also tends to be characterized by distinctive process. As in the case of the Unconscious, when we refer to this process we shall capitalize and refer to the Repressed. The Repressed emerges as a kind of private Unconscious in the ego. These views are expressed in *Beyond the Pleasure Principle*[1] and they indicate that Freud has found a place of a sort for such phenomena as "ideal masochism."

In the Repressed area it is assumed that all the material is unconscious. In the ego, however, there is conscious, preconscious and unconscious material.

The exposition of the reality-principle required Freud to be more explicit about the perceptual aspects of the ego. Consciousness, i.e. the perceptual part of it, explained Freud, is ". . . a rind . . . which would finally have been burned through by the effects of stimulation such that it presents the most favourable conditions for the reception of stimuli and is incapable of any further modification."[2] Freud then postulated certain physiological ". . . defenses against stimuli." These are the ". . . sense organs, which essentially comprise arrangements for the reception of specific stimuli, but also possess special arrangements adapted for a fresh protection against an overwhelming amount of stimulus, and for warding off unsuitable kinds of stimuli. It is

179

characteristic of them that they assimilate only very small quantities of the outer stimulus, and take in only samples of the outer world; one might compare them to antenae which touch at the outer world and then constantly withdraw from it again."[3]

The external "rind" then is the window upon reality. Incoming stimuli are filtered or sampled by the sense organs. Next to the sense organs there is a ". . . cortical layer . . . differentiated as the organ for reception of external stimuli."[4] This latter structure is the main Conscious system which also receives stimuli or excitations from within. ". . . the position of the system," says Freud, "between outer and inner and the difference in the conditions under which this receptivity operates on the two sides become deciding factors for the functioning of the system and of the whole psychic apparatus. Towards the outer world there is a barrier against stimuli, and the mass of excitations coming up against it will take effect only on a reduced scale; towards what is within no protection against stimuli is possible, the excitations of the deeper layers pursue their way directly and in undiminished mass into the system, while certain characteristics of their course produce the series of pleasure-pain feelings."[5]

Freud constructed a favorite model here, one in which dynamic forces converge upon an inert element. The old relation between the Ucs and the Cs is reasserted with the addition of another dynamic force which presses upon the Cs from the outside through the organs of perception. In the present anatomical model Freud has separated the Conscious system as such from the forces of selection and rejection. He has attached these to the sense organs themselves. The defense which the Conscious system has outwardly is not due to any power of its own but to the structure of the sense organs. There being no such organs inwardly the Conscious system is pictured as defenseless.

Freud now proposed to show how forces ". . . beyond the pleasure-principle" operate in the mind. "Such external excitations," he says, "as are strong enough to break through the barrier against stimuli we call traumatic. In my opinion the concept of trauma involves such a relationship to an otherwise efficacious barrier. The pleasure-principle is to begin with put out of action here. The flooding of the psychic apparatus with large masses of stimuli can no longer be prevented: on the contrary, another task presents itself—to bring the stimulus under control, to 'bind' in the psyche the stimulus mass that has broken its way in, so as to bring about a discharge of it."[6] It appears that in the case of trauma the normal defenses furnished by the sense organs themselves have broken down. No reason is given us for this at present. But in any event the mind must furnish some kind of emergency defense. "What are we to expect as the reaction of the psychic life to this invasion? From all sides the 'charging energy' is called on in order to create all round the breach correspondingly high 'charges' of energy. An immense 'counter-charge' is set up, in favour of which all the other psychic systems are impoverished, so that a wide-spread paralysis or diminution of other psychic activity follows."[7]

At first Freud held that the Conscious system was inert, dependent on the sense organs to repel external stimuli and quite powerless with relation to the stimuli coming from inside the psyche. But then it appears that in an emergency the Conscious system can muster up quite a fund of energy. It would seem that this fund of energy would have to be attached as "free-floating" energy to the Conscious system and that it should be available not only to repel borders from without but also from within.

Freud assumed that there is an *automatic force* attached to external stimuli. The quanta of these forces can ordinarily be repelled or reduced by the sense organs. In certain cases, however, the amount of the force in the stimulus is sufficient to overwhelm the sense organs. Then the external force moves directly into the mind.

This view probably suggested itself to Freud because of its resemblance to his earliest representations of the relation between libido-quantum and the mind, and the production of neurasthenia by a "flooding" of the mind. Here the "flood" comes from a physical force from the outside, instead of a somatic source on the inside.

But certainly the quanta of force associated with stimuli *per se* are not the quanta associated with psychic disturbance in the typical case. Individuals withstood the discharge of 5-inch and 16-inch guns during World War II without mental disturbance. Yet, on other occasions, individuals cannot stand the sight of a mouse or a horse's "widdler." The physical impact of a stimulus has but a low correlation with its reception by the psyche.

The stimulus does not carry the energy with which Freud is concerned. The mind furnishes the critical energy to the stimulus. The problem of the deployment of psychic energies is therefore not avoided any more than it was avoided in the earlier cases of sexual innervation.

This model appeared so unsatisfactory, even to Freud, that he despaired of proceeding very far with it. His doubts extended to quantitative analysis in general. "The indefinite nature of all the discussions that we term metapsychological," he said, "naturally comes from the fact that we know nothing about the nature of the excitation process in the elements of the psychic system and do not feel justified in making any assumption about it."[8]

TRAUMATIC NEUROSIS AND
REPETITION-COMPULSION

Freud examined some of the mechanics of repetition-compulsion and their relation to the reality-principle in an analysis of traumatic neurosis. "I think," Freud reported, "one may venture (tentatively) to regard the ordinary traumatic neurosis as the result of the extensive rupture of the barrier against stimuli. . . . We seek to understand the effect of the shock by considering the breaking through of the barrier with which the psychic organism is provided against stimuli, and from the tasks with which this is thereby faced."[9] He considered fright to be the central factor in the neurosis and suggested that, "What conditions it [fright] is the failure of the mechanism of apprehension to make the proper preparation, including the overcharging of the systems first receiving the stimulus. In consequence of this lower degree of charging these systems are hardly in a position to bind the oncoming masses of excitation, and the consequences of the breaking through of the protective barrier appear all the more easily."[10] So it appears that ". . . the apprehensive preparation, together with the overcharging of the receptive systems, represents the last line of defense against the stimuli."[11]

Freud applied these views to the traumatic neuroses. "When the dreams of patients suffering from traumatic neuroses so regularly take them back to the situation of the disaster they do not thereby, it is true, serve the purpose of wish fulfillment, the hallucinatory conjuring up of which has, under the domination of the pleasure-principle, become the function of dreams." Here is the familiar restatement of the dream as a kind of regressive mechanism in which the pleasure-principle is deluded into accepting an image as object. This view of course does not fit the dreams in question. "But we may assume," continued Freud, "that they [dreams] thereby subserve another purpose, which must be fulfilled before the pleasure-principle can begin its sway. These dreams are attempts at restoring control of the stimuli by developing apprehension, the pretermission of which caused the traumatic neurosis."[12]

In this passage Freud again attached a purpose, a function, to the repetition of the "situation of disaster." The dream he thought, was trying to gain control of the stimuli by developing "apprehension." This reasserts the mastery impulse that Freud suggested with reference to the child's game.

In transference, the "resistance" that Freud speaks of strongly resembles the repetition here. Certainly there is a strong inference that in the repetition of transference the ego is trying to "restore control" of the stimuli. In this case, however, the stimuli may be internal stimuli.

Freud's hypothesis that apprehension is developed is an attempt to maintain the fiction that there is a real external threat. In any event, "apprehension" refers to one of the concrete ways in which free-floating energy in the ego may be employed to bring about psychic stability.

Freud was of the opinion that the traumatic neuroses ". . . afford us an insight into a function of the psychic apparatus, which without contradicting the pleasure-principle, is nevertheless independent of it, and appears to be of earlier origin than the aim of attaining pleasure and avoiding 'pain.' "[13] So Freud held tenaciously to the view that a psychic mechanism wags the ego. Referring to the traumatic dreams that bring back the recollection of the psychic traumata of childhood, he said, "They obey . . . the repetition-compulsion, which in analysis, it is true, is supported by the (not unconscious) wish to conjure up again what has been forgotten and repressed."[14]

Refusing to grant to the ego the therapeutic power that is suggested by the evidence, Freud preferred to assume the repetition-compulsion and to establish a principle of mental functioning that was independent of the reality-principle and the pleasure-principle.

Freud's reasoning about the war neuroses is curious. He conceded that there are traumatic neuroses ". . . which have arisen the more easily on account of an ego-conflict."[15] This line is not pursued, however. He felt that an important factor about the traumatic neuroses was that ". . . a severe injury inflicted at the same time as the trauma lessens the chance of a neurosis arising."[16] Explaining this he said: ". . . a mechanical concussion must be recognized as one of the sources of sexual excitation." Furthermore, ". . . a painful and feverish illness exerts for the time it lasts a powerful influence on the distribution of the libido."[17] He concluded that, ". . . the mechanical force of the trauma would set free the quanta of sexual excitation which, in consequence of the lacking preparation by apprehension, has a traumatic effect; but, on the other hand, the contemporaneous bodily injury would bind the surplus excitation by the putting in of a claim to a narcissistic overcharging of the injured part."[18]

Freud employed two theories here to serve his purposes. He could have applied them to one event and come up with the same result. He maintained that a trauma released energy in the mind. This is generally in line with his most recent theory of the impact of an external stimulus. But the bodily injury, which is also an external stimulus, puts in a claim for narcissistic overcharging. So it uses up the energy created by the trauma and equilibrium is maintained. By applying the two points of view to the bodily injury alone Freud could have come up with the same result. It is the "yield" of opposed theories that furnished the "explanation" here.

In the analyses we have examined Freud reduced ego process to an essentially mechanical and "primal" type. The repetition-compulsion was shaken loose of any function. Mental activity was reduced to the opposition of organic or mechanical quantities. The subjective experiences were reduced to hallucinatory phenomena.

Freud's theory has accumulated any number of mechanisms and processes with strangely perverse tendencies. The dream process, we remember, was "regressive." Childhood dreams had a peculiar need to *repeat* themselves. In punishment dreams the organism turned on itself, as it were, and forced itself to feel pain. In the earliest time there was a primal repression, the establishment of a state of primal neurosis. Mental events have again and again appeared as hallucinations. The libido theory assumed that object-cathexis was the result of the overflowing of libido in the mind. Later considerations led Freud to feel that this flow in the direction of object-cathexis might deplete the mind. Thus the "normal" object interests of the individual appeared to work toward his weakening and eventual destruction. Since the repetition-compulsion was associated with pain and suffering its insistence on this pain and suffering appeared to indicate a feverish press toward the destruction of the organism. This press seemed general, instinctive. Yet it was broader than an instinct. It was a general tendency.

"In what way," asks Freud, "is the instinctive connected with the compulsion to repetition? At this point the idea is forced upon us that we have stumbled on the trace of a general and hitherto not clearly recognized—or at least not expressly emphasized—characteristic of instinct, perhaps of all organic life. According to this, an instinct would be a tendency innate in living organic matter impelling it toward the reinstatement of an earlier condition, one which it had to abandon under the influence of external disturbing forces . . . the manifestation of inertia in organic life."[19]

This is indeed a master assumption. It tends to bring together under one head *all of those errant processes in the mind which have neither served the interests of the Unconscious nor been assigned to the ego.* This is the master mechanism which provides a rationale for the various local mechanisms that Freud has postulated from time to time. Those mechanisms made it possible for Freud to maintain the equilibrium of his system without granting dominance to the ego and without expressly organizing and analysing a category of motivation resulting from the socialization of the individual.

When life first was awakened in lifeless matter ". . . the first instinct was present, that to return to lifelessness. The living substance at that time had death within easy reach; there was probably only a short course of life to run, the direction of which was determined by the chemical structure of the young organism."[20] It follows that ". . . we are obliged to place all the results of organic development to the credit of external, disturbing and distracting influences."[21] The earliest creatures would not have wanted to change, they would ". . . if circumstances had remained the same, have always merely repeated the same course of existence. But in the last resort it must have been the evolution of our earth, and its relation to the sun, that has left its imprint on the development of organisms."[22] These influences worked so as to ". . . compel the still surviving substance to ever greater deviations from the original path of life, and to ever more complicated and circuitous routes to the attainment of the goal of death. These circuitous ways to death, faithfully retained by the conservative instincts, would be neither more nor less than the phenomena of life as we know it now."[23] Seen in this light "The theoretical significance of the instincts of self-preservation, power, and self-assertion, shrinks to nothing . . . they are part-instincts designed to secure the path to death peculiar to the organism and to ward off possibilities of return to the inorganic other than the immanent ones . . . the organism is resolved to die only in its own way; even these watchmen of life were originally the myrmidons of death. Hence the paradox comes about that the living organism resists with all its energy influences (dangers) which could help it to reach its life-goal by a short way (a short circuit, so to speak); but this is just the behaviour that characterizes a pure instinct as contrasted with an intelligent striving."[24]

Thus we see the development of the death instinct. It is really a theoretical postulate to employ along with the Unconscious and the Ego. Earlier mechanisms, of the same nature, have been local. They have not been theoretically on the same level with the Conscious-Preconscious or the Unconscious. They have applied to material which has been removed from either category. In the death instinct all these mechanisms or assumptions are joined in a new category. This category is a residual category, i.e. it holds material that does not fit the other two categories. And in that sense it is a confession of the theoretical inadequacy of the other two categories. Since Freud has spun his theory so close to organic processes it has, from the beginning, been convenient to transform these categories *into organic processes*. This has been done with the Unconscious and the Conscious-Preconscious. Once they have been looked upon as organic processes they have had an independent right to exist. The death instinct, since Freud has postulated it as an organic process, also has an independent right to exist. But this organic process has been assumed merely for the purpose of extricating Freud from a very grave theoretical problem. Large segments of data are not falling conveniently into the logical categories of the Unconscious and the Conscious-Preconscious. Radical revisions have been made in these categories. They have now become the ego and the repressed. But Freud has refused to grant to the category of the ego therapeutic powers, or motivations based on internalized standards. And he has also refused to grant to the ego the tendency to cathect organic impulses, with the extensive theoretical alterations that result from that assumption. This leaves many processes unmotivated. Since Freud has become concerned with ego processes, with the reality-principle and traumatic neuroses, these processes have appeared more dominant than ever before. The assumption of a death instinct recognized the existence of new psychic functions. However, by relegating these processes to the category of instinct Freud made it extremely difficult to isolate them. As I see it he has absorbed three ego processes into the death instinct: (a) Those ego processes tending to work toward personality "equilibrium" or mastery. (b) Ego tendencies toward self-therapy. (c) The formation and influence of the ego-ideal.

In the concept "cathexis" Freud has already presented us with a means of at least suggesting a typology of the metapsychological forces in the mind, and their relation to external stimuli. In the first place there are three sets of organic impulses. (We are not considering ego-ideal "impulses" here.) Using Freud's terminology they are the "sexual impulse," the "nutritional impulses" (hunger and thirst; they are not examined extensively by Freud), and the "self-preservative instincts." Freud has granted almost exclusive significance to the sex-impulse but it is clear that all of these impulses are represented by a variable amount of mental "press." In other words they have a variable amount of cathexis. As Freud has pointed out, in certain circumstances of maximum or nearly maximum cathexis the mental energy of these impulses may overwhelm the ego and take command of the means of mobility. In the vast number of cases however the instinct representative is not strong enough to commandeer the ego. Nevertheless, *the impulses mentioned are sources of energy imput at the ego level.*

The energy-value of a stimulus, as Freud has been considering it, is not dependent on the absolute amount of somatic impact it has on the organism, but on its "index-value" as the object of cathexis or anti-cathexis. An object-impulse formation tends to mobilize energy. In the case of sex the relation of the stimuli to the impulse often must be learned. In the case of fear, a self-preservative impulse, the stimulus may be cathected without the interposition of the learning process.

The impulse, then, varies along the following dimensions in terms of its mental significance: (a) It varies along the lines of the intensity of its psychic representative. In other words, it varies in its maximum and minimum cathexis potential, as well as in its average and modal cathexis potential. It is clear that the nature of these potentials is so influenced by cultural conditioning that the two cannot be successfully separated. (b) The impulse varies in object-cathexes along the dimension of learned and unlearned responses. (c) The impulse, upon cathecting an image or object varies in the amount of its cathectic "mobilization." The presentation to the sexual impulse of an image of a naked person of the opposite sex will bring about a marked inflammation of the cathexis potential without ordinarily breaking down the resistance of the ego. On the other hand, the presentation of certain stimuli to the impulse of fear may so inflame the energy potential of this self-preservative impulse as to temporarily demolish the rule of the ego.

There is, then, a constant input into the ego of impulse-energies that vary in proportion to the somatic states which they represent. The cathexes of stimulus-presentations result also in a continual alteration in their energy states.

Freud's research supports the view that there is a fund of free-floating energy which can only be conceived as attached to the coherent ego. This energy may resist or advance the tendencies of the organic impulses. If it resists we speak of anti-cathexis. If it reenforces we speak of hyper-cathexis.

The phenomenon of repression may be distinguished from denial by the fact that in repression there is a factor of hyper-cathexis added to organic cathexis. This makes the formation harder to hold down, to repress. In denial it would seem that the hyper-cathexis of the organic energy does not take place and therefore the particular formation is "normally" not a psychic problem. The process of denial appears to be the act of withdrawing hyper-cathexis from the mental formation.

This approach may throw some light on sublimation and dream formation. Sublimation appears to be the redeployment of a mental formation in terms of an ego objective, even though appreciable amounts of impulse-energy are assumed to be in the formation. Sublimation tends to show that the amount of ego energy in libidinal formations must be very large. In a similar manner the "gratification" obtained in the usual dream is a gratification of the hyper-cathexis furnished by the ego to the libidinal formation. It seems clear that the ego is by no means the Puritan that Freud once imagined it to be.

Freud mentioned an "immense countercharge" that surrounds the "breach" in cases where the mind is flooded with stimulus energy. Our analysis has indicated that the threatening energy is not attached to the stimulus as such. It is a result of the tumescence, as it were, of the organically based energy upon cathexis of the stimulus. The ego energy does not surround the breach in the perceptual system but deploys itself against the mobility threat involved in the increase of organic energy, i.e. it withdraws hyper-cathexis and employs anti-cathexis. It is quite conceivable that the ego might hyper-cathect the organic energy formation. This should lead to an abnormally intense formation.

Freud's insistence on maintaining the passive quality of the ego has stood in the way of moving toward theoretical synthesis. At the same time it has kept him from making the best use of one of his most important insights—the reality principle. The accumulation of residual mechanisms and primal urges—being substantially "unreasonable" in the framework of the Freudian system—have been subsumed under a "death-instinct." We have tried to show that Freud's data pointed to a more active ego—one that could absorb the activities assigned to the death-instinct. In an earlier chapter our analysis showed that Freud masked the activity of important variables in the ego by reducing them all to libidinal currents. Under the rubric of the death-instinct he has concealed a new set of important ego activities.

Chapter XIV

THE PRINCIPLE OF

OUTGOINGNESS—EROS

A PHILOSOPHY

FOR THE UNCONSCIOUS

THE DEATH-INSTINCT "explained" why people engage in senseless and self-destructive behavior. It remained for Freud to try to integrate this concept into his larger theory. He must in particular relate the death-instinct to the ego-instincts and his views on sexuality.

First, Freud explained the sexual impulse. He said that the reproductive cells, after a given time, detach themselves from the parent organism, and ". . . under favourable conditions they begin to develop . . . to repeat the same cycle to which they owe their origin, the end being that again one portion of the substance carries through its development to a finish, while another part, as a new germinal core, again harks back to the beginning of the development."[1] These cells confer a potentiality on the living substance, ". . . although perhaps it only means a lengthening of the path to death." The sexual instincts are the ". . . actual life-instincts."[2]

One of the peculiarities of these "life-instincts" is that they have been able to resist development. ". . . the reproductive cells . . . retain the original structure of the living substance and, after a given time, detach themselves from the parent organism. . . ."[3] These cells are, then, similar to those organisms which have not ". . . yielded to the external compulsion driving to an ever further development." They

189

resemble those forms of life that have ". . . succeeded in maintaining themselves on their low level up to the present time. . . ."[4]

The sexual instincts have a dual aspect—they maintain the earlier simple biological organization and are therefore nearer death, and they encourage the union of cells which results in a new organism and in this they are furthering the life of organisms. Thus the sexual instincts actually have a life aspect and a death aspect. Freud used the sexual instincts to isolate a biological death-instinct and this, of course, obscured his development of these instincts as life-instincts. The sexual instincts were the most rudimentary organizations he could find in advanced organic life. This attempt at isolation was not completed to his satisfaction. It left the ego-instincts as psychic death-instincts that could not be matched by an organic instinct of the same nature.

Freud pushed forward with the idea of the sexual instincts as life-instincts. They help the reproductive cells, and look after the destinies of those ". . . elementary organisms which survive the individual being"; they ". . . concern themselves with sheltering them." This continues ". . . as long as they are defenseless against the stimuli of the outer world." The sexual instincts ". . . bring about their conjunction with other reproductive cells."[5] At the same time these sexual instincts or life-instincts are "Conservative in the same sense as the others are . . ." but ". . . they are so in a higher degree."[6]

It seems that the life-instincts, themselves, have a rather nostalgic feeling about death. Freud maintained that ". . . when life first was awakened in lifeless matter the first instinct was present: that to return to lifelessness. The living substance at that time had death within easy reach. . . ."[7] The reproductive cells have kept death within easy reach. They have resisted development, they have maintained themselves "on their low level."

On the other hand the ego-instincts or the death-instincts actually work mightily to avoid death. They insist on a ". . . lengthening of the path to death." However, it is true that this action seems to have been forced upon them by exterior circumstances.

The difficulties in reconciling the life-instincts and the death-instincts are compounded when we think of the way the energies are distributed among these instincts. The sexual instincts are governed by the "pleasure-principle" and, as Freud has already pointed out, the tendency of this principle is to restore a tensionless state, or a state of death. On the other hand, the ego-instincts are governed in part by the "reality-principle." This principle guards the organism by having regard for the "danger signal" and controls and limits the satisfaction striven for under the pleasure-principle. So the reality-principle tends to preserve the organism, while the pleasure-principle tends to destroy the organism.

Beyond the Pleasure Principle is one of the most persuasively recondite of Freud's works. His sallies into myth and biology contribute little to a clear picture.

The target of Freud's thought, as it seems to us, was the relation between the categories Conscious and Unconscious. His formulations of the life-instincts and the death-instincts restate the dynamics he found in the relations of the Conscious and the Unconscious. The Conscious through a strange constitutional moment of force worked against the Unconscious. The Unconscious, striving for libidinal discharge and "death" in that way, was hampered by the restrictions of the Conscious system. The Conscious system was set on the "death" of the Unconscious. In this sense the life-instincts and the death-instincts constitute a philosophy for Freud's theoretical categories.

This philosophy makes pretty much of a mockery of psychic process. It is fundamentally "defective" and "hallucinatory." "The development of man up to now," said Freud, "does not seem to need any explanation differing from that of animal development, and the restless striving towards further perfection which may be observed in a minority of human beings is easily explicable as the result of that repression of instinct upon which what is most valuable in human nature is built. The repressed instinct never ceases to strive after its complete satisfaction which would consist in the repetition of a primary experience of satisfaction: all substitution- or reaction-formations and sublimations avail nothing towards relaxing the continual tension; and out of the excess of the satisfaction demanded over that found is born the driving momentum which allows of no abiding in any situation presented to it, but in the poet's words ". . . urges ever forward, ever unsubdued."[8]

REFORMULATION OF THE
DEATH INSTINCTS—EROS

Freud decided that the ego-instincts were even more conservative than the life-instincts. Only for the ego-instincts, he said, ". . . can we properly claim the conservative, or better, regressive-character corresponding to a repetition-compulsion." He emphasized the "creative" aspects of the sexual instincts. He called attention to the process of conjugation, ". . . the temporary mingling of two unicellular entities," and said that this ". . . has a preservative and rejuvenating effect on both."[9] This pervasive influence of the sex instinct leads directly to the use of libido theory. "The attempt might consequently be made to transfer the libido theory yielded by psychoanalysis to the relationship of the cells to one another and to imagine that it is the vital or sexual instincts active in every cell that take the other cells for the 'object,' partially neutralize their death-instincts, i.e. the processes stimulated by these, and so preserve those cells in life, while other cells do the same for them, and still others sacrifice themselves in the exercise of this libidinous function."[10] Thus libido takes on an entirely new dimension: "The libido of our sexual instincts would coincide with the Eros of poets and philosophers, which holds together all things living."[11]

Freud, in a number of earlier concepts, has provided for the production of libido. He has emphasized the discharge of libido and its tendencies toward cathexis. But the co-operative aspect of libido is something distinctly new. This aspect was sorely lacking in Freud's earlier analysis of object-cathexes. Although Freud has derived the concept of Eros from the union of the sex cells, the function of Eros is particularly apt for the ego. It stands for the tendency toward outgoingness which could not be handled in the early libido analysis.

Certainly libido-quantum would no longer recognize itself. First it acquired the ability to seek out images and now it is sacrificing itself for the common good. Compared to libido, Proteus had but a pedestrian imagination in his creation of new forms.

Freud then libidinized the ego with Eros, in this way tending to identify Eros with the death instincts. "We are the more compelled," said Freud, "now to accentuate the libidinous character of the self-preservative instincts, since we are venturing on the further step of recognizing the sexual instinct as the Eros, the all-sustaining, and of deriving the narcissistic libido of the ego from the sum of the libido quantities that bring about the mutual adherence of the somatic cells."[12]

In the above statement the reader will readily recognize a restatement of the proposition, familiar to us in earlier libido theory, that the erotic instincts are supported upon the self-preservative instincts. But this is a new kind of libidinal quality concerned not only with the survival of the self-ego but with the egos of others. It thus enthrones the variables of esteem and altruism that were not isolated under the old libido theory. This makes possible the following position. "If the self-preservative instincts are also of a libidinous kind," said Freud, "then perhaps we have no other instincts at all than libidinous ones. There are at least no others apparent."[13]

However, this whole investigation was originally set in motion by the phenomenon of repetition-compulsion. If we do away with all instincts but Eros we have eliminated the possibility of explaining repetition-compulsion. Freud, therefore, takes a cautious stand. "It remains an awkward fact that analysis up to now has only put us in the position of demonstrating libidinous impulses. The conclusion that therefore there are no others is one to which we do not assent."[14] But he now explicitly separates the death instincts from the self-preservative instincts. "We were prepared indeed to reckon even the alleged self-preservation instincts of the ego among death instincts, a position which we have since corrected and withdrawn from."[15]

All other devices having failed it remained for Freud to postulate a death instinct *de novo*. "We have," he said, "long recognized a sadistic component of the sexual instinct: it can, as we know, attain independence and as a perversion dominate the whole sexual trend of a person. . . . But how is one to derive the sadistic impulse which aims at the injury of the object, from the life-sustaining Eros! Does not the assumption suggest itself that this sadism is properly a death-instinct which is driven apart from the ego by the influence of the narcissistic libido? so that it becomes manifest only in reference to the object? It then enters the service of the sexual function; at the oral stage of organization of the libido, amorous possession is still one and the same as annihilation of the object; later the sadistic impulse separates itself and at last at the stage of the genital primacy it takes over, with the aim of propagation, the function of so far overpowering the sex-object as the carrying out of the sexual act demands. One might even say that the sadism expelled from the ego has acted as guide to the libidinous components of the sexual instinct; these later press on towards the object. Where the original sadism experiences no abatement or fusion, the well-known hate-love ambivalence of the love-life is set up."[16] Thus both the life-instincts and the death-instincts are derived from libido. The emphasis on the self-preservative instincts as insisting on a roundabout way to death is much lessened. In fact, the entire analysis appears as a tortuous struggle toward the formulation of Eros to supplement the functions previously given to libido.

EROS AND THE DEATH-INSTINCT
AS COMPONENTS OF
SOCIAL CONDITIONING

In the old libido theory Freud had no satisfactory explanation of object-cathexes. Eros fills this need. And as it does fill this need it alters the base of the Freudian system. It gives up the attempt to reduce ego motivation to somatic excitation. *Now sexual somatic excitation appears as but one aspect of Eros.* In the older view ego activity was seen as but one aspect of sexual somatic excitation. And we encountered those awkward mechanisms, primal cathexis of the ego and homosexual cathexis of the ego-ideal.

Both the ego-ideal and the super-ego could have been employed to motivate the organism in the direction of object-cathexis and co-operation. But both of these concepts were reduced to sexual somatic components and their usefulness was much reduced. Freud derived the ego-ideal and the super-ego from social conditioning but made them palatable to himself only by minimizing their relation to social experience. When he tied them to homosexual libido or the Oedipus complex he destroyed their effectiveness as concepts. Major trends of the organism could not be satisfactorily reduced to these concepts as they were finally defined. Eros, then, is a new approach. Instead of specific mechanisms we have a general, "primal" trend of the organism. Homosexual libido and the Oedipus complex are superceded by larger concepts. The social components of human action no longer have to be reduced to sexual somatic excitation. *They are in themselves sexual in the broader sense, in the sense of Eros.* Thus at last Freud made room in his system for individual motivation which cannot be specifically related to the pleasure-principle, and the reduction of somatic excitation. In this sense Eros fills a gap that has been present from the beginning. The pleasure-principle refers to one type of motivation. Eros now refers to another type of motivation, the motivation to conform to the standards and norms of the society, to join in co-operative action with others. In this aspect we see the reality-principle in a new light. The reality-principle refers to the behavior of the ego. The reality-principle suggests that the ego mediates between the satisfaction of these two ego-interests, the pleasure-principle and Eros, with reference to external reality and *with reference to their claims upon each other.* Since the organism is assumed to be motivated for co-operative activity which is reduceable only to Eros and not to sexual somatic excitation, it follows that all mental energy cannot be reduced to somatic energy. We must assign an energy component to Eros. Eros then permits us, once and for all, to remove sexual energy from the super-ego or the ego-ideal and to power these formations with "Eros-energy." Looking back to "Mourning and Melancholia" we see that some suggestions made there can now be carried out, *within the framework of the Freudian system.* Components of Eros-energy were involved. Eros, then, is an organic concept to fill theoretical needs in a biological frame of reference.

Eros is a definite improvement in Freudian theory. But on Freud's view this tendency, represented by Eros, toward co-operative or altruistic behavior would have been present from the beginning. This contradicts the learned aspects of the super-ego or the ego-ideal. It contradicts the assumption of the egoism of childhood. So perhaps we could think of Eros as a maturation factor. But this would not account for the differences in the form of Eros between individuals, or between societies. We see here the serious problems that arise from postulating mechanisms to explain motivation derived from social experience.

It is in a way curious that the repetition-compulsion should have led to the life-instincts or Eros via the death-instincts. Perhaps this betrays the fact that Freud was not searching so much for a destructive element in the mind as he was for a general category of motivation. He was thus sensitized to mental behavior that did not fit his established concepts. In this broader framework the life-instincts and the death-instincts are complementary. They supplement each other in handling behavior that does not fit established categories.

The view is often advanced that the life- and death-instincts are not an integral part of Freud's thought. The position seems to be that these concepts are philosophical in nature and not any proper part of Freud's established system of concepts. It is, in this view, perfectly feasible to reject the life-instincts and the death-instincts while accepting the rest of the Freudian system. To be sure Freud approached his present position through biological analogy and a sort of cosmic ethics. But the position that he took is definitely a theoretical position and it is designed to improve the validity of the system. *Eros is Freud's long delayed confession that the ego is theoretically dominant over the Ucs and that there is a strong component of motivation in the ego that is not organic in the traditional sense.*

Although this whole inquiry started over the repetition-compulsion Freud has not successfully indicated how the repetition-compulsion is related to the sadistic impulse or death-instinct. These concepts lead us no further than the facts of repetition or sadism or self-destruction. Yet these are puzzling facts. We have pointed out that in some cases the repetition-compulsion appeared to have a therapeutic function. But Freud felt there was "enough left over" to warrant the assumption of a death-instinct. However, when he reached this conclusion he had not posited the existence of Eros. Eros formed a new category of motivation.

It followed that in any particular course of action the pleasure-principle and the Eros-principle may take different sides. If in these circumstances the ego favors the side of Eros the resulting action violates the pleasure-principle and appears as destructive *to that principle*. The death-instinct is a principle of destruction only so long as the pleasure-principle is seen as the sole motivational force in the mind.

However, Eros established a new system of motivation that was not based on the pleasure-principle and did not destroy the organism. Action motivated by Eros might be consistent or not consistent with the aims of the pleasure-principle. Before the formulation of Eros the tendencies against the pleasure-principle seemed to be destructive. After the formulation of Eros these tendencies fulfill the needs of Eros and are not destructive. The death-instinct can no longer claim status as an independent principle. It is a variety of Eros behavior where the action runs counter to the pleasure-principle. (The death-instinct was also used to compensate for certain functions of the ego, as I have pointed out. Those functions are not considered here.)

This view does not indicate that destructive tendencies do not exist in individual motivation. Freud's mechanisms of sadism, masochism, aggression, etc. are among the most useful but they relate to empirical situations that result from associations of motivation and energies and not to any "primal" principle of their own.

The "resistance" that Freud discovered in his early career led to various explanations. They all emphasized some perverse process injecting "conflict" into the psychic system. These all fell under the death-instinct when it was formulated. But then Eros admitted new motivation into the ego which explained these resistances. The death-instinct is doomed to wither on the vine.

Chapter XV

EROS AND

SOCIAL MOTIVATION

FREUD, IN ORGANIZING the ego, first called up the supporting concept of erotogenicity and out of erotogenicity he produced the cathexis of the ego and the suffusion of the ego-ideal with homosexual libido. These two trends were analyzed in a fairly satisfactory manner. They did not account for object-cathexis. Freud supported the sexual instincts on the self-preservative instincts. He then explained how the self-preservative instincts would be concerned with objects that secured and maintained the safety of the organism. Since the sexual instincts were attached to the self-preservative instincts, object-cathexis represented the outflow of libido. The way for this was prepared by the self-preservative instincts. In terms of quantities Freud held strongly to the position that libido only flowed outward from the ego to avoid illness. This view proved generally unworkable and Freud returned to it only for the gains it offered in particular situations.

Generally, the outgoingness of the ego was not satisfactorily explained. Eros, as we have said, has been postulated as a given trend to explain this outflow of libido. In the older theory ego activity was twice removed from sexual somatic excitation. First, the concept of erotogenicity was analogical. There was no measureable or testable excitation involved. In the second place, the ego processes were far removed from anything like sexual somatic discharge. Ego-cathexis involved a new system of dynamics. The same was true of the homosexual cathexis of the ego-ideal. And the third category, object-cathexis, likewise represented a whole category of ego action which Freud sought to reduce to an awkward alliance between the sexual and the self-preservative instincts.

Eros removed these systems of ego motivation even further from sexual somatic excitation. This is indicated in the following passage. "Libido is an expression taken from the theory of the emotions. We call by that name the energy (regarded as a quantitative magnitude, though not at present actually measurable) of those instincts which have to do with all that may be comprised under the word "love." The nucleus of what we mean by love naturally consists (and this is what is commonly called love, and what the poets sing of) in sexual love with sexual union as its aim. But we do not separate from this—what in any case has a share in the name "love"—on the one hand, self-love, and on the other, love for parents and children, friendship and love for humanity in general, and also devotion to concrete objects and to abstract ideas. Our justification lies in the fact that psychoanalytic research has taught us that all these tendencies are an expression of the same instinctive activities; in relations between the sexes these instincts force their way towards sexual union, but in other circumstances they are diverted from this aim and are prevented from reaching it, though always preserving enough of their original nature to keep their identity recognizable (as in such features as the longing for proximity and self-sacrifice)."[1]

In the earlier view the three categories of ego behavior were reduced to sexual libido through tortuous channels. In the present passage the same three categories are reduced to Eros (love, "co-operation"), and *this* in turn is reduced to sexual somatic excitation by tortuous channels. In the earlier view the outgoingness of the ego was explained in terms of a composite of established categories. In the present view a new assumption has been made, and the new assumption, the Eros trend, is looked upon as dominant. It explains not only friendship (object-cathexis), love of humanity and devotion to abstract ideas (ego-ideal), but also self-love (cathexis of the ego).

Freud's insight did not lead him to see clearly the relation between these factors and the social environment. Instead, he thought of Eros as working automatically and he derived it from sexual instincts that had been diverted in their aims. The familiar view of sexual "injury" is thus suggested again. He approached the question of Eros dynamics in this fashion: ". . . our interest now leads us to the pressing question as to what may be the nature of these ties which exist in groups. In the psychoanalytic study of neuroses we have hitherto been occupied almost exclusively with ties that unite with their objects those love instincts which still pursue directly sexual aims. In groups there can evidently be no question of sexual aims of that kind. We are concerned here with love instincts which have been diverted from their original aims, though they do not operate with less energy on that account."[2] Freud drew his inference from the Oedipus. "A great deal has been said in this paper about directly sexual instincts and those that are inhibited in their aims, and it may be hoped that this distinction will not meet with too much resistance. . . . The development of the libido in children has made us acquainted with the first but also the best example of sexual instincts that are inhibited in their aims."[3] Freud was referring to the childhood fixation on the parent (usually of the opposite sex), of the child's desire: ". . . to kiss them (the parents), touch them, and look at them; it is curious," Freud went on, "to see their genitals, and to be with them when they perform their intimate excremental functions. . . . Direct observation, as well as the subsequent analytic investigation of the residues of childhood, leave no doubt as to the complete fusion of tender and jealous feelings and of sexual intentions, and show us in what a fundamental way the child makes the person it loves into the object of all its incompletely centered sexual tendencies."[4]

If these new aims are merely diversions they indicate no essential change in the instincts, although it is strange to see them "gratified" by such diversions. But Freud meant to reach deeper than this. "This first configuration of the child's love," he said, "which in typical cases is co-ordinated with the Oedipus complex, succumbs, as we know, from the beginning of the period of latency onwards to a wave of repression. Such of it as is left over shows itself as a purely tender emotional tie, which relates to the same people but is no longer to be described as 'sexual.' " Psychoanalysis, which illuminates the depths of mental life, has no difficulty in showing that the sexual ties of the earliest years of childhood also persist, though repressed and unconscious. It gives us courage to assert that wherever we come across a tender feeling it is the successor to a completely 'sensual' object tie with the person in question or rather with the person's prototype (or image). It cannot indeed disclose to us without a special investigation whether in a given case this former complete sexual current still exists or whether it has already been exhausted. . . . It is quite certain that it is still there as a form and possibility and can always be charged with cathectic energy and put into activity again by means of regression; the only question is (and it cannot always be answered) what degree of cathexis and operative force it still has at the present moment. Equal care must be taken in this connection to avoid two sources of error—the Scylla of underestimating the importance of the repressed unconscious, and the Charybdis of judging the normal entirely by the standards of the pathological."[5] Here is the basic sexual current again which is expressed or repressed. Freud had something further in mind, however. "We are justified in saying," he concluded, "that they [tender emotional ties] have been diverted from these sexual aims, even though there is some difficulty in giving a representation of such a diversion of aim which will conform to the requirements of metapsychology. . . . If we choose we may recognize in this diversion of aim a beginning of the sublimation of the sexual instincts, or on the other hand we may fix the limits of sublimation at some more distant point."[6]

Obviously Freud cannot identify this diversion of instincts with repression. Much about Eros is conscious, and much is not under repression. However, since Eros is derived by Freud from the sexual instincts, there is no alternative but to divide the sexual instincts into two parts. This does not mean diverting the sexual instinct from its aim, as is suggested in some of the above passages. It means diverting the instinct as such, i.e. producing a qualitatively different type of instinct. This is no easy task and Freud performed it with a deceptive sleight-of-hand. When the usual sexual instinct goes under repression during latency—or at the time of the development of the secondary ego—some kind of alchemy takes place and the aim-inhibited instincts arise from the repression like the Phoenix from the ashes. Freud's remarks indicated that he was uncertain whether to assign this miracle to the maturation process of each individual, or handle the whole matter at once by assuming that this change took place in prehistory.

These classifications of sexual instincts in terms of object-cathexes and the assumption of an unexplained "diversion" at least appears to have justified, in Freud's mind, the assumption of Eros in the ego. He proceeded to further analysis on the basis of his assumptions. "Those sexual instincts," he said, "which are inhibited in their aim have a great functional advantage over those which are uninhibited. Since they are not capable of really complete satisfaction, they are especially adapted to create permanent ties; while those instincts which are directly sexual incur a loss of energy each time they are satisfied, and must wait to be renewed by a fresh accumulation of sexual libido, so that meanwhile the object may have been changed."[7] This view raises more acutely than ever the problem of the first diversion. What occasioned this neurotic or defective trend in object-catheixs? This, of course, is the perennial problem where the motivation of Eros and the "superego" is reduced to the pleasure-principle.

Since we have no adequate reason for the diversion of the sexual instincts Freud was not surprised that it may not take place, or, having taken place, may cease. "The inhibited instincts are capable of any degree of admixture with the uninhibited; they can be transformed back into them, just as they arose out of them. It is well known how easily erotic wishes develop out of emotional relations of a friendly character, based upon appreciation and admiration . . . and especially in the case of women. . . . On the other hand it is also very usual for the directly sexual tendencies, short-lived in themselves, to be transformed into a lasting and purely tender tie; and the consolidation of a passionate love marriage rests to a large extent upon this process."[8] Freud here looked for support in the empirical world. Although the facts he has reference to are clearly true they only throw his instinct theory into confusion. In the earlier libido theory we pointed out that the theory was made to fit the facts in an excellent illustration of circular reasoning. The same is true here. The empirical data forced Freud into assumptions about the relations of his two classes of instincts which are inconsistent with their definition. At one moment Freud assumed that the inhibited instincts derived an advantage from the fact that they could not be gratified. They could serve as the basis of lasting social relationships. But the next moment we see them blithely turning back into the other class of erotic instincts. The "press" of socially-derived motivational factors is outstripping Freud's undoubted facility in fashioning physical models. We have no better illustration than Eros of the fact that Freud seldom felt that he has a clear grasp of an insight until he has restated it in biological terms. And then it may not be able to exercise the functions for which it was devised.

APPLICATION OF THESE CONCEPTS TO

GROUP PSYCHOLOGY

Eros "catches" data that refers to social behavior. Thus Freud is led to the analysis of group behavior. He held that ". . . a group is clearly held together by a power of some kind . . . to what power could this feat be better ascribed than to Eros, who holds together everything in the world?"[9] In ordinary relations, said Freud, ". . . men give evidence of a readiness for hatred, an aggressiveness the source of which is unknown, and to which one is tempted to ascribe an elementary character."[10] Freud observed, however, that the situation may be quite different in the relations of individuals composing a group. ". . . the whole of this intolerance vanishes, temporarily or permanently, as the result of the formation of a group, and in a group. So long as a group formation persists, or so far as it extends, individuals behave as though they were uniform, tolerate other people's peculiarities, put themselves on an equal level with them, and have no feeling of aversion towards them."[11] Freud then made this interesting comment: "The same thing occurs in men's social relations as has become

familiar to psychoanalytic research in the course of the development
of the individual libido. The libido props itself upon the satisfaction
of the great vital needs, and chooses as its first objects the people
who have a share in that process. And in the development of mankind
as a whole, just as in individuals, love alone acts as the civilizing
factor in the sense that it brings a change from egoism to altruism."[12]

Here is our first indication of Freud's view of the dynamics of the
"society." There is something in the relations of men that is similar to
the development within men. There is some Eros-effect in the relations
of people, as there is in the behavior of individuals. We notice that
Freud reinstated the idea of the sexual instincts attaching themselves
to the self-preservative instincts. However, now the self-preservative
instincts become the "great vital needs."

This widening of the terms of discourse dimly suggests an organization of personal relationships, of cooperative activity, which could
become the base for the cooperative "need" in the individual. Thus,
Freud gives us a view of his developing interests. Eros permits him to
see human relationships in an aspect slightly different from the eroti-
cally tinged super-ego. In the passage immediately following the one
quoted above, Freud made a feeble attempt to reduce this altruistic
force to something vaguely sexual. He stated that this change from
egoism to altruism is true ". . . both of the sexual love for women,
with all the obligations which it involves of sparing what women are
fond of, and also of the *desexualized, sublimated, homosexual* love
for other men which springs from work in common."[13] (Italics ours.
Notice the resort to old libido theory in the reference to homosexual
energy.)

Continuing with his analysis of social groups Freud said that the
aim-inhibited instincts although ". . . not really capable of complete
satisfaction" nevertheless need an outlet. ". . . it appears that where
a powerful impetus has been given to group formation neuroses may
diminish and at all events temporarily disappear. Justifiable attempts
have also been made to turn this antagonism between neuroses and
group formation to therapeutic account."[14] The facts, as Freud alleges
them, do not appear very consonant with the assumptions Freud has
made. He has powered Eros with aim-inhibited instincts and has informed us that they can have no real satisfaction. He has in fact praised
this state of things. It is passing strange then than these instincts "need
an outlet." Clearly we cannot be talking in tension-reduction terms at
all. Even stranger is the fact that these distorted instincts, employing
this outlet, may cause the diminishing or disappearance of neurosis.

Freud has fastened upon the therapeutic value of the group. He has
not, however, perceived the possibility of the same type of force op-

erating here as in the war neuroses or in the phenomenon of transference, i.e. social acceptance.

Freud offered a description of neuroses in terms of the aim-inhibited
instincts. "Neurosis," he said, "makes its appearance wherever the
advance from directly sexual instincts to those that are inhibited in
their aims has not been completely successful; and it represents a conflict between those instincts which have been received into the ego
after having passed through this development and those portions of the
same instincts which, like other instinctive desires that have been
completely repressed, strive, from the repressed unconscious, to attain
direct satisfaction."[15]

Freud is concerned here with the two types of motivation which we
have referred to as Eros-motivation, cooperation, love of humanity,
devotion to standards, etc. and instinct motivation or pleasure motivation. It is clear that these two types of motivation may be in conflict and
that this conflict may be the efficient cause of neurosis. Freud's model,
however, permits only the most awkward presentation of this idea.
The additional assumption that a sexual instinct may be partly repressed
and partly turned into an aim-inhibited instinct is completely *ad hoc*.

In passing, however, it might be well to point out an earlier phase
of Freud's thought where he employed an approach similar to the one
used here. In the present case he was trying to power the ego on a
base broader than he had before attempted. The general problem of
trying to energize the ego is an old one. In his first interpretation of the
"thirteen cases of hysteria" Freud tried to energize the ego with sexual
energy that had been deflected or diverted as the result of sexual assault
upon the person at an early age. The reader will perceive how the
same point of view has extended from that time to this.

Accepting Freud's view that group relations often reduce neuroses,
and that neuroses themselves are caused by conflict between the repressed and the diverted or aim-inhibited aspect of the same sexual
instinct, we must inquire how this reduction of the neurosis takes
place. This involves a further inquiry into group relations. Freud
started this inquiry by consideration of the processes of identification
and the ego-ideal.

While object-cathexis is related, in the manner we have brought
out, to the sexual instincts, the phenomenon of identification ". . .
has nothing to do with a passive or feminine attitude."[16] Freud pointed
out the distinction between identification and object-choice: in the
former the object is what one would like to be; in the latter the object
is what one would like to have. "The former is therefore already possible before any sexual object-choice has been made."[17] Freud conceded that "It is much more difficult to give a clear metapsychological

representation of the distinction. We can only see that identification endeavors to mould a person's own ego after the fashion of the one that has been taken as a 'model.' "[18]

Freud did not attempt to apply here the kind of analysis he employed in "Mourning and Melancholia." He was unwilling to make full use of the Eros concept, but he apparently also realized that the earlier libido analysis was quite inadequate. He perceived that identification and the ego-ideal are closely related. "On previous occasions," he said, "we have been driven to the hypothesis that some such faculty develops in our ego which may cut itself off from the rest of the ego and come into conflict with it. We have called it the 'ego-ideal,' and by way of functions we have ascribed to it self-observation, the moral conscience, the censorship of dreams, and the chief influence in repression."[19] This is an outright avowal that the ego-ideal is the "moral conscience" in part at least. In the following passage he conceded again the *social* origin of this conscience. The ego-ideal ". . . gradually gathers up from the influences of the environment the demands which that environment makes upon the ego and which the ego cannot always rise to."[20] Proceeding to sociological analysis he added, "But we have not forgotten to add that the amount of distance between this ego-ideal and the real ego is very variable from one individual to another, and that with many people this differentiation within the ego does not go further than with children."[21] This tolerance of social influence is due in part to the fact that even though the ego-ideal is caused by social experience, it is also "caused" by sexual instincts through a devious system of reduction. For the ego-ideal rests upon Eros, which rests upon the aim-inhibited instincts, which rest on the sexual instincts, which reduce to sexual somatic excitation. These speculative physical processes fail as conceptual means of dealing with external, social "trauma." The qualities of these external social "stimuli" "flood" Freud's perceptual system.

The Eros type of motivation led Freud to alter the view he formerly advanced with reference to the distinction between identification and "fascination." "In the former case," he said, "the ego has enriched itself with the properties of the object, it has 'introjected' the object into itself, as Ferenczi expresses it. In the second case it is impoverished, it has surrendered itself to the object, it has substituted the object for its most important constituent. Closer consideration soon makes it plain, however, that this kind of account creates an *illusion of contradistinctions that have no real existence*. Economically there is no question of impoverishment or enrichment; it is even possible to describe an extreme case of being in love as a state in which the ego has introjected the object into itself."[22] (Italics ours.) Economically, of course, there *was* a question of impoverishment under the old libido theory which permitted no outpouring of this nature. Eros, however, being aim-inhibited can have no "gratification." Its "outlet," therefore, although in some manner appropriate to it, cannot impoverish it. For *it,* the object cathexis is its own type of gratification.

With reference to social groups, Freud suggested that ". . . a primary group . . . is a number of individuals who have substituted one and the same object for their ego-ideal and have consequently identified themselves with one another in their ego."[23] This explanation recognized a common universe of esteem. The esteem centered on the leader and gave the rest of the group "something in common." If Eros is employed to represent this esteem then a straightforward sociological description can be made. Then, of course, Eros seems an unnecessary concept. If Eros is to be employed as a concept in the libido galaxy then explanation becomes more than difficult. How can we explain this common object-cathexis on the part of the separate aim-inhibited instincts? And what kind of further object-cathexis is this collateral "identification?" Looked at from this point of view we must agree with Freud that, "We cannot for long enjoy the illusion that we have solved the riddle of the group with this formula."[24] In the next section we shall see how Freud tried to solve this problem.

THE MECHANISM OF THE
"HORDE INSTINCT"

Freud proposed to bring his instinct theory into line by the assumption of yet another mechanism. But now he must look to the social environment for it is here that we see the forces that the mechanism must take into account. "Let us venture, then," he suggested, "to correct Trotter's pronouncement that man is a herd animal and assert that he is rather a horde animal, an individual creature in a horde led by a chief."[25] In the horde the individual is motivated by tender feelings toward the leader and "group feeling" is an identification with others in the group caused by ". . . a similar love for the same object."[26] The tendency of the individuals in the group is to be jealous of the other members, but, ". . . in face of their numbers and the consequent impossibility of their reaching the aim of their love, they renounce it, and, instead of pulling out one another's hair, they act as a united group. . . ."[27]

We can see that Freud's intuition has taken him to a new kind of mechanism—a mechanism of concrete social organization. In this case it is the horde. How are we to bring this ancient situation into relation with a contemporary group? Freud suggested the hypothesis of ". . . regression to a primitive mental activity."[28] These "regressions" are familiar to us from the study of Freud's analysis of dream-process. "Human groups," said Freud, "exhibit once again the familiar picture of an individual of superior strength among a troop of similar companions, a picture which is also contained in our ideas of the primal horde."[29] The group, then, revives the primal horde. "Just as primitive man virtually survives in every individual, so the primal horde may arise once more out of any random crowd. . . ."[30] This conception is reenforced in Freud's mind by the fact that "Even today the members of a group stand in need of the illusion that they are equally and justly loved by their leader; but the leader himself need love no one else, he may be of a masterly nature, absolutely narcissistic, but self-confident and independent."[31] (Freud's relations to his followers have been described in these terms.)

With the social mechanism of the horde Freud tried to explain not merely the internal psychic processes, not merely the behavior pattern of the individual, but the interactive process between individuals in a group.

However, libido dynamics cannot be applied to the horde mechanism. The instincts must have gone through their amazing transformation before even this early time. The ultimate explanation is that the primal father ". . . had prevented his sons from satisfying their directly sexual tendencies; he forced them into abstinence and consequently into the emotional ties with him and with one another which could arise out of those of their tendencies that were inhibited in their sexual aim. He forced them, so to speak, into group psychology."[32] Here then is the ultimate social mechanism that produced the aim-inhibited instincts out of which Eros developed. All fancy and myth to be sure. But, on the point of theory, it bears witness to the complete breakdown of libido analysis. For this analysis only applied to the primal scene. Since that remote time the instincts have been fixed as Freud showed in his description of the horde structure.

Freud's group psychology required a leader and Freud therefore made short work of Trotter. "Trotter's exposition" he said, "is open to the objection that it takes too little account of the leader's part in the group. . . . The herd instinct leaves no room at all for the leader; he is merely thrown in along with the herd, almost by chance. . . ."[33]

Both Trotter's and Freud's views on group psychology appear somewhat archaic in view of the advances made in this field. Yet both the "herd" view and the "horde" view emphasize an aspect of group relations. Freud postulated an original leader of which all subsequent leaders are prototypes. He also postulated the leader as the condition precedent to the existence of a group. Thus his group psychology was narrowly limited. Needless to say Trotter's view was equally limited in a different direction. The limitation which Freud imposed upon his analysis of group activity was that he sought to show the *rise of Eros* rather than *the activity of Eros*. In the passages we have referred to above Freud did not consider that he had invented Eros as a concept to deal with the outgoingness of the individual, his cooperative tendencies. Yet it was the invention of Eros, itself, which legitimated Freud's researches in social psychology. However, once he got out "in the field" he reverted to his old libido-theory which was singularly deficient in its ability to account for object-cathexis. In other words, he tried to employ a type of explanation that, in actuality he had already given up by the assumption of Eros. Thus he was required to root his explanation in purely libidinal considerations. He had to postulate some kind of sexual cathexis. But when he had done this he had no way of transforming the sexual cathexis into a group psychology. So, as I have pointed out, he announced it as a matter of fiat, as a fact of history. Why did Freud seek to "derive" Eros instead of relying on it for explanation of the group situation? At one time it seemed that physical mechanisms could explain mental events. Here he toyed with the idea that libidinal social structures could explain mental events. This is a "circuitous route" to explanation, but it should be remembered that Freud had few concepts of social structure available to him that might have indicated the tendency for social behavior to persist through time.

It is really the Eros type of social activity in which Freud is mainly interested. After the development of the aim-inhibited instincts something new had happened to mankind and Freud should have approached the problem of modern social relations armed with Eros and the ego ideal. With these concepts he could have suggested that the leader might conform to standards which were important in terms of the ego-ideal. The outgoingness of the individual could be referred to Eros and the assumptions involved in this concept. In regard to relations between the "followers" it would have appeared that they must have much the same ego-ideal since they "cathected" a common leader. Thus there would appear to be a mutual identification based upon a community of *standards*. The leader would be subject to separate linear identifications on the basis of his superior embodiment of these standards. This view, clearly indicated by Eros and the ego-ideal, makes possible a reconciliation with the leaderless group, for in that case the group would have a community of standards without any single individual cathected as superior to the rest.

This would of course in no sense constitute a typology of groups.

But Freud has really been concerned here with an aspect of group solidarity. He has failed to make the best use of his concepts in this regard because of his persistence concern with equilibrating the instinctive system.

In fact, after this circumlocutory attention to history, myths and instincts, Freud fastened on the precise issue. He stated that the individual gives up his ego-ideal and substitutes for it the group ideal as embodied in the leader. And, avoiding the issue of libidinal cathexis, he emphasized the importance of "typical qualities." He said, "In many individuals the separation between the ego and the ego-ideal is not very far advanced; the two still coincide readily; the ego has often preserved its earlier self-complacency. The selection of the leader is very much facilitated by this circumstance. He need only possess the typical qualities of the individuals concerned in a particular clearly marked and pure form, and need only give an impression of greater force and of more freedom of libido.[34] Here is simple "Eros analysis."

Again we see in this study of groups that Freud cannot successfully reduce the inhibited sexual instincts, the Eros, to libido dynamics. No matter how this category of motivation may be designated, or what devices are employed to reduce it to an instinctive pattern, it constitutes a theoretically autonomous category of motivation. Eros is closely allied to the ego-ideal and the ego-ideal, and, as Freud concedes in more than one passage, consists of a selection of standards from the social environment. We have mentioned Freud's tendency to weld libidinal love and esteem into an inseparable mass. He has the concepts to force them apart and these concepts are based on empirical requirements. But even yet the category of social motivation is not freely received by Freud or by his system of thought.

Chapter XVI

ORGANIC INNERVATION

IN THE MIND—THE ID

FREUD HAS MENTIONED that perhaps the most satisfactory categories of mental process are (a) the ego, and (b) the Repressed. However, for some time Freud did not address himself specifically to the matter of categories. His suggestions with reference to them were collateral. His interest was in mechanisms, processes, motivations. The so-called metapsychological approach, however, just about demolished the earlier topological structure. It became necessary to rethink the entire matter of the categories.

THE REFORMULATION OF GENERAL
CATEGORIES. THE GENESIS OF THE ID

In *The Ego and the Id* Freud gave us at first little intimation of the structural change that he had in store. He restated the former categories of the Cs, the Pcs and the Ucs. (Cs stands for Conscious; Pcs for Preconscious; Ucs for Unconscious.) Then, in a manner the more startling for its being so offhand, he suggested quite a different point of view. Referring to the distinctions between the Ucs, Pcs and Cs he said: "In the further course of psychoanalytic work, even these distinctions have proved to be inadequate and, for practical purposes, insufficient. This has become clear in more ways than one; but the decisive instance is as follows. We have formulated the idea that in every individual there is a coherent organization of mental processes which we call his ego. This ego includes consciousness and it controls the approaches to motility, i.e. to the discharge of excitations into the external world. . . . From this ego proceed the repressions, too, by means of which an attempt is made to cut off certain trends in the mind not merely from consciousness but also from their other forms of manifestations and activity. . . . Now we find that during analysis when we put certain tasks before the patient, he gets into difficulties; his associations fail when they ought to be getting near to the repressed. We then tell him that he is dominated by a resistance; but he is quite unaware of the fact, and, even if he guesses from his feelings of discomfort that a resistance is now at work in him, he does not know what it is nor how to describe it. Since, however, there can be no question but that this resistance emanates from his ego and belongs to it, we find ourselves in a unforeseen situation. We have come upon something in the ego itself which is also unconscious, which behaves exactly like the repressed, that is, which produces powerful effects without itself being conscious and which requires special work before it can be made conscious. From the point of view of analytic practice, the consequence of this piece of observation is that we land in endless confusion and difficulty if we cling to our former way of expressing ourselves and try, for instance, to derive neuroses from a conflict between the conscious and the unconscious. We shall have to substitute for this antithesis another, taken from our understanding of the structural conditions of the mind, namely, the antithesis between the organized ego and what is repressed and dissociated from it."[1]

In this passage Freud took his stand upon the general unconscious state of the mind. We have observed this view gradually unfolding. He also now officially accepted the tentative hypothesis advanced by him at least twice before, namely, that the significant distinction to be made is not that between the Pcs and the Ucs but that between the organized ego and the repressed. Since in this passage he stipulated that the repression *proceeds from the ego* it is clear that the key to the structure of the repressed is to be found in the exclusion policy of the ego. Thus the ego at last becomes the strategic category.

Freud has altered his meaning of ego somewhat. In the earlier formulation that he suggested the ego referred to the entire mental area other than the repressed. Thus, within the ego you could distinguish a coherent ego. In the present formulation the ego refers to the "coherent organization of mental processes." At the moment no concept covers the mental material that is neither repressed nor organized. Note also that the ego "includes consciousness."

Freud made use of an earlier concept in order to fill in the gap here. "Experience," he said, "shows . . . that a mental element (for instance, an idea) is not as a rule permanently conscious. On the contrary, a state of consciousness is characteristically very transitory; an idea that is conscious now is no longer so a moment later, although it can become so again under certain conditions that are easily brought about. What the idea was in the interval we do not know. We can only say that it was latent, and by this we mean that it was capable of becoming conscious at any time."[2] He then suggested that, "That which is latent, and only unconscious in the descriptive sense, we call preconscious; the term unconscious we reserve for the dynamically unconscious repressed. . . ."[3] Freud proceeded to revise drastically his ideas of the "dynamically unconscious repressed." "For our conception of the unconscious . . ." he said, "the consequences are even more important. Dynamic considerations caused us to make our first correction; our knowledge of the structure of the mind leads us to the second. We recognize that the Ucs does not coincide with what is repressed; it is still true that all that is repressed is Ucs, but not that the whole Ucs is repressed. *A part of the ego too—and heaven knows how important a part—may be Ucs, undoubtedly is Ucs.* And this Ucs belonging to the ego is not latent like the Pcs; for if it were, it would not be activated without becoming Cs, and the process of making it conscious would not encounter such great difficulties. When we find ourselves thus confronted by the necessity of postulating a third Ucs which is not repressed, we must admit that the property of being unconscious begins to lose significance for us. It becomes a quality which can have many implications so that we are unable to make it, as it should have hoped to do, the basis of far-reaching and inevitable conclusions."[4]

Freud has at last presided over the dissolution of the Ucs. The doom of the Ucs was originally pronounced by the repetition-compulsion and the "resistance" to say nothing of ideal masochism. Much of ego process cannot become conscious. In his earlier thinking Freud experimented with the assumption that the Ucs penetrated into the Pcs. In the present instance, Freud recognized the logical heterogeneity of the concept, unconscious. He has given up the region Ucs. And he has recognized that material which possesses the common quality of not being able to penetrate into consciousness may yet be different in other respects.

The forces operating in the mind—as distinct from the dynamics of mental formations and their association—are now seen in quite a new light. The organized ego emerges as the dominant category. This category has a characteristic process that is largely unconscious. Some elements of the organized ego are admissible to consciousness, but many are not. There are many mental formations that are not "bound" into the organized ego and yet are not repressed. Then there is the category of the Repressed. At the moment the Repressed is divided into two parts. First, there is the repressed material that resembles the former Unconscious material in that it is the source of sexual press. There there is the repressed material which is part of the ego, such as repetition-compulsion. We would think that Unconscious process (the "index value") has been absorbed into the Repressed and that, therefore, the Unconscious denotes merely material that is innervated by organic "press." The organized ego includes the conscious ego.

It has appeared from the beginning that the ego was a developmental phenomenon. It was therefore superimposed upon an existing situation. At the beginning, then, we can only imagine that the mind was suffused with the mental representations of organic press. The "aim" of the mind would be tension reduction. Out of these representations of organic tensions the ego must develop. It cannot be supposed that the ego brings a new and original quantity of energy. It must reallocate the old. And its development is largely unconscious. The metapsychological view has rendered obsolete the tidy compartmentalization involved in the Meynert overlay. Freud's formulation starts with a statement by Georg Groddeck, who, said Freud, ". . . is never tired of pointing out that the conduct through life of what we call our ego is essentially passive, and that, as he expressed it, we are 'lived' by unknown and uncontrollable forces."[5] On this cue Freud proposed that, "We shall now look upon the mind of an individual as an unknown and unconscious id, upon whose surface rests the ego, developed from its nucleus the Pcpt-system."[6] Freud added, ". . . the ego is not sharply separated from the id; its lower portion merges into it."[7] The id then is the unorganized mind out of which the crystalization of the ego develops. This is followed or attended by the development of the Repressed. Freud said: ". . . the repressed merges into the id as well, and is simply a part of it. The repressed is only cut off sharply from the ego by the resistances of repression."[8]

The formulation of Eros has influenced the geography of the mind, as Freud saw it. The ego develops out of the perceptual system. Very likely Freud was thinking of the stimulus value of outer influences as he analysed it in his study of the war neuroses. He was thinking of the reality-principle as it related to the self-preservative instincts. But by emphasizing the role of the perceptual system he has also made possible the view that the development of the ego is influenced by all material coming into the mind through this channel. This includes the socialization process and the individual's experiences in interpersonal relations. We would emphasize not only the influences from the external physical world but also the influences entering the mind from the community of other individuals. We have pointed out that the ego-ideal introduces new principles of orientation into the mind. Since the ego-ideal influences mental formations and the dynamics of the Repressed and even the attitudes of the ego toward itself it seems that it has a critical importance in the development of the ego. However, the reorganization of the mind, which we call the development of the ego, must employ existent mental energy and recognize the organic press for tension reduction. To this extent the ego merges with the id.

Of the ego Freud said, "The ego has the task of bringing the influence of the external world to bear upon the id and its tendencies, and endeavours to substitute the reality-principle for the pleasure-principle which reigns supreme in the id. In the ego perception plays the part which in the id devolves upon instinct. The ego represents what we call reason and sanity, in contrast to the id which contains the passions."[9] Thus, as we have said, the id represents the instinct presentations in the mind. The id then refers to organic tension but not organization.

However, we should bear in mind that Freud has not advanced us very far with reference to the categories of material flowing into the mind through the Pcpt system. His reality principle was largely a physical reality principle. It remained for him to recognize sufficiently and organize a *social* reality principle. This social reality principle involved three important elements: (a) the general values and orientations that are current in the community and to which conformity is required by the community, (Freud has talked of instinct presentations or representations. The social reality principle, to use Durkheim's phrase, requires the recognition of "collective representations.") (b) the internalization of the collective representations, (Freud has admitted many times that culture and breeding get into the individual and form part of his personality. These factors have been seen as limiting factors with reference to a "true psychic reality." The formulation of the id can encourage Freud to think of internalized collective representations as basic factors in the refurbished ego.) and (c) the process whereby the internalized collective representations become attached to energy and influence mental dynamics. (In our analysis of Eros and the death instinct we have tried to simplify Freud's thinking and indicate the ego's relation to these elements. This analysis would look vainly for Freud's stamp of approval.)

Freud was no devotee of free-floating energy in the mind. Thus ego development would have to employ only organic energy. When the ego used this energy for other purposes Freud partly purified it. It would have been easier and more in accord with the behavior of energy to have assumed a fund of free-floating energy as an endowment of the mind, itself. This would make possible the whole process of ego-cathexis, hyper-cathexis and anti-cathexis. But Freud had to deal with his "reductive" commitment. The following well known passage indicates how Freud saw ego process: "The functional importance of the ego is manifested in the fact that normally control over the approaches to motility devolves upon it. Thus in its relation to the id it is like a man on horseback, who has to hold in check the superior strength of the horse; with this difference, that the rider seeks to do so with his own strength while the ego uses borrowed forces. The illustration may be carried further. Often a rider, if he is not to be parted from his horse, is obliged to guide it where it wants to go; so in the same way the ego constantly carries into action the wishes of the id as if they were its own."[10] The coining of the concept id has to a large extent preempted the use of the word "wish." But old customs in thinking die hard. The id is fundamentally a body of somatically related tension as represented in the mind. Thus wishes cannot be attributed to it. But the higher the tension situation of the id the more the employment of the pleasure principle, rather than the reality principle, recommends itself to the ego. Consequently, instead of developing the figure of speech on the basis of the wishes of the id it would be more helpful to consider that the higher the id-tensions the more the ego is motivated to discharge these tensions. It would be more accurate and more prosaic to say that organic or id tensions may find their representation in any or all of three "areas": the "bound" ego, the "unbound" ego or the repressed.

With the new attitude toward the ego, Freud was willing to concede the dream-forming power of the ego. ". . . we have evidence," he said, "that even subtle and intricate intellectual operations which ordinarily require strenuous concentration can equally be carried out preconsciously and without coming into consciousness. Instances of this are quite incontestable: they may occur, for instance, during sleep, as is shown when someone finds, immediately after waking, that he knows the solution of a difficult mathematical or other problem with which he had been wrestling in vain the day before."[11] Freud also indicated how the internalized "standards of the community" may work unconsciously. "Accustomed as we are to taking our social or ethical standard of values along with us wherever we go, we feel no surprise at hearing that the scene of the activities of the lower passions is in the unconscious; we expect, moreover, that the higher any mental function ranks in our scale of values the more easily it will find access to consciousness assured to it. . . . In analysis we discover that there are people in whom the faculties of self-criticism and conscience—mental activities, that is, that rank as exceptionally high ones—are unconscious and unconsciously produce effects of the greatest importance."[12]

This emphasizes the dynamic functioning of the organized ego below the level of consciousness.

THE CONSCIOUS SYSTEM

The advent of the reality-principle emphasized the importance of perception and this in turn required a new attention on the Conscious system. This new study was also indicated by the demise of the Unconscious and the assignment of so many functions to the organized ego. The reader will remember that Freud said the coherent ego included consciousness. This coherent ego, however, was able to "cut off certain trends from consciousness." Therefore the coherent ego has an "index value." It is a molar process.

But what of consciousness? Is it wagged by the unconscious ego? It seems that the conscious has some function, for Freud pointed out that preconscious material would not be activated unless it became conscious. It seems that we have no alternative but to recognize the Conscious as a distinct area of process and to capitalize it as we have the Unconscious. When we refer to the state of the material we refer to it as conscious.

What kinds of functions and properties does the Conscious have? We must piece together what evidence we can find. We know, for one thing, that the Pcpt (the perceptual system) is grafted on to the Conscious. Closely connected with this is the control of motility. Perception and control are two properties of the Conscious. And in addition there are the properties of cognition and volition which Freud often referred to as the "institutions of the mind." The Conscious system has some initiative in the recall of ideas and in the retention of ideas. But mental elements, as a rule, seem to dart in and out of the Conscious system. Yet, as we have said, the Conscious can activate material. The Conscious cannot pluck material out of the unconscious section of the coherent ego. On the other hand it may take a hand in refusing to admit material from the coherent ego that proposes to get in the Conscious. We are forced to recognize in the descriptions that Freud gives us of the coherent ego and the Conscious system that both of these systems are adept at retaining material they do not want to give up and rejecting material which they do not propose to admit. Thus they both seem to have the power of *repression proper* and *retention*.

Freud's emphasis on the "true psychic reality" which now seems to be in the coherent ego and was formerly in the Unconscious leads him to a calculated underemphasis on the Conscious system. We will remember, however, that in the case of little Hans Freud mentioned the power of condemnation that was exercised by consciousness. The potentiality of "insight" on the part of the Conscious system is widely used in psychoanalysis. If bringing psychic material into the Conscious is not to be tied to a mechanical result it must be assumed that the Conscious can "redistribute cathexes" and "institute connections" that may extend some distance into the unconscious coherent ego. (Freud's self analysis indicated that the Conscious system may develop skills for wide exploration of the coherent ego and the Repressed.)

Studies of hypnosis, sleep-walking, etc. indicate that the same processes that are carried on in the Conscious system may be carried on while the individual is in an unconscious state. The employment of initiative appears to be maximized in the Conscious system, however. Coherence is more efficiently striven for in the Conscious system although the achievement here is strictly limited. Faculties of cognition and volition are not exclusively employed by the Conscious system but they are most effectively employed there.

Thus, from the clues furnished by Freud we conclude that the Conscious system is not qualitatively distinct from the coherent ego, but that it represents an intensification of process and greater inner mobility. It is indeed difficult to see, in the potentialities of the Conscious system, anything but a phylogenetic development which not only improved the adjustment of the organism but also made practical the whole system of social conditioning on which group life depends.

THE SUPER-EGO AND THE OEDIPUS

COMPLEX

We have seen that Freud insisted on the "derivation" of Eros as a category of "altruistic behavior." This derivation, of course, only sought to account for something in the "primal" past. Once the change took place the quality of "altruism" became a human potential. But its past was libidinal. This analysis, however, had to do with a kind of group Eros. It had to do with a sociological generalization.

But how about the psychological generalization? How does the psychological Eros develop? Out of what libidinal forces shall it be formed? The super-ego turns out to be the psychological Eros and the Oedipus complex is the means of its libidinal derivation.

"At a very early age," said Freud, "the little boy develops an object-cathexis of his mother, which originally related to the mother's breast and is the earliest instance of an object-choice on the anaclitic model; his father the boy deals with by identifying himself with him. For a time these two relationships exist side by side, until the sexual wishes in regard to the mother become more intense and the father is perceived as an obstacle to them; this gives rise to the Oedipus complex."[13]

The conjunction of identification and object-cathexis is based on the analysis in Freud's group psychology. But in that analysis identification grew out of the employment of the instincts that were "inhibited in their sexual aim." In this situation there is a straight libidinal cathexis of the mother that is anaclitic in nature, i.e. it rests upon the mother's function in sheltering and protecting the child. Little Hans was not aim-inhibited as we well remember. On what basis, then, does the identification with the father become bound in with the cathexis of the mother? Furthermore, in view of the famous Freudian position that the child is "polymorphous perverse" why is there an invariable sexual cathexis of the mother?

Whatever the explanation of the original situation—and we shall come back to it—it does not long prevail. The sexual wishes with regard to the mother become more intense. "The identification with the father . . . takes on a hostile colouring and changes into a wish to get rid of the father in order to take his place with the mother. Henceforward, the relation to the father is ambivalent . . ."[14]

Here, then, is the "package deal" with reference to the Oedipus complex. It is difficult, however, to hold it together. For instance, during the break-up of the Oedipus the male child usually increases the identification with the father. However, there may be an identification with the mother. In the case of the girl there may be an intensification of identification with either parent. Thus, at the close of the Oedipus, the girl may absorb the abandoned object, the father, into the ego.[15] If, as Freud is led to believe, the Oedipus necessarily consists of a libidinal cathexis plus an identification with the other partner the random distribution of identification that appears at the end of the Oedipus raises a difficult problem. The problem comes up in this form: if the girl sometimes identifies with the former sex-object, then, in Freud's view *there must have been a matching libidinal cathexis of the other parent.* This necessity arises from the assumption of the package mechanism, and it requires that the mechanism be further complicated. Referring to the situation in females, Freud said, "Analysis very often shows that a little girl, after she had to relinquish her father as a love-object, will bring her masculinity into prominence and identify with her father, that is, with the object which has been lost, instead of with her mother. This will clearly depend on whether the masculinity in her disposition—whatever that may consist of—is strong enough."[16] This leads him to the conclusion that ". . . in both sexes the relative strength of the masculine and feminine sexual dispositions is what determines whether the outcome of the Oedipus situation shall be an identification with the father or with the mother. This is one of the ways in which bisexuality takes a hand in the subsequent vicissitudes of the Oedipus complex."[17] This position does not remain tenable for long. For if there is a bisexuality that operates with reference to identification there also must be a bisexuality that operates with reference to libidinal cathexis. So Freud suggested that "closer study usually disclosed the more complete Oedipus complex, which is twofold—positive and negative—and is due to the bisexuality originally present in children: that is to say, a boy has not merely an ambivalent attitude towards his father and an affectionate object-relation towards his mother, but at the same time he also behaves like a girl and displays an affectionate feminine attitude to his father and a corresponding hostility and jealousy towards his mother."[18]

Then Freud took an interesting step. Having assumed bisexuality and the resulting cathexes in order to explain identification he found himself in a position in which he could eliminate identification. For now the ambivalence of the boy toward his father is based on his desire for his father on the one hand and his hostility toward his father as a result of the impediment he offers to the boy's enjoyment of his mother on the other. So Freud stated: "It may even be that the ambivalence displayed in the relations to the parents should be attributed entirely to bisexuality and that it is not, as I stated just now, developed out of an identification in consequence of rivalry."[19] Thus Freud recognized the inadequacy of his explanation of identification in the Oedipus complex just as he did in the analysis of the human group. This elaboration of the Oedipus seems to be reducing its usefulness. As Freud said, it makes it difficult to ". . . obtain a clear view of the facts . . . and still more difficult to describe them intelligibly."

To make matters rather worse there is another hypothesis lingering in the last passage we quoted. Freud talked of an "identification in consequence of rivalry."[20] This appears to be a suggestion that identification may be explained in terms of the original Oedipus by the boy's imitation of the father in an attempt to be more desirable to the mother. (We saw this in the case of little Hans.) All of these "theories" can be applied to the empirical situation so long as we do not use identification as it was employed in the case of the aim-inhibited instincts. But the use of these theories, bisexuality and rivalry, does not furnish us with a determinate mechanism. It gives us a fluid type of mechanism *which can adjust to whatever the empirical facts happen to be in a given case.* Actually the concept of bisexuality can be reduced to simpler terms. In terms of *Three Contributions to the Theory of Sexuality* we remember that the sexual instinct is characterized by tension not direction. Its aim is tension reduction. It would appear then that classifications of objects do not warrant classifications of sexual tension. The child has a general libidinal tension which may be gratified by either parent. Thus, depending on the circumstances, the libidinal cathexis may develop in one way or the other or for that matter in both ways at once. Thus the Oedipus loses its structure and re-solves into a matter of libidinal tension as related to learned methods of gratification. Identification may then be seen as imitation of the non-cathected parent. Or identification may be removed entirely from the libidinal syndrome. This latter course was suggested by Freud in *Group Psychology and the Analysis of the Ego.* "A little boy," he said there, "will exhibit a special interest in his father; he would like to grow like him and be like him, and take his place everywhere. We may say simply that he takes his father as his ideal."[21]

We may wonder why Freud was at such great pains to establish the structure of the Oedipus complex, although, in fact, he was not suc-cessful in establishing it as a unit. We see that the Oedipus complex is closely related to the ego-ideal, although Freud tried to separate the two. In *The Ego and the Id* he stoutly resisted an interpenetration of the ego-ideal *into* the Oedipus. The object is to form a primal, sexual mechanism which can interpenetrate the ego-ideal or the super-ego.

Freud's purpose becomes clear in the following passage. "The broad general outcome of the sexual phase governed by the Oedipus complex may, therefore, be taken to be the forming of a precipitate in the ego, consisting of these two identifications in some way combined together. This modification of the ego retains its special position; it stands in contrast to the other constitutents of the ego in the form of an ego-ideal or super-ego."[22] The super-ego is seen by Freud as the result of the Oedipus. The assumption of bisexuality permits the inference that the child desires to "possess" each parent. This desire is matched by an identification with each of them. The Oedipus is then the sexually possessive side of this syndrome, and the super-ego is the identifica-tion side of the same syndrome. Here we see again that the libidinal estimation of an object is welded to the "value" estimation of an object such that all value estimations must proceed from some aspect of a libidinal cathexis. As Freud saw the sexual instincts supporting them-selves on the self-preservative instincts, he now sees the "value in-stincts" supported on the sexual instincts.

We have seen previously that, in the case of the ego-ideal, Freud tried to invest it with homosexual libido in order to reduce it at least termino-logically to sexual somatic excitation. However, he also recognized that the ego-ideal was the basis of the standards of action that guide a large part of the behavior of individuals. In the present situation Freud has returned to the attack with far greater vigor. But now the "reduction" does not consist of an investment of homosexual libido. It consists of the construction of a sexualized framework, the close affectional relationships of the conjugal family; the main structure—the internal standards, value orientations, love of humanity, culture and breeding, etc.—is then constructed on this framework. This is a much improved solution over the first one. As in the case of group relations Freud has centered on a crucial social situation, the human family, but, as a result of his assumption that there is a mechanical continuity of a primal situation he has robbed himself of the possibility of analysing the dynamics of groups and recognizing their differential influence on individuals.

The road from the Oedipus complex to the super-ego is difficult, however. "The parents," says Freud, "and especially the father, were perceived as the obstacles to realization of the Oedipus wishes; so the child's ego brought in a reinforcement to help in carrying out the repression by erecting this same obstacle within itself."[23] The reality principle brought this about. There is libidinal cathexis of a parent which constitutes a danger signal in view of the external situation, especially the presence of the other parent. Therefore, the child "introjects" the parent as obstacle and presumably feels the same resistance within himself to his desire for his mother as his father feels about this same desire.

So the child feels the parent's disapproval as binding on himself. He has taken over the values of the parent—at least so far as they apply to a specific situation. This interpretation fits the facts, without a doubt. But it cannot be fitted into the mechanics of the Oedipus. The values of the super-ego have to be derived from the libidinal cathexis or the identification. There is ample reason to believe that the child may want to imitiate the successful parent to increase his chances of success with the other. In bisexuality this could work both ways. And it is clear that the opposition of one parent to libidinal interests in the other can operate as a danger signal. On the theory of bisexuality which Freud too glibly took over from Fliess the child should be quite busy with imitations, danger signals and libidinal cathexes. But there is no basis here for the internalization of standards which is an important aspect of the super-ego. To say that the child erects the super-ego within himself to keep himself out of trouble with his father has no standing in theory or fact. It is an assumption that libidinizes the super-ego, just as a similar assumption libidinized Eros.

The super-ego can not be successfully derived from the Oedipus complex although it may be closely associated with it. The parents must be recognized as the basis of a system of orientation not grounded on an immutable association with libidinal interest. At the same time the empirical association between libidinal interests and value internalization in the family group is not denied. It is one of Freud's most valuable insights. But the relation is not fixed, immutable.

The human faimily is a relatively closed system of concentrated interaction. This is especially true of the "nuclear" family. The tendency for profound disturbances to grow from this situation supports Freud's statement that the super-ego ". . . is also the expression of the most powerful impulses and the most important vicissitudes experienced by the libido in the id."[24]

Freud gave the impression of describing an inevitable psychological experience in his analysis of the Oedipus and the super-ego. But then, as in the case of Eros, we get the suggestion of a primal state. He said that the super-ego ". . . answers in every way to what is expected of the higher nature of man." It is the source of "self-judgment," and it produces the "sense of worthlessness."[25] The super-ego thus seems to divorce itself from a concrete relation to a particular Oedipus.

In Freud's "group psychology" we remember that after a difficult derivation of Eros Freud gave a straightforward, sociological description of group cohesion based on common principles. This is worth repeating: "In many individuals the separation between the ego and the ego-ideal is not very far advanced; the two still coincide readily; the ego has often preserved its earlier self-complacency. The selection of the leader is very much facilitated by this circumstance. *He need only possess the typical qualities of the individuals concerned in a particular clearly marked and pure form, and need only give an impression of greater force and of more freedom of libido.*"[26] (Italics ours.)

Freud does much the same thing with the super-ego. With some suggestion of the primal Oedipus he said: "Religion, morality and a social sense—the chief elements of what is highest in man—were originally one and the same thing. According to the hypothesis which I have put forward in *Totem and Tabu* they were acquired phylogenetically out of the father-complex; religion and moral restraint by the actual process of mastering the Oedipus complex itself. . . ."[27] This constituted the libidinal derivation. The post-primal situation can then be described by a simple statement. "Social feelings rest on the foundation of identifications with others on the basis of an ego-ideal in common with them."[28] All in all social relations and group relations can be reduced to the common values held by the interacting individuals.

Libidinal reduction legitimized Eros both in terms of the social group and the individual. But it by no means helped in the analysis of the varieties of social experience or the vicissitudes of social experience in the mind. Basically, Freudian "love" is a mosaic of different "qualities" that are strategically of great importance. The attempt to handle them all in a similar, mechanical, manner has impeded the development of theory.

Chapter XVII

REFORMULATIONS

OF THE

LAST YEARS

TIME IS RUNNING out for Sigmund Freud. We do not find any extensive and systematic re-examination of his system in the later years. However, there are specific or partial reconsiderations which now merit our attention. They indicate that Freud threw off to a striking extent the bondage in which his "system" had held him. We should bear in mind, however, that this bondage could not shake off the insights of genius. These insights kept him moving ever toward the crucial variables, processes, relations. And they carry him on now.

EGO-LIBIDO AGAIN

We can take our departure from some ideas in *The Ego and the Id*. That study markedly enlarged the powers and the initiative of the ego. It remained to furnish it with some component of energy suitable to its new estate. "We have reckoned," Freud stated, "as though there existed in the mind—whether in the ego or in the id—a displaceable energy, which is in itself neutral, but is able to join forces whether with an erotic or with a destructive impulse, differing qualitatively as they do, and augment its total cathexis."[1] The frank recognition of this would have aided some of Freud's earlier analyses. Freud added, "Without assuming the existence of a displaceable energy of this kind we can make no headway. The only question is where it comes from, what it belongs to, and what it signifies." A sizeable question.

How could such an energy serve the ego? This energy was neutral and yet it could not but reflect its libidinal origin. "It would seem to be characteristic of the ego to be more particular both about the choice of an object and about the path of discharge."[2] For, after all, this energy is employed to ". . . obviate accumulations and to facilitate discharge."[3] It looks as though this neutral energy is nothing but a front for libido-quantum. Freud made use of the concept of Eros to extricate himself from this problem. ". . . this neutral, displaceable energy, which is probably active alike in the ego and in the id, proceeds from the narcissistic reservoir of libido, i.e. it is desexualized Eros."[4] This being so the energy would have lost its more vulgar tendencies, and ". . . it would still retain the main purpose of Eros—that of uniting and binding," and thus would appear to help ". . . towards establishing the unity, or tendency to unity, which is particularly characteristic of the ego. If the intellectual processes in the wider sense are to be classed among these displacements, then the energy for the work of thought, itself, must be supplied from sublimated erotic sources."[5] The desexualized energy assigned to Eros is a definite improvement over the homosexual energy assigned to the ego-ideal.

There are now, at last, two qualitatively different energies in the mind. Id energy has been proved beyond doubt. And Eros energy has grown out of primal individual and social scenes. Eros can now perform the object-cathexes that so vexed Freud in earlier analyses.

Freud was once quite willing to indenture the ego to the id. But he is not at all anxious to indenture the ego to Eros. At the same time the source of ego energy is not clear. We remain uncertain how the ego moves in the first place, but having moved it proceeds to capture energy from Eros. It also steals energy from the id which it desexualizes and thus sets itself up in business. This indicates that the ego is a psychic independent. ". . . this throws light," said Freud, "upon an important function of the ego in its relation to Eros. By thus obtaining possession of the libido from the object-cathexes, setting itself up as sole love-object, and desexualizing or sublimating the libido of the id, the ego is working in opposition to the purposes of Eros and placing itself at the services of the opposing instinctual trends."[6]

As I said we do not know where the energy came from that moved the ego in the first place. Freud dealt with the problem as follows: ". . . at the very beginning," he said, "all the libido is accumulated in the id, while the ego is still in process of formation or far from robust. Part of this libido is sent out by the id into erotic object-cathexes, whereupon the ego, now growing stronger, attempts to obtain possession of this object-libido."[7]

Still we have not energized the ego in the first place. Finally Freud suggested an ego energy ". . . which is itself neutral, but is able to join forces either with an erotic or with a destructive impulse . . . and augment its total cathexis."[8] Eros, then, has led the way to an interdependent ego energy. This energy can be looked upon as sublimated sexual energy in the same sense that Eros is derived from aim-inhibited sexual instincts. Thus there takes place a ". . . transformation of erotic libido into ego-libido."[9]

This new ego-libido has many advantages over the old. The present concept does not refer to any direct psychic representative of somatic excitation. It does not refer to a process that invests an inert ego. It is an assumption of motive power in the ego process. It can add to or subtract from libidinal or Eros energies. And it seems the ego is not unalterably opposed to the id. "The separation of the ego from the id seems justified," said Freud, "indeed is forced upon us, by certain findings. Yet on the other hand the ego is identical with the id, is only a specially differentiated portion of it. . . . The same with the relation of the ego to the super-ego; as regards many situations they are one and the same."[10] As Freud said, ". . . we have been taking abstractions too rigidly."[11]

By the time of the publication of *The Problem of Anxiety* (1926) Freud was indicating his feeling that id, super-ego and ego were in a sense interdependent forces where the line-up could not be predicted in advance. This negates the instinctual dominance which has followed Freud's thought from the beginning.

THE POWERS OF THE EGO

The emergence of the ego gave Freud occasion to chide those who might think that it had ever been otherwise. He regretted that, "Many opinions have forcibly emphasized the weakness of the ego in relation to the id, of the rational against the demonic in us, and are on the point of making this pronouncement into a pillar of a psychoanalytic Weltanschauung."[12] Freud now sought to correct this. One of the requirements is that the economic view be given up. Referring to repression and the formation of anxiety he stated that these developments ". . . are not to be explained on an economic basis."[13]

Freud now assumed that the ego is *sui generis* and powered by an energy appropriate to its nature. This altered his view of repression. We learn that in repression the instinct energy is not converted into unpleasure. "We hope," Freud stated, "that we shall clarify the situation if we lay it down definitely that in consequence of repression the excitation arising in the id altogether fails of discharge: the ego succeeds in inhibiting or deflecting it. . . . We have thereby conceded to the ego the ability to exert so far-reaching an influence upon the processes taking place in the id, and have now to learn to understand the way in which this surprising manifestation of power becomes possible to the ego."[14]

Anxiety is no longer seen as the result of some kind of somatic-psychic block. In repression, said Freud, "The ego withdraws (preconscious) cathexis from the instinct representative which is to be repressed and utilizes it in the release of unpleasure, (anxiety)." While the mechanics of this process are not clear he felt that it is justifiable to ". . . hold the view that the ego is the real locus of anxiety."[15] Thus Freud was led to surrender the old view with considerable reluctance. "It is not pleasant," he said, "to think of it, but there is no use in denying that I have repeatedly put forward the thesis that through repression the instinctual representative is distorted, displaced, and the like, and the libido of the instinctual impulse transformed into anxiety."[16]

Repression and anxiety are, then, not processes that can be reduced to somatic excitation. Furthermore, they cannot be reduced to primal psychic mechanisms. It is therefore necessary to motivate the ego, to give it a reason for action. This is the peculiar function of the castration complex. By means of this complex Freud was able to tie together the factors of anxiety, the super-ego, and the reality principle. "We do not want to lose sight . . . of the place that anxiety occupies," said Freud. "We have said that as soon as the ego has recognized the danger of castration, it gives the signal of anxiety, and through the medium of the pleasure-pain mechanism it inhibits, in a manner still obscure to us, the threatening cathectic process in the id."[17] The method whereby this takes place is not, of course, entirely obscure. As Freud has stated it involved ". . . the withdrawal of (preconscious) cathexis."[18] The castration complex is thus projected from the Oedipus complex into the outer world and constitutes the important prototype of social reality orientation. The castration complex also sufficiently dramatizes the Oedipus complex by indicating the specific factor which leads the boy to see his father as an obstacle to the boy's libidinal cathexis of the mother. Castration thus occupies a dual position. It applies to a fear that can be grounded in some type of primal mechanism. Or on the other hand it can be related to the social situation where the father actually threatens the boys with castration. In this second case there is not the same necessary connection between the threat of castration and the libidinal cathexis of the mother as there is in the first case.

There is a third interpretation of the castration complex also. Castration may be used symbolically to indicate paternal sanction in general. The difficulties with such conceptualization are now familiar. They do not cover the available data although they may be peculiarly apt for the explanation of specific important data. We have seen that the superego cannot rest solely on the Oedipus. So also external sanction cannot rest solely upon the castration complex, and thus serve as the basis for the social reality-principle. Again it should be noticed however that these concepts emphasize the frequent empirical conjunction of important affective and cognitive elements.

Since Freud is so rapidly shifting his theoretical interests from the Ucs to the ego what is he to do with the repetition-compulsion? The original view of the repetition-compulsion formed the basis of the death-instinct. In *The Problem of Anxiety* we see how that original view of a senseless mechanism working to cause "pain" in the psyche has, by slow gradations, changed into something rather different. The vexing situation is that repression may persist even when the danger situation is altered so that the ". . . ego is without incentive to defend itself against a newly arisen instinctual impulse analagous to the one which has been repressed."[19] Let us say that the boy has formed a libidinal cathexis of the mother and has been diverted from overt behavior by the threat of castration. But the father dies or leaves the home. Now, why does the repression persist with reference to the libidinal interest? There is no longer any danger in the external situation and therefore there is no reason for repression. This, says Freud, is a situation where we must have recourse to the concept of repetition-compulsion. "The new instinct," he says, "pursues its course in automatic fashion—I should prefer to say, under the influence of the repetition-compulsion; it follows the same path as did the instinct which had previously been repressed, as though the successfully surmounted danger situation were still in existence. The fixating factor in repression is thus the repetition-compulsion of the unconscious id, which normally is put an end to only through freely mobile ego-functioning."[20] This is a view very similar to the original exposition of repetition-compulsion. The fact that it is in the "id" does not mean, I think, that it is in the "Unconscious." Freud was referring here to that part of the ego which has "grown out of" the id; i.e. to the repression of a libidinal component.

In the present view the repetition-compulsion consists of a rather unpredictable and automatic continuation of repression when the ego is not motivated to continue this repression. The necessity for the assumption rests, of course, on the certainty that the ego is not motivated to continue the repression. After all, a good deal of "repetition" is required for repression. As Freud said: "It is an important element of the theory of repression that this process is not one which takes place on a single occasion but is one demanding a continuous expenditure of effort. Should this effort be intermitted, the repressed impulse, which receives a continuous influx from its sources of origin, would thereupon strike out upon the same path off which it has been forced, and the repression would have failed of its purpose or would have to be repeated an indefinite number of times. Thus, from the uninterrupted character of the instinctual impulse there arises the demand of the ego to insure its defense by an unremitting expenditure of effort."[21] The repetition-complex, then, is a perverse persistance of the ego.

Freud thought there might be some other repressing agency. He worked, I think, on analogy with a former hypothesis. The reader will remember that Freud earlier suggested that the Unconscious exercised "attraction" on material in the Preconscious. "We experience the fact," said Freud, "that the ego still finds it difficult to nullify its repressions even after it has resolved to give up its resistances, and we have designated the phase of strenuous effort which follows upon this laudable resolution as the period of 'working through.' Now it is easy to recognize the dynamic factor which makes this working through necessary and intelligible. It can but be that after the cessation of the ego-resistance there is still the power of the repetition-compulsion, the attraction exerted by its unconscious prototypes upon the repressed instinctual process, to be overcome; nor is it in any way inconsistent with this to designate this factor as the resistance of the unconscious."[22]

This view does not come to grips with the fact that the repetition-compulsion, as Freud now describes it, continues in operation a process started by the ego. And if this resistance of the unconscious does exist how does "talking through" help matters?

This resistance must be due to something in ego structure. In our discussion of mental energies and their relationships we suggested that repression requires us to consider that ego energy is employed to bring about a repression of material that also may be cathected by other ego energy. Another process of the same type seems visible here. A part of the ego is motivated to undo the repression, but another part of the ego is motivated to continue it. In the type of case that Freud is concerned with, the motivation to undo the repression is conscious and the motivation to continue the repression is unconscious. So Freud refers to it as the resistance of the unconscious.

What is the basis for the ego motivation to continue the repression? We do not find the answer in *The Problem of Anxiety*, with which we have been presently concerned, but rather in *The Ego and the Id*. In the latter work Freud suggested that the solution of ego ambivalence toward the undoing of a repression is to be found in the influence of the super-ego. Commenting on the fact that there is in some people a factor that sets itself against their recovery he said: ". . . we come to see that we are dealing with what may be called a 'moral' factor, a sense of guilt, which is finding atonement in the illness and is refusing to give up the penalty of suffering. . . . This sense of guilt expresses itself only as a resistance to recovery which it is extremely difficult to overcome. . . . The description we have given applies to the most extreme instances of this state of affairs, but in a lesser measure this factor has to be reckoned with in very many cases, perhaps in all severe cases of neurosis. In fact, it may be precisely this element in the situation, the attitude of the ego-ideal, that determines the severity of a neurotic illness."[23] The reader will find here I think considerable confirmation of the views we put forward in the case of little Hans.

Thus the repetition-compulsion at last takes on a function which seems to remove it from the category of the death-instinct. And we find confirmation of our view that the repetition-compulsion and the death-instinct do represent, in part, conceptual equivalents for influence resulting from social conditioning.

THE THEORY OF NEUROSIS

In *The Problem of Anxiety* Freud tried to bring his theory of neurosis in line with his new theoretical views. Old ideas of "primal repression" and "after-expulsion" are obsolete. And yet Freud was ambivalent. He pointed out that the act of repression ". . . has demonstrated to us the strength of the ego. . . ." But he added, ". . . but it also bears witness at the same time to the ego's impotence and to the uninfluenceable character of the individual instinctual impulses in the id."[24] On the whole, however, the ego holds the dominant position. ". . . the process which through repression has become a symptom now maintains its existence outside of the ego-organization and independent of it. And not it alone, but all its offshoots, enjoy the same privilege of extra-territoriality, as one might put it; and where these come into associative contact with parts of the ego organization, it becomes a question whether they will not win the latter over to their side and batten on this success at the expense of the ego."[25]

In energy terms, of course, this does not imply that the repressed material possesses decisive amounts of energy, but that repressed material may seek to attract energy from the ego. Thus repressed material may struggle for hyper-cathexis. Again we see the possibility that the ego may be divided between those forces maintaining the repression and those forces seeking to cathect the repressed material and upset the repression.

Formerly, Freud referred the "symptom" to the instinctual presentation. In most cases, however, it is difficult to see how the symptom has a sensible relation to the instinct need for discharge. We have pointed out that in dreams the "gratification" appears to be an ego gratification. Is it not possible that the dream symptom and the neurotic symptom are alike in this regard?

Freud inclined to this solution. He said that the symptom is ". . . *ab initio* an integral part of the ego," and that it often represents a ". . . fulfillment of a demand on the part of the superego."[26] He was not willing, however, to concede that the symptom is ego-procured. He suggested rather that it is something the ego comes to accept and take advantage of. ". . . the ego," he said, "behaves as if it were swayed by the consideration that the symptom is there and cannot be got rid of, and that therefore the thing to do is to make the best of the situation and extract the greatest advantage possible from it. . . . Thus the symptom is gradually entrusted with the representing of important interests; it acquires a value for self-assertion; it becomes intertwined more and more intimately with the ego, becoming ever more indispensable to the latter."[27] Freud was quite against the idea that the ego invented the symptom in the first place. He said, "One would exaggerate the significance of this secondary adaptation if one were to say that the ego acquired the symptom for the sole purpose of enjoying its advantages. This would be to advance a view as correct or as erroneous as the opinion that a maimed war veteran had had his leg shot away only that he might thereafter live in indolence on his pension."[28] The symptom is the result of repression which is procured by the ego. The question is, did the symptom arise vicariously from the repression or was it in some sense intended by the repressive agent?

If the symptom is random and only *used* by the ego it would appear that there was only a chance possibility of the symptom being associated with the repression. Only the employment of the symptom would be clinically significant. In describing his theory of phobias Freud suggested, however, that the symptom itself is created by the ego. He tells us that he has previously ". . . ascribed to phobias the character of a projection since they substitute for an internal, instinctual danger an external perceptual one." He altered this position. "This statement of mine is not incorrect, but superficial. For the instinctual demand is not in itself a danger, but is so only because it entails a true external danger, that of castration. So that fundamentally we have in the phobias, after all, merely the substituting of one external danger for another."[29] Although Freud did not expressly say so, this substitution of external dangers appears to be not a random process but an organized plan of the ego.

We also see in the above passage that Freud has given up the view that the ego has no defense against internal stimuli and that it therefore transfers internal dangers to external dangers in order to make use of the "barrier against stimuli." The frank admission of the ego powers in repression have made the earlier view untenable. Furthermore, Freud now assumes that the ego is not necessarily set against instinct presentations as such. In fact, from this passage we would infer that the ego is inclined to grant object cathexis to instinctual presentations unless there is some kind of "external" obstacle. The obstacle in this case is the castration complex. The ego appears by the symptom to substitute for the real external danger a substitute, dramatized danger exercising more compulsion upon the mind. This suggests that the mobile ego-energy is deployed both in hyper-cathexis and anti-cathexis at the same time and that the phobic symptom is an attempt to buttress the anti-cathectic forces.

The originating power of the ego is finally admitted by Freud in his treatment of agoraphobia. "The symptomatology of agoraphobia," he says, "is complicated by the fact that the ego is not content with renouncing something; in addition to this, it takes steps to deprive the situation of its danger. This additional measure is usually a regression to childhood (in extreme cases, to the uterus, to a period when one was protected against the dangers which threaten today); the regression constitutes the condition under which the renunciation need not be made. Thus the agoraphobic may go on the street provided that, like a small child, he is accompanied by a person in whom he has full confidence."[30]

The ego's function with reference to neurotic symptoms is similar to the generally therapeutic and homeostatic functions of the ego that we mentioned in the discussions of the dream process, transference, and repetition-compulsion.

LATER VIEWS
ON PERSONALITY PROCESS

The castration complex, as a price of its specific advantages, had the disadvantage that it did not sufficiently distinguish the real castration complex from the symbolic castration complex. The latter would be of course the fear of the disapproval of the father rather than the fear of physical injury from the father. In addition, the castration complex was not easily extended to the sanction of social disapproval as exercised by other individuals in the society. Yet, as we have seen, it was increasingly evident to Freud that the field of social disapproval was an important ingredient of the reality-principle.

The internal situation was similar. The super-ego is limited by its attachment to the Oedipus complex. Thus both with reference to the external and the internal situation it remained for Freud to tie his views to the conditioning effect of the social environment. In the last years of his life he indicated that his theoretical interest had in fact centered on the social environment.

We find a specific indication of this new interest in his *Autobiographical Study* where he put forward a somewhat revised view of latency. "The period of latency," he said, "is a physiological phenomenon. It can, however, only give rise to a complete interruption of sexual life in cultural organizations which have made the suppression of infantile sexuality a part of their system. . . ."[31] This emphasis upon "cultural organizations" points to a "cause" that cannot be well confined to the framework of the Oedipus complex or the castration fear. It requires that these "organizations" themselves be considered, that the variety of their characteristics be investigated and the lines of their influence determined. But on what basis could these cultural organizations be considered "real"? Since they were evidenced by the behavior of individuals how could they also be seen as external to the individual? This problem had faced Freud before. But his changing orientation indicated that an important key to personality dynamics could be found in cultural influences. Freud proposed the hypothesis that *cultural* development was in some sense a *biological* process. ". . . we must not forget," he reminded us, "that the mass of mankind, subjected though they are to economic necessities, are borne on by a process of cultural development—some call it civilization—which is no doubt influenced by all the other factors, but is equally independent of them in its origin; *it is comparable to an organic process,* and is quite capable of itself having an effect upon the other factors. *It displaces the aims of the instincts,* and causes men to rebel against what has hitherto been tolerable." (Italics ours.) Freud proceeded to outline the field of social science. "If any one were in a position to show in detail how these different factors—the general human instinctual disposition, its racial variations, and its cultural modifications—behave under the influence of varying social organization, professional activities and methods of subsistence, how these factors inhibit or aid one another—if, I say, any one could show this, then he would not only have improved Marxism but would have made it into a true social science."[32] Here we can see that Freud is clarifying the social component in his system of theory. By assuming that the cultural tradition is an organic type of process it could be viewed as external to the individual. For Freud, this served to legitimize the study of cultures as distinct from the study of the maturation and genesis of social mechanisms in individuals.

Following this line of thinking Freud developed his own theory of the "social contract" which is very close to that of Hobbes.[33] "But how ungrateful, how short-sighted after all, to strive for the abolition of culture! What would then remain would be the state of nature, and that is far harder to endure. It is true that nature does not ask us to restrain our instincts, she lets us do as we like; but she has her peculiarly effective mode of restricting us; she destroys us, coldly, cruelly, callously, as it seems to us, and possibly just through what has caused our satisfaction. It was because of these very dangers with which nature threatens us that we united together and created culture, which, amongst other things, is supposed to make our communal existence possible. Indeed, it is the principal task of culture, its real raison d'être, to defend us against nature."[34]

We would conclude from this passage that Freud must rethink the problem of the genesis of Eros. Eros, the love of humanity, the devotion to standards, has been derived from the sex cells and later from the aim-inhibited instincts. It appears that Eros works to some extent against nature, and helps to make our "communal existence possible." Is it not possible then that Eros does not belong within the individual at all but should be installed in that other organism, the social organism? Freud does not tell us this in so many words but he does say that ". . . culture obeys an inner erotic impulse which bids it bind mankind into a closely knit mass . . ."[35] and since this is the function of Eros we must conclude that Eros has been extended to the society. Thus socialization is a study of the process whereby the Eros of the society is communicated to the individual constituting the Eros in the individual. The super-ego and ego-ideal are the Eros components of motivation as it finds dynamic representation in the mind.

When we take this point of view the phylogenetic social mechanisms are no longer necessary. "It is not really a decisive matter," says Freud, "whether one has killed one's father or abstained from the deed; one must feel guilt in either case, for guilt is the expression of the conflict of ambivalence. . . ."[36] It is possible, Freud thought, that there may have been a rudimentary guilt mechanism. Culture then proceeded to build upon it. "When mankind tries to institute wider forms of communal life, the same conflict continues to arise—in forms derived from the past—and is intensified so that a further reinforcement of the sense of guilt results."[37]

Freud has viewed the cultural tradition as generally repressive since it may act contrary to the aims of the instincts. Thus, within the individual, Eros has appeared to Freud as a movement toward self-destruction. In earlier thinking the death-instinct represented, in part, the dynamics of Eros within the personality. Although Freud recognized that one component of Eros represented "love of humanity" he did not examine the motivations derived from Eros that were associated with pleasurable affect. Thus he disregarded or discounted the affirmative contributions of the cultural tradition. In one of his last works, however, he turned to this more affirmative aspect and again opened a field for further investigation. Time was running out now and Freud was not permitted to continue his labors in the new fields of inquiry which he was opening up. But in *Civilization and Its Discontents* he showed us that culture not only defends us against nature but also may make possible a delicate exploitation of the pleasure principle. "We are so constituted," said Freud, "that we can only intensely enjoy contrasts, much less intensely, states in themselves." Yet ". . . a method of guarding against pain is by using the libido-displacements that our mental equipment allows of, by which it gains so greatly in flexibility." This reference is probably to the "mobile" ego energy. "There is, then," he continued, "one means of transferring the instinctual aims into such directions that they cannot be frustrated by the outer world. Its success is greatest when a man knows how to heighten sufficiently his capacity for obtaining pleasure from mental and intellectual work. Fate has little power against him then. This kind of satisfaction, such as the artist's joy in creation, in embodying his phantasies, or the scientist's in solving problems or discovering truth, has a special quality which we shall certainly one day be able to define metapsychologically. Until then we can only say that it seems to us 'higher and finer,' but compared with that of gratifying gross primitive instincts its intensity is tempered and diffused; it does not overwhelm us physically."[38]

This is, at once, an hypothesis and a new philosophy. I would think that the metapsychological foundation to support it had already been established by the assumption of Eros energy. Here we have the suggestion that Eros energy has some kind of qualitatively distinct gratification potential. Thus, at long last, Freud has suggested that social influence is not necessarily psychic hurt. Eros gratification is an interdependent pleasure-principle along with organic gratification.

Chapter XVIII

SUMMARY

AND CONCLUSION

THE DEVELOPMENT OF FREUD'S
THOUGHT

FREUD'S THOUGHT HAS been divided into three stages which correspond to the three parts of this study. We have mentioned that he thought rather consistently within the limits of an organic frame of reference. He thus committed himself to the proposition that a satisfactory system of concepts could be worked out within the limits of the organism as such. Other factors would then operate on the "system" in the form of conditions. Freud was strongly inclined to reject causative sequences that appeared to lead in the direction of these "conditions."

It should be pointed out also that, with reference to personality, there are two orders of data. There is an "objective" order of data which refers to somatic events and their relation to personality process. Freud, of course, was deeply concerned with the relation between personality and sexual somatic excitation. Then there is a "subjective" order of data which includes ideas, emotions, and motivations. Whichever order of data is employed, the concepts must "fit" this data. A concept like libido-quantum was based on the "objective" data. On the other hand, a concept like identification is based on the "subjective" data. Freud's concept-building moved from the first order of data to the second order of data rather early in his career.

The first stage of Freud's thought involved a number of sub-stages that reflect the various views he experimented with in testing concepts based on the "objective" order of data. He flirted with the idea that mental events were something in the nature of hallucinatory phenomena attending the changes in somatic states of the body. The early theory of anxiety as a subcortical expenditure of libido-quantum is a good example of this early conceptualization. The treatment of the mind as an hallucinatory process at this time was, of course, largely a methodological assumption.

Freud encountered insuperable difficulties with this approach. They reduced to the fact that hallucinatory phenomena in the mind, i.e. the "subjective" order of data, were rich and varied in their manifestations and these manifestations could not be paralleled by equivalent somatic states. The mind seemed to have "a mind of its own." In addition to being influenced by somatic states, the mind also influenced them. This counter-influence was not consistent with a hallucinatory hypothesis. Freud tried to "explain" it by an "objective" assumption. Employing an electrical analogy he referred to the "resistance of the subcortical conduction." This did not advance his theory very far.

It appeared, therefore, that the subjective order of data could not be disregarded as mere phantasm. Freud proceeded to consider it on the assumption that if it could not be dismissed as hallucination it could be satisfactorily explained by somatic states. The dominant concepts could still be concerned with the "objective" order of data. An example from some of the early concepts will illustrate how Freud proposed to work out this approach. Freud employed the concept ego-libido (not to be confused with his use of the same term but with a different meaning in *The Ego and The Id*) with reference to certain mental events. But this concept was by definition referable to another concept, libido-quantum, which referred to the energy value of sexual somatic excitation. In this approach Freud was recognizing the legitimacy of subjective data. But he did not propose to organize and explain this data by a system of concepts directed to the subjective data. He proposed instead to translate this subjective data into somatic terms and to ground his systematic theory on somatic states. The concepts libido-quantum and ego-libido constituted a prototype of this method. The relation between ego-libido and libido-quantum was assumed to be such that changes in the quantity of libido-quantum (due to alterations in the amount of sexual congestion) caused changes in the activity of ego-libido within the mind. In this way certain behavior designs of the mind could be explained in terms of variations in the quantity of libido-quantum and consequently in the quantity of sexual somatic excitation. This particular model proved far too simple, however. The necessary equivalence between libido-quantum and ego-libido could not be established. The "resistance of the subcortical conduction" intervened sometimes to ward off the libido-quantum so that it expended itself subcortically and was not translated into ego-libido. Freud felt that this fate of the libido-quantum was important in distinguishing between certain psychoneuroses.

Freud proceeded to a more sophisticated conceptualization of mental events. We find the genesis of his famous categories, the Unconscious, the Preconscious and the Conscious. Somatic states were not forgotten, however. The Unconscious was designed expressly as the mental representative of somatic tension. The reductive model had an important position, for Freud assumed that the Unconscious had a private pipe-line to sexual somatic excitation. Thus the theoretical priority of the Unconscious was a heritage from earlier theory and from certain interpretations of clinical evidence that derived from this earlier theory. There was an important difference between the new approach and the old, however. In the earlier and simpler theory Freud had tried to trace somatic excitation into the mind, into the field of subjective events. The concepts Conscious, Preconscious, and Unconscious, nevertheless, disclose a forthright attempt to organize the subjective order of events, to treat them in all their complexity. In other words, Freud shifted his theory from the somatic or objective field to the mental or subjective field. He did not give up the conviction that crucial causative effects operated from the somatic. But, with the new type of theory, instead of starting with somatic tension, he proposed to work back to it. Libido-quantum was a somatic concept. The Unconscious was a mental concept. Yet the Unconscious connected back to the somatic just as the libido-quantum connected forward to the mental. With better and sharper tools than he had employed before Freud proposed to establish three hypotheses: (1) Sexual excitation found its mental representation in a discrete mental system known as the Unconscious. (2) The energy increments of these mental representations of somatic states were the dominant if not the exclusive quantum of energy available in the mind. (3) The dynamics of mental proceedings were related in a crucial manner to the accumulation of somatic tension and the discharge of this tension.

The tools proved to be better but still not good enough. Investigations that culminated in *The Interpretation of Dreams* indicated that mental concepts did not reach backward into the somatic with much more success than somatic concepts had reached forward. The libido-quantum had been caught in only one quandary, however. It could not reach forward. The Unconscious, on the other hand, was in a double quandary. It could reach neither forward nor backward. No clear relation was established between the Unconscious and somatic sexual excitation. Furthermore, nothing but confusion resulted from the attempt to organize mental proceedings on the basis of the Unconscious.

There was no escape from entering upon a new field of theoretical inquiry. That elusive force, "the resistance of the subcortical conduction," had to be further examined. Freud had many terms for this force. He called it the "censor," "ideal masochism," "the unsuspected contrary sexual," or just "the resistance." Freud's attempt to critically examine the effects of this force on mental events and to devise concepts that would integrate with the theory already fashioned takes us into the second stage of his thought. *The Interpretation of Dreams,* published in 1900, bridges these two periods.

Freud had, of course, referred to the "ego" and he had put forward numerous ideas as to how the Preconscious figured in dream processes. The requirement now, however, was for some sort of systematic advance that would establish the status of the ego as a theoretical category. A formulation of the ego was required that could explain the outgoingness of certain human activity. Freud needed a fuller explanation and treatment of the variety of object-cathexes.

There was a further advantage to be gained in this quest. It raised the hope that some of the furniture of the Unconscious could be moved to other quarters. Consider, for example, the whole field of ego-centered motivation. This had been inherited from Meynert when Freud accepted his overlay theory as applied to the maturation of personality. The theory seemed quite right. The child developed a "primary personality" which was dominantly egoistic. Only later was there a gradual development of a "secondary ego" which tended to overlay the primary ego. In taking over this view Freud had tended to identify the primary ego with the Unconscious. Thus, the Unconscious had been stocked with many heterogeneous elements. Freud now had an opportunity to clarify and simplify the Unconscious even while he was strengthening his theory by the elaboration of a new category.

Freud removed the "self-preservative" instincts from the unconscious and placed them in the ego. They became central factors in ego activity. In the Unconscious these instincts had been servient to the libidinal "currents" existing there. In the ego, however, they were able to realize their theoretical potential, to serve as the basis for a large range of object-cathexes.

This was hardly sufficient, however. The self-preservative instincts presented a reason for object cathexis only so long as the object was related to the self-preservation. Clinically, it appeared that object-cathexis need not coincide with this period of dependence. In addition, the ego might not cathect an object at all. It might cathect itself. Freud introduced a component of libidinal energy into the ego by the assumption that the sexual instinct "supported itself upon" the self-preservative instincts. This quantum of sexual energy could now explain the extensions of cathexes. An original cathexis might relate to the self-preservative instincts, might result from the protection and care furnished by some person, but the extension of this cathexis after the security threat was over could be explained as a libidinal cathexis. The attachment to the self which was another kind of frequent cathexis could not be explained on the same basis. Freud assumed a primary rite, a libidinal cathexis of the ego, through which this attachment took place. In terms of these assumptions there must be constant demand for libidinal energy which in turn required that there be a continuous condition of sexual somatic excitation. This requirement led to the formulation of "erotogenicity" in terms of which many organs of the body were assumed to be productive of libido.

The above assumptions constituted the basis for Freud's "libido theory" which dominated the second period of his thought. Personality process was to be largely explained by the behavior of energy arising out of somatic excitation and flowing either in the direction of anaclitic object-cathexis or into ego-cathexis. The dominant variable was libidinal energy. Its amounts were considered decisive in personality proceedings.

Although Freud set up two theoretical categories, the Unconscious and the ego, he "reduced" them both to quantitative libidinal factors. Libidinal energy in the ego "caused" different events than it did in the Unconscious. The model that Freud followed here is similar to that employed in the "thirteen cases of hysteria." He considered in those cases, that there was damage done to the sexual instincts and that the "resistance" of the ego could be traced to these damaged instincts. This view was, of course, given up when it became apparent that the sexual injuries had not really taken place in these cases of hysteria. However, the same model was employed not only in "libido theory" but also later in the assumption of "aim-inhibited instincts."

Freud made thorough-going attempts to carry out the full implications of libido theory. The problem of quantification proved insuperable. The assumption of erotogenicity destroyed whatever possibility might have existed for the measuring of somatic excitation. Freud proposed to set up some kind of measuring system in the mind itself. He assumed that the libidinal energy of the ego cathected the ego as a matter of preference. All libidinal object cathexes were then to be explained as the draining away of surplus energy. As Freud put it, ". . .

in the last resort we must begin to love in order that we may not fall ill, and [we] must fall ill, if, in consequence of frustration, we cannot love." This view proved untenable in the empirical test reported in "Mourning and Melancholia."

Although libido theory extended the field of "legitimate" object-cathexes there was need for further extension. It appeared for example that individuals became motivated to conform to general principles of action, certain norms, which were "internalized" and that in accordance with these norms individuals cathected objects that were not necessarily anaclitic. Freud brought both of these trends into focus under the concept of the ego-ideal. He suggested that the ego-ideal might be "explained" in libido theory on the ground that it was suffused with a charge of homosexual energy. Since there was no claim that measurable quantities of homosexual libido were involved here, there was an almost irresistible temptation to circular reasoning. Clinical data was assumed to be associated with such a distribution of libido quanta as could "cause" the data in question.

The introduction of the ego-ideal gave the *coup de grace* to libido theory. While Freud was struggling with methods of accommodating it he was also testing means of altering the body of theory itself. The "metapsychological" approach to mental events was to an important degree an alternative approach to strict libido analysis although it incorporated that analysis as one of its elements. This approach was rather far advanced as early as the *Metapsychological Supplement to the Theory of Dreams*. However, the data requiring the formulation of the ego-ideal also indicated that Freud required something more than the multiplication of "approaches" such as the dynamic, economic, and topological. Freud embarked on a reformulation of his system of thought as such. The beginning of this reexamination may be somewhat arbitrarily set at the publication of *Beyond the Pleasure Principle* in 1920, and constitutes the third stage of Freud's thought. In general we may say that Freud's systematic theory at this time proved unsatisfactory in that (a) it failed to take into account a sufficiently wide segment of human behavior, (b) it failed to make clear the relations between the two categories, the ego and the Unconscious, and (c) it was unable to demonstrate the usefulness of a libidinal-quantitative approach to ego dynamics.

In the third period Freud addressed himself to the following problems:

1) What is the "instinctual" basis for "ego-ideal" type of motivation? This inquiry led to the formulation of repetition-compulsion, and finally to the assumption of the life and death-instincts. These mecha-

nisms were supplemented and explained by organic mechanisms which were assumed to have become imbedded in the organism by mutation on the occasion of a "primal" social experience. The "aim-inhibited" sex instincts serve as an example of this process. This theoretical position, as can be seen, was awkwardly attained. It also required the abandonment of certain views of the sexual instinct advanced in "Three Contributions to a Theory of Sexuality" which had served as a pillar of the Freudian system.

Freud found it extremely difficult to apply this kind of theory to the analysis of concrete social relations. He was required to reduce social groups to one type, that modeled on his assumption of a primal patriarchal family group. His thinking was thus severely circumscribed and his analysis, as in many other situations where he is hard pressed, was a mixture of scholasticism and opportunism here combined with the creation of an ingenious mythology. Libido theory appeared at its weakest in this type of analysis. The mythology illustrated that "pseudo-anthropology" which is frequently the object of criticism.

Although the specific concepts produced to deal with social motivation were not integrated in Freud's thought and although the assumptions of aim-inhibited instincts and primal mutations arising from social situations were far from satisfactory, nevertheless Freud's concepts, taken together, greatly enlarged the field of social motivation that was open for theoretical consideration. The death-instinct applied in very large measure to that component of internalized social motivation that is opposed in some sense to the organic tensions of the organism *qua* organism. By means of the death-instinct, therefore, Freud came to consider social experience and its effect on the individual but he got at it in reverse, as it were. Eros constituted a decisive advance in the consideration of social motivation. By means of Eros the outgoing "altruistic" behavior of individuals was granted a legitimate and qualitatively distinct place in Freud's thought. Freud went on to postulate an Eros not only in the individual but also in the society. To the sociologist this must remain as one of his greatest insights for it suggested that the outgoingness of the individual was not based on organic facts but on the influence of another Eros: the cultural system and the interpersonal experience of the individual in this system. Freud, maintaining his frame of reference to the bitter end, saw this larger Eros as part of still another organic system, the social system as such.

2) In what manner shall we account for the phenomenon of repression? This problem had persisted throughout all of Freud's thinking. It was a reference point for almost all aspects of his theory. The clinical data concerned with repression indicated that it was a funda-

mental dynamic element in mental process and thus no theory could hope to be satisfactory that did not account for it. We shall mention in a later section some of the devices that Freud employed to explain repression. We wish to emphasize now that the view of the ego which we have discussed above furnished Freud with quite a new approach to this phenomenon. If we take any one of the "mental formations" that Freud discussed in *Interpretation of Dreams* and use it as a co-ordinate system we find that Freud's description of mental formations in general furnishes a striking example of the processes in repression.

Freud only gradually constructed the mental formation. First there were "trains of thought" in the preconscious. Then there might be certain "ideas which have their source in our unconscious and ever-active wishes." When the train of thought was cathected by the idea it received the energy of the wishes. Here we see the rudimentary beginnings of the mental formation. Later it took on more specific form and appeared able to influence other formations. Thus it was able to "institute connections" or enter into other formations, perhaps absorb them. This, of course, implied that a formation could be penetrated and perhaps absorbed by another mental formation. If we look at this process from the view of one formation as a coordinate system, repression would be the elimination of a penetration by another formation; in other words, one aspect of a larger dynamic system. The implications of this dynamic process for repression were not clear at an earlier date. But the analysis of repetition-compulsion showed the same process at work at a higher and more general level. The unconscious ego resisted the attempts of the conscious ego to eliminate a type of ego behavior. This was an example of resistance exercised by the unconscious ego against the conscious ego. On the other hand it was already clear that the conscious ego could resist and cast out material from the unconscious ego. Here then was a reciprocal process of mutual expulsion, rejection, and penetration that Freud had discovered in the dynamic relations of smaller mental formations. Repression as such would appear to be the description of this process, taking the Conscious system as a coordinate system.

Freud did not come to a completely clear statement of this position. But his increasing reliance on the ideas of cathexis and hyper-cathexis indicated a strong tendency to explain repression in terms of the mutual give and take between the various levels of mental activity. It is a simplification of theory since it reduces repression to processes already postulated and consequently does not require the assumption of additional mechanisms as was the case in earlier Freudian thought. However, the full significance and usefulness of these views remain to be examined.

3) In view of the implications of repetition-compulsion and the life- and death-instincts, what are the theoretically tenable "divisions of the mind"? This problem was explored to considerable depth in *The Ego and The Id*. This work represents a determined attempt to do away with topological commitments. The task proved to be exceedingly difficult because of the "index value" (to use Freud's phrase) that attached to these regions. These index values or "normal" behavior trends of the regions formed a basis for explaining dynamic processes in the mind. When these regions are vacated the "index values" associated with them must be given up. The question then arises, what are the index values in mental processes, i.e., what are the fundamental factors, in terms of which, mental interaction takes place? This was the underlying quest in *The Ego and The Id*.

The solution is not presented with utmost clarity. It appeared, however, that one basic factor was the ego's employment of mobile energy. This implied that the ego could act as a unit and that it had at its command a quantum of free-floating psychic energy with which it could control motility and arbitrate the demands of reality, the super-ego and the id. There were two other basic factors, the tensions resulting from somatic congestion and the compulsions engendered by the super-ego.

These factors were not new although Freud gave increasing attention to the initiative of the ego and its employment of mobile energy. Is there any other basic factor at work? In topological thinking Freud had held that there was another factor. It consisted in the characteristics of regions and the settled types of interaction between them. Was Freud to give up this additional factor or substitute for it in some manner?

The solution suggested by Freud was a new regionalism and one which was better founded both empirically and theoretically. The new region consisted of the "coherent" ego. This coherent ego was not a phylogenetic mechanism but an association of similar psychic "formations" resulting from the interaction of the mind with its internal and external environment. It was a product of one's living and not of the living of one's ancestors in some primal past. The formulation of the coherent ("bound," "organized") ego, although hinted at frequently, actually developed from libido theory and from what we have termed "cathexis analysis" as applied to "psychic formations."

These formations were first treated extensively in *The Interpretation of Dreams,* and in "The Metapsychological Supplement to the Theory of Dreams." They possessed a cathexis-potential and were also characterized by combinations of affect, images, and ideas. They constituted units and interacted on the basis of their energy-potentials. They were in fact psychic molecules. However, in earlier thinking the association of these units into larger units was not stressed, for their dynamic relations were overshadowed by the dominant characteristics of the psychic regions. With the demise of topology, however, these formations warranted examination. The "union" of some of them into a somewhat homogeneous group took on added significance. Such a line of analysis, I think, led to the formulation of the coherent ego as another basic dynamic factor in mental process. This was a most important mutation in Freudian theory. It made of the ego not only a "body" ego, not only a libidinal ego, but also an experiential ego. It made not a primal ego but a present ego, and it indicated that not only the content of the ego but its very principle of organization depended in part on its internal dynamics (the cathectic changes in the organized and unorganized ego and between them) and in part on the environmental forces, including the social, that impinged upon this system.

Freud's position, in *The Ego and The Id,* that the ego penetrated the id indicated the theoretical change I have mentioned. His further demonstration that the state of unconsciousness was distributed between the ego and the id indicated his steadfast, if reluctant, decision to give up the old Unconscious as a theoretical category. It should be noted that consciousness is not co-terminus with the ego.

This theoretical change was, of course, brought about not by any great enthusiasm for society's influence on personality but by the substantial impossibility of organizing a conceptual system that did not take this influence fully into account.

Although the emphasis on the coherent ego emphasized the importance of factors formerly outside the system, it also indicated the transformations that overtake external material in the process of mental ingestion. It indicated that the "social self," so to speak, has little psychological validity, that the "looking-glass self" is a dangerous oversimplification. The social self has a "natural history" of its own within the mind. At this point Freud forged the theoretical links connecting his theory not only with somatic tension but also with the social experience of the individual. It will readily occur to the reader that there is an interesting similarity between the mental formation as Freud thought of it and the concept of role as it is used in sociology and anthropology. It would be inaccurate to say that these advances were clearly formulated in Freud's mind. He lapsed frequently into topological thinking and was wedded to reductive mechanisms. But the views I have mentioned were the fresh insights. Freud did not live to implement them satisfactorily but it appears to the writer that they constitute an initial foothold in exploring that area where the human organism and the culture meet.

THE TYPES, FUNCTIONS AND DEVELOPMENT
OF MECHANISMS IN FREUDIAN
THOUGHT

Freud not only devised large categories such as the Unconscious or the Preconscious, he also formulated an imposing array of more specific concepts that mediated in some manner between the categories and certain empirical processes. The object was to absorb the data of mental life into the ordered compartments of the theoretical system and to so relate the compartments as to emphasize the most important dynamic relations in personality process.

Among the more specific concepts is a general class that may be referred to as Freudian "mechanisms." They are found at the "crisis-points" of Freud's thought. These concepts may have been devised mainly in answer to some theoretical requirement or in answer to some empirical consideration. Or both types of interest may have been involved. The common characteristic of these concepts is that they had no clear relation to the body of systematic thought. They constituted a wide variety of residual assumptions about the nature of somatic or mental processes. Accordingly, they also placed limitations and conditions upon mental processes. They were required only because the processes referred to appeared meaningless otherwise, i.e., they did not fit the establish body of related concepts and categories.

These mechanisms, then, disguised, or compensated for, some theoretical inadequacy. They plugged the theoretical interstices. Instead of helping the system to work as a whole, they tended to act as temporary palliatives and to present stumbling blocks to further change or improvement in the general system. Thus, they are very sensitive indicators of the strategic weaknesses in Freud's system of thought.

Let us take for example the assumption that "childhood dreams crave reproduction for their own sake." Freud observed that the dreams both of children and of adults were full of reconstructions of childhood experiences. Trips might be repeated in dreams that had been taken during childhood. Delicious meals, or particular foods, might be eaten and enjoyed in dreams that had been relished in youth. How did this come about? It was clear that the "wish" for the trip or the meal was the efficient cause of the dream. This wish must then be a wish of the Unconscious since it was one of Freud's major assumptions that only a wish from the Unconscious could furnish the motive power for a dream. However, this interest in trips and foods showed none of the libidinal coloring that characterized Unconscious motivations. To admit this interest as typical of the Unconscious would be to violate basic assumptions about the Unconscious. Yet, as we have mentioned, this wish could not be relegated to the Conscious-Preconscious system because Freud assumed that nothing in this system could cause a dream. Here was a dilemma. Freud solved it by the assumption of an isolated mechanism at work in the unconscious, a craving for reproduction attributed to childhood memories. (For the same reasons he made a similar assumption about "nakedness-dreams.") Such isolated wishes became Unconscious needs, although not theoretically assimilable in the Unconscious, and the reproduction of the memories through dreams became in itself a "gratification."

This assumption was a one-way street. It led to no fruitful hypotheses and it formed connections with no other parts of the Freudian system. In fact, it substituted for theoretical adequacy. It formed a serious obstacle in Freud's thinking because it discouraged meeting head-on the real problem which was the adequate formulation of the major categories of Freud's thought, the Unconscious (Ucs) and the Conscious-Preconscious (Cs-Pcs). Furthermore, since Freud assumed this characteristic to be inherent in the mind, it became something to take into account in further theorizing. It became part of the data rather than part of the theory about the data.

Freud's theory is strewn with assumptions of this nature and doubtless only in the process of time will they be totally ripped from the fabric of his thought. Since these mechanisms have important functions their absence must be compensated for by satisfactory alterations in the general system of thought. At the moment it may be noted that some of Freud's undoubted pessimism about the fate of the human mind and the urgency of somatic tensions is based upon the array of assumptions that he made about mental processes. Since one assumption was not repealed when another was made the human mind came to be a hodgepodge of regressive, libidinal, primal mechanisms that often worked against each other and often against the best interests of the organism. For this reason Freud referred to many of them as "defective" or "regressive."

These mechanisms may be divided into certain cross-classifications: first, they were either somatic or psychic in their nature. A somatic mechanism was one which Freud deemed to have existence in the "body" rather than the "mind" of the individual. Its influence extended to the mind. Such a mechanism was erotogenicity. It denoted a libidinal potential in the organs of the body which was reflected in the flow of libido into the mind. As Freud's thought matured he came to prefer psychic mechanisms which were assumptions about the functioning of the mind itself. Primal repression is an excellent example of such a mechanism.

Secondly, these mechanisms may be distinguished by their functions of supplementing the category Ucs or supplementing the category Cs-Pcs. We have mentioned Freud's assumption that childhood memories craved reproduction. The mechanism producing the "reproduction" and gratifying the "wish" served to supplement the powers of the unconscious. Other mechanisms with the same function of supporting the Ucs were the "need for transference" on the part of repressed material and the assumption of "unconscious formations." The first mechanism explained why certain Unconscious material attached itself to recent Conscious experiences in dreams. The second assumption related to Preconscious affects and attributed their origin to unknown and unknowable causes in the Unconscious which Freud called "unconscious formations."

On the other hand there were many devices that supported or supplemented the Conscious-Preconscious system. One of these was primal repression with its complement, after-expulsion. This mechanism was one of the many solutions to the problem of repression. In view of Freud's theoretical commitments it was necessary to explain repression without assigning dominant power to the preconscious system. Yet no kind of formulation of the Unconscious could solve the problem. Freud, therefore, postulated a mechanism which "explained" repression without any reconstruction of the major categories. This mechanism had a dual aspect. First, as primal repression it performed an *a priori* act of sorting certain types of material and assigning them to the Pcs-Cs or the Ucs. For this no action on the part of the categories themselves was required. Secondly, as after-expulsion, the mechanism continued the sorting process. After-expulsion took place when the Pcs-Cs and the Ucs had come into existence and it consisted of a continued sorting of mental material such that material in the Pcs-Cs could be "expelled" from that system and would therefore enter the Ucs system. A peculiar advantage of after-expulsion was that it did not rely on the expulsion power of the Pcs-Cs. It assumed in the Ucs a power of "attracting" certain material out of the Pcs-Cs. Through this mechanism, then, Freud established the Ucs by fiat and he "explained" repression without increasing the energy potential of the Pcs-Cs system.

A third important cross-classification of Freudian mechanisms has to do with the type of data, if any, which was their referent. We have pointed out that sometimes there was no such body of referent material. This would be the case where the mechanism was required merely to establish an equilibrium in the "system." I am referring to such mechanisms as the primal cathexis of the ego. This mechanism had no empirical referent but actually amounted to a theoretical reconstruction of the Conscious-Preconscious category. In other cases, however, the mechanism referred to some kind of perplexing empirical situation which served as its "exciting cause." (Freud sometimes lost track of the immediate situation that prompted his inquiry however. This occurred in the case of repetition-compulsion.) This referent situation may be either biological (somatic or mental) or social (resulting from the influence on the individual of his inter-personal experience). Classification of the Freudian mechanisms on this base is useful in that it brings out the awkwardness involved in translating social influences into workable biological mechanisms. It also shows the improvement that took place in this regard and the striking advance involved in the formulation of Eros.

We recall that Freud was concerned at first to explain mental events in terms of somatic events. His first concerted effort to take social experience into account occurred with reference to the "thirteen cases of hysteria." Here Freud considered that the early experience of seduction caused some kind of damage to sexual apparatus that was reflected on the mental side by the phenomenon of resistance. He found later that the social experiences of seduction had not taken place in these cases and the theory associated with them was accordingly permitted to lapse.

With the castration complex we see an early "response" to data which in part refers to inter-personal experience. The castration complex is a biological mechanism that in a dim and unsatisfactory manner "reflects" inter-personal experience.

The Oedipus complex had the same general construction as the castration complex but it was more complicated and sought to accept a wider segment of social experience. The ego-ideal, as originally formulated, showed a kind of sudden advance which was later repeated with Eros. The ego-ideal was seen as a real social category, it referred directly to social influences as they impinged upon the personality. Freud made this concept theoretically "respectable" by infusing it with homosexual libido and reduced its usefulness by making it servient to libido-type analysis. The super-ego was closely related to the ego-ideal. The dominant empirical referent for this concept was also social. But where the ego-ideal succumbed to homosexual libido, the super-ego became the "heir of the Oedipus complex" and thus fell heir also to the limitations involved in biological "mechanization."

We can see the core of this problem clearly. Freud recognized more and more definitely that there was a large body of data involved in the relation of the individual to his social environment that was pertinent to personality process. This material could be treated only with the greatest difficulty within the biological frame of reference, however. Freud invented biological mechanisms that were designed to have approximately the same effects on personality as the pertinent social data. Thus, as we can see in the castration complex or the Oedipus complex, these mechanisms suffer from two main defects. As mechanisms they are highly elusive. As concepts for the treatment of social influences they are too rigid and too narrow.

Timid experimentation with the ego-ideal and the Oedipus complex resulted in the unconstrained inventions leading to Eros. In his pursuit of a concept that would do justice to the crucial social material Freud was at length prepared to embark upon a series of really preposterous mechanical assumptions. He assumed "primal" situations of interpersonal experiences that suited his theoretical needs. Thus his needs gave birth to his "pseudo-anthropology." He translated these interpersonal experiences into the organism by the assumption of a biological mutation. He met his requirements for some kind of libidinal relationship by assuming that the mutations involved consisted of a sort of damage to the sexual instincts giving rise to the aim-inhibited instincts. Thus the aim-inhibited instincts took on a social aspect. These mutations and alterations were given wider significance through consideration of the germ cells. Freud discovered in them, in their tendency to union, a sort of "altruism." Thus Eros, as the "heir" of the aim-inhibited instincts and the fanciful "other-orientation" of the sex cells, developed as a full-blown "sociological" concept with reference to personality.

It remained for Freud to construct a mechanism that would be receptive to the social history of the individual rather than his "primal" history. For this to take place within Freud's frame of reference the social milieu must itself become a type of mechanism which can have a continuing contemporary influence on personality. It would, of course, be necessary also to extend the libidinal unity which Freud had discovered in the personality to the society at large. This next major advance was clearly indicated by Freud in his later work. He considered that culture came ". . . to obey an inner erotic impulse." He saw civilization as "comparable to an organic process." And in those last years he set down a program for himself that could as well serve as a program for the social psychologist or the sociologist. (We can see how Freud's quest tended to repeat Durkheim's—in reverse.)

FREUDIAN THOUGHT AS A GENERAL
SYSTEM OF THEORY

There were, of course, three Freudian systems of thought. There was the first "somatic" system, the second "topographical" system, and the third "social" system. Freud showed a pronounced tendency to "close" each system during the period that he worked on it. He was not only an indefatigable researcher but he had a keen sense of the usefulness of systematic theory. The movement from period to period in his thought was prompted by the search for greater and greater theoretical adequacy. Seen in this light Freud's third period is the legitimate "heir" of the first two. It represents the high-water mark of his theory. It also represents definite departures from earlier models. The full extent of these departures has not been given sufficient attention. It may well be that from a clinical point of view the concrete conceptualization of the second period is more useful. Yet it cannot be gainsaid that the departures from this second period conceptualization were prompted by what Freud considered to be substantial inadequacies in the theory.

In estimating this third period we do not have the concrete material available earlier. Freud moved swiftly in new directions. He cut out his theoretical forms in the rough. He was in haste. It remains to us to see the significance of these forms and to suggest the more concrete alterations in theory that are required by them. We shall consider some of the more important aspects of this third-period theory.

a) The promise of a social referent for
personality analysis.

Mechanisms like the Oedipus complex acquired a certain amount of biological respectability precisely because they restricted the dimensions of social motivation which they took into account. When Freud extended these dimensions it was necessary to construct a different order of biological mechanism. Thanatos (the death-instinct, the repetition-compulsion) and Eros (the aim-inhibited instincts) are thus more generalized biological assumptions. They are so general they merge into myth, and disclose that you cannot hope to account for social motivation through biological concepts. (A reading of the literature demonstrates that this bifurcation has persisted, however. Psychoanalytic "explanation" often hovers between reliance on suggestions of biological determinism and unintegrated innuendoes of social determinism.)

This indicated that the biological frame of reference was no longer tenable. Freud, as we have seen, did not exactly give it up. Instead, he reduced it to a fiction, a fiction of the organic nature of culture. This served to open up the whole field of inter-personal experience as a vital consideration in this matter of personality process. In this frame of reference. Thanatos applied to that portion of social motivation that was of significant impact on the individual but which also was opposed to the operation of the "pleasure-principle." The super-ego was for that reason closely associated with the death-instinct. The death-instinct in fact tied in with all those binding forces operating on the individual as a result of the socialization process which run counter to libidinal, egoistic and self-preservative tendencies in the organism. Thus, at last, such concepts as "resistance of the cerebral conduction," "influence of culture and breeding," "ideal masochism," "unsuspected contrary sexual," etc. found a master assumption in the death-instinct.

On the other hand, Eros applied to quite a different component of social motivation, that component dealing with the outgoingness of the individual, his capacity for rewarding self-sacrifice. This dimension of social influence had not been apparent to Freud. It was perhaps the considerations that rose out of *Group Psychology and the Analysis of the Ego* and certain persistant problems left over from "Mourning and Melancholia" that led Freud gradually to accept the "normality" of social-cohesive behavior. This type of behavior had to be legitimated, of course, and thus we find the development of Eros out of the somatic sex cells and the aim-inhibited instincts. But Eros, in its social matrix, represented that component of social motivation that opened up new avenues for "pleasure" and thus did not run directly counter to the other pleasure-principle operating in the individual. Freud turned more and more to "culture" as an organized system of cause and he suggested that society was in a sense organic and that there was a social Eros. This disclosed the possibility that culture might be more than a semi-pathological resistance to nature. It might be the basis for a new order of experience, a new "pleasure-principle." Thus, Eros explained behavior formerly attributed to the death-instinct.

b) The escape from topology: the categories.

The import of Freud's final considerations was that the coherent ego was the dominant element in mental processes. However, it did not have the "index value" that Freud had striven to associate with such a dominant element. The coherent ego was not homogeneous with reference to the state of consciousness or unconsciousness. It was not homogeneous with reference to the qualities or quantities of energy which were concerned in its formation. And it was not homogeneous with reference to the opposition or confluence of these energies. Obviously the coherent ego was, like the secondary ego of Meynert, a developmental ego. But, because of the influence of inter-personal experience on this coherent ego, it was not an organic development as Meynert and Freud originally proposed. The development of the coherent ego must then be the result of the interaction of the components of motivation finally developed by Freud: first, the egoistic motivations by which we refer to the libidinal and "self preservative" motivations; second, the Thanatos type of social motivations; and third, the Eros type of social motivations. Since the emphasis was on a "bound" ego, it was clear that the principle of organization of the ego must be a Thanatos type or an Eros type of social motivation or a combination of the two. For neither libidinal nor self-preservative forces constituted a basis for organization, although they might be important and at times decisive in the influence and effectiveness of that organization. This view was clearly indicated in Freud's last works. The coherent or organized ego was than a social-organic product. Once formed, however, it tended to operate holistically in terms of the organization it had developed. It was also internally dynamic, being composed of "mental formations" whose cathectic relations were continually changing, both in the Repressed and the coherent ego.

The coherent ego developed as the main category of analysis. Two other categories were meaningfully related to it, the "unorganized ego" and the Repressed. The "unorganized ego" represented mental formations of no particular concern to the coherent ego. Their structure could quickly change, however, and make them subject to further psychic disposition. The Repressed was a category of active but "imprisoned" material with special significance for the dynamics of the mind. There was a last major category that Freud did not develop as completely as the others, the Conscious system. This system had certain survival functions and perceptual functions. The coherent ego was only partly in the Conscious system. There was a mutuality of censorship between the coherent ego and the Conscious system and it seemed also that the coherent ego had the power of *retention,* i.e., of withholding material from the Conscious system. On the other hand, there is evidence from many sources that the Conscious system gains efficiency from the fact of consciousness and can develop skills for wide explorations into the coherent ego and the Repressed. I would suggest that the Conscious might be termed the "supra-ego." These categories had significant inter-relations. They were in turn composed of "psychic formations" that were dynamic internally and externally with reference to other psychic formations.

c) The universal strategic variables.

Freud had sought for a universal and rigid personality system. It was to be rigid in that its dynamics were to take place within clearly marked channels. As we have pointed out, the major channels which were to guide this interaction proved quite untenable. In the third period, therefore, Freud's thought appeared to have lost much of its organization. This indicated, however, that personality must be analysed without the help of "props" from the first and second periods. Personality did not reduce to a number of mechanisms and it did not reduce to a system like the Unconscious that controlled process. The analysis must be carried forward in terms of a number of important variables.

1. *Drives, norms and social or physical reality testing.* These constituted the basic reasons for action or motivations in any personality system. The most nearly "given" in these basic variables were the drives. Freud saw them as of two types, the libidinal drives and the self-preservative drives. Although in the maturational and inter-personal context they were interpenetrated by other factors, they could be thought of as fundamentally "primal."

Norms, of course, constituted another basic reason for action but these norms (as interiorized) would vary among societies, among sub-cultures and among individuals. The word norm as employed here would refer to any generalized basis for preferring one act over another as a result of social learning.

Reality testing should be understood as applying not only to the external environment but also to the internal environment, i.e., the interrelations in personality itself. It could be thought of as given, yet in any "human" context it was completely penetrated by the "social" basis for action.

2. *The Capacities.* Freud referred frequently to the "institutions of the mind," but so far as I am aware he did not explicitly examine them in any study. They formed part of the assumptions in terms of which he thought. We may refer to them without trying to render them logically compatible or exhaustive. They consisted of such qualities as cognition, affect, ideation, volition, imagery and cathexis, and they formed the basis of the dynamic relations between the categories and the "psychic formations."

A homeostatic capacity should also be attributed at least to the coherent ego. It is our contention that repetition-compulsion, transference, the dream process, and "symptom procurement" in neurosis, are three important examples of equilibrating behavior, or self-therapy, on the part of the coherent ego. In the body of the study we have indicated how these processes are related to a social "reality principle" or an internal disequilibrium.

3. *The Energies*. The basic motivations to which we have referred require energy components to "power" them. We have separated motivation from energy here for the reason that they were split in the development of Freud's thought. At the beginning, he relied on sexual tension as the prime motivation and this motivation, of course, furnished its own energy component. But when Freud analysed ego dynamics he found it necessary to assume a reality-orientation. How was the energy for this to be furnished? By such devices as the primal cathexis of the ego and erotogenicity Freud furnished a "sexual" energy for this purpose. Then, when a new type of motivation became apparent in the ego-ideal Freud furnished components of "homosexual libido." In fact, Freud merely recognized a *fait accompli* in reality motivation and "normative" motivation and suggested an unhappy wedding between these motivations and sexual energy. It appears that we must assume not only organic energy, as in sex and the self-preservative instincts" but another type of organic, free-floating energy available to support ego behavior and socially-learned behavior. This free-floating energy becomes "bound" into ego-energy and what we have termed "Eros energy." It should be remembered that bound energies and formations have relative, not absolute, stability.

d) *Emphasis on holistic functioning.*

The breakdown of regionalism radically changed the structure of Freud's thought. Mental formations and categories were not to be distinguished on the basis of any *innate* qualitative or quantitative differences. They tended to interact holistically as units. They also tended to interact internally in terms of their component smaller units. They were thus both externally and internally dynamic. Freud indicated that these types of dynamic processes extended from the organized ego as the largest formation to the smallest formations.

e) *The experiential ego.*

The views we have mentioned re-instated a type of Meynert overlay. There was indeed a secondary ego that came to overlay the primary ego. But this process could no longer be looked upon as an organic development. Nor could it be controlled and ordered by means of the assumption of a number of organic compartments and conduits which served to maintain the dominance of the organic system by parcelling out the new factors according to pre-determined criteria. The very essence of the personality was now the developmental process itself. Uniformities in personality structure were thus to be related to uniformities in inter-personal experience (if the uniformities of organic press were to be taken as a constant). The largest formation that tended to grow from the experience of the person was the coherent ego. This formation could vary from society to society on the basis of the basic reasons for action that constituted its core. Only in the limiting case of the unsocialized human organism could we imagine the organized ego to be composed solely of organic reasons for action. There are ample reasons for doubting whether these organic bases could constitute a "coherent" ego.

One of Freud's most fruitful demonstrations was that the individual was seldom in contact with moral norms in any "pure" sense, for norms were only one element in the social context. The growth of the organized ego was related to the contact of the person with "social formations" and to the selective interiorization of the multiple aspects of these social formations. The relevant social formations would appear to be the "roles" which already have been abstracted for use by sociologists. Moral norms tended to be interiorized selectively in terms of the total norms presented by the "situation" and in relation to the "needs" of the then existing personality system.

We have mentioned that the organized ego, once it starts to develop, is influenced by its own development. Freud mentioned how the ego "put forth" its own cathexes and "instituted connections." In this regard it should be emphasized that personality not only "reflects" the social matrix, it also exercises a counter pressure upon the social environment and is a vital factor in role performance, role deviation, and social change. It appears likely that the sociologist cannot complete a satisfactory system of social theory until he can encompass the action potential of personalities into his system. Since the social milieu is refracted within personality, and since the result of this refraction is evidenced by social action, the sociologist requires some method of translating the social input into some reasonable prediction of social output.

f) *Some possibilities for conceptual parsimony.*

It is evident that Freud did not define his concepts carefully. He seemed to fear that the freshness of the insight might be lost through over-laborious concentration on the mechanics of definition. And, although he applied himself to the crucial theoretical issues, he left his concepts strewn about as a workman might leave his tools. Much can be done to relate and where necessary to annul Freud's concepts. We have not made a rigorous attempt to do this in the present study since it lies on the periphery of our interests. However, it is worthwhile to indicate certain main lines along which we think greater conceptual simplicity might be obtained.

1) When Freud suggested that there was a social Eros he was opening up the entire field of inter-personal relations for study so far as they influenced personality dynamics. This view supplanted others so far as they delimited social influences. I refer to such concepts as the castration complex, the Oedipus, the ego-ideal, and the super-ego. These latter concepts remain, however, as important empirical formations; they are likely combinations of variables in a particular socio-cultural system.

2) In the third period Freud gave up the idea of regionalism or topology and he likewise gave up the fundamental dichotomy that was expressed in the Pcs and Ucs (whatever concepts were employed to express this dichotomy). On this basis a number of concepts appear to have very limited usefulness in the Freudian system. There is no reason to preserve those postulates having to do with unintegrated processes in the Ucs, such as the craving for reproduction that was attached to childhood memories. In addition, those concepts that secured the dominance of the Ucs in its long struggle with the Pcs are superfluous, for example, unconscious formations. We recall, also, that Freud found it necessary to libidinize the ego or the Pcs-Cs in order to "legitimize" his approach to this category. The mechanisms making this possible are no longer required. Such concepts as the cathexis of the ego and erotogenicity became functionless in the light of third period thinking. Finally, the concepts Eros and the death-instinct were connected with Freud's biological frame of reference through a system of assumptions. We see, however, that this frame of reference gradually "withered away" in the third period, or, what is much the same, it was so expanded as to become essentially meaningless. Since the true source of Eros was not the biological organism but the society (as Freud recognized when he implied the existence of Eros in the individual and in the society) there is no necessity to maintain such conceits and extravagances as the pseudo-anthropology and the assumption of aim-inhibited instincts.

3) The assumption of repetition-compulsion stands in a peculiar position. It came to signify a meaningless regularity in the unconscious, an inertia. However, the early researches that gave rise to the assumption of repetition-compulsion had quite a different focus. These re-

searches were concerned with a certain "masterful" tendency on the part of the organism, a problem-solving trend. Repetition-compulsion as finally formulated masked this early, significant interest. In *Beyond the Pleasure Principle* Freud recounted the case of the young child who overcame his insecurity at the daily loss of his mother for a number of hours by playing a game. In this game the child symbolically repeated the departure and return of the mother over and over again. Freud held that this repetition was creative, therapeutic, cathartic. We think immediately of the cathartic nature of speech as Freud developed this view in his early researches. Freud also attached this same cathartic function to "dramatic and imitative arts." He recognized the dream as meaningful, indeed the psychonanalytic methodology was based on this assumption. And yet Freud was also willing to hold that the dream represented a "regressive current" in the apparatus leading to hallucination. Although the dream was meaningful, it was not sensible. This conclusion was required by the assumption that the dream produced satisfactions or fulfillments that were not somatic. The maturest thinking of Freud recognized the possibility of ego satisfactions and largely divorced ego energy from libidinal energy. On this basis the hallucinatory process in the dream could represent ego fulfillment. So far as it was fulfillment it reminds us of the case of the child's game above, a situation of cathartic discharge and therapeutic fulfillment. This view of the dream is more consistent with its meaningful nature. It suggests also that the dream process strives not only for fulfillment but also for the preservation of the fundamental equilibrium of the psyche.

This hypothesis of "mental homeostasis" seems, then, to bring into focus certain facets of Freud's thinking and to "explain" what have remained as inconsistencies in his thinking. The base for this hypothesis is the assumption that ego satisfactions or fulfillments represent, or may represent, a different qualitative order of gratifications than Freud was inclined to admit.

Repetition-compulsion, as it finally developed, did not really center on the problem of the child's game. It centered rather on the resistance of the unconscious ego to the conscious ego. As such, at the time of the analysis, it appeared as a non-functional, non-consummatory process similar in nature to the "craving for reproduction" that characterized childhood memories. However, if in line with the indications present in Freud's third period thinking, we admit to a qualitatively distinct order of gratifications (distinct from the reduction of somatic tensions) then the repetition compulsion may be meaningful with reference to that order of interest. In this view the repetition compulsion would be functional and homeostatic in nature and would not require the assumption of a *deus ex machina.*

This hypothesis with reference to repetition-compulsion is logically consistent with the subsequent formulation of the death-instinct. Generally, the qualitatively different order of ego-interests we have referred to resulted from the internalization or interiorization of social expectancies, so that they became normative commitments of the personality. So far as the mind strove for equilibrium with reference to them it appeared to violate the pleasure-principle and work toward its own destruction.

If we entertain the view of repetition-compulsion here suggested, our attention is immediately attracted to the phenomenon of transference. Is not this process related intimately to this hypothesis of mental homeostasis? In this case, however, the focus of the process is not in the mind but outside the mind. In transference, the external social situation appears to be crucial to the condition of homeostasis (whether in threatening it or preserving it). Freud certainly had no tools with which he could explore this view. His libido analysis appears strikingly forced and circular not only in relation to transference, but also in relation to the war neuroses. The threat to mental equilibrium in each case, we think, was largely in the relation of the individual to the social environment. The social scientist has tools for the analysis of this relationship at the present time. We called attention to the role of the analyst in legitimizing the personality orientation of the patient and in protecting the patient from the adverse judgments of the larger social group. Transference thus appears to have a function similar to repetition-compulsion although in a different context.

In the formulation of the "reality principle" Freud did recognize the adjustive orientation of the mind. Considerations mentioned above suggest that much might be done to bring all of the data of this nature together with a view to conceptualizing more adequately the homeostatic nature of mental processes and the types of adjustment characteristic of them.

4) Freud persisted in "reducing" energy to sexual energy. This obscured some of the variables operating in personality and required ingenious assumptions to perform the reduction. If we recognize the simple need for ego-energy and Eros energy as biological potentials, then such mechanisms as the primal cathexis of the ego and erotogenicity have no further use. The same applies to the cathexis of the ego and the homosexual investment of the ego-ideal. In addition, if we recognize the coherent ego as the strategically basic category with sufficient quantities of energy to accomplish repression then the devices used by Freud to maintain the power of the old Unconscious are out-

moded. I refer to such mechanisms as primal repression and after-expulsion.

An important dimension of the dynamics of the mind is found in cathexis. Sexual cathexis and cathexis arising from the "self-preservative" instincts are assumed. However, Freud's work demonstrated that it is not ordinarily decisive in personality. Energy available to the ego in a free-floating form, and energy bound to the ego or Eros and employed for cathexis, hyper-cathexis and anti-cathexis are usually decisive. Repressed material is subject to anti-cathexis but the repressed material itself may possess hyper-cathexis. Since "drive" cathexis does not appear to be usually coercive in the mind it follows that the dynamic potential of repressed material must ordinarily come from hyper-cathexis of the repressed material which is at the same time subjected to anti-cathexis. In the "normal" case, "drive cathexis" would be supplemented by hyper-cathexis except in cases of reality orientation or normative orientation.

This view suggests the basis for the distinction between "denial" and "sublimation." In denial the ego hyper-cathexis is removed from the repressed formation which thereupon becomes inactive. In sublimation the hyper-cathexis is not withdrawn but the organism is directed into behavior that "gratifies" the ego component of energy if not the "drive" component.

CONCLUSION

The body of the study must, of course, speak for itself. It is the writer's hope that the reader will find the present chapter useful in presenting an overall view of what this study contains by way of "finding." In each case, we think these findings are required to achieve the maximum "coherence" in Freudian theory and to render it most responsive to the clinical data with which Freud was concerned. The Freudian system is an unfinished system.

It appears that Freud in at least a part of his third period was engaged upon substantially the same undertaking that many social scientists have been engaged upon since—the conceptual organization of the relation between the organism and the social environment as it strikes into the organism. We hope that Freud's contributions to this problem —and they were many—may become more evident in the light of this study. We hope that perhaps the study may render Freud more "translatable" into social-scientific terms. There must be a road from the libidinized ego to the "collective representations" of Durkheim. Perhaps it is clearer now how far Freud went along that road.

NOTES

NOTES TO CHAPTER I

1. See Paul W. Tappan, *Juvenile Delinquency* p. 86.
2. Antoine Lavoisier, "Reflections on Phlogiston," 1783, as quoted in McKie, Douglas, *Antoine Lavoisier* (New York: Henry Schuman, 1952).
3. Albert Einstein, *The World as I See It* (New York: Covici Friede, 1934) pp. 53–54.

NOTES TO CHAPTER II

1. Sigmund Freud, "A Phobia in a Five-Year-Old Boy," *Collected Papers* (London: The Hogarth Press, 1953), III, 279.
2. *Ibid.*, p. 279.
3. *Ibid.*, p. 280.
4. *Ibid.*, p. 269.
5. *Ibid.*, p. 228.
6. *Ibid.*, p. 264.
7. *Ibid.*, p. 260.
8. *Ibid.*, p. 260.
9. *Ibid.*, p. 278.
10. *Ibid.*, p. 168.
11. *Ibid.*, p. 169.
12. *Ibid.*, p. 169.
13. *Ibid.*, p. 168.
14. *Ibid.*, p. 171.
15. *Ibid.*, p. 171.
16. *Ibid.*, p. 268.
17. *Ibid.*, pp. 269–70.
18. *Ibid.*, p. 275.
19. *Ibid.*, pp. 261–2.
20. *Ibid.*, p. 285.
21. *Ibid.*, p. 262.
22. *Ibid.*, p. 226.
23. *Ibid.*, p. 226.
24. *Ibid.*, p. 239.

NOTES TO CHAPTER III

1. Sigmund Freud, "The Interpretation of Dreams," *The Basic Writings of Sigmund Freud* (New York: Modern Library, 1938), p. 287.
2. *Ibid.*, p. 498.
3. *Ibid.*, p. 499.
4. *Ibid.*, p. 276.
5. *Ibid.*, p. 392.
6. *Ibid.*, p. 542.
7. *Ibid.*, p. 299.
8. *Ibid.*, p. 312.
9. *Ibid.*, p. 299.
10. *Ibid.*, p. 251.
11. *Ibid.*, p. 497.
12. *Ibid.*, p. 500.
13. *Ibid.*, pp. 252–53.
14. *Ibid.*, p. 253.
15. *Ibid.*, p. 499.
16. *Ibid.*, p. 499.
17. *Ibid.*, pp. 499–500.
18. *Ibid.*, p. 538.
19. *Ibid.*, p. 538.
20. *Ibid.*, p. 538.
21. *Ibid.*, p. 537.
22. *Ibid.*, p. 537.
23. *Ibid.*, p. 537.

NOTES TO CHAPTER IV

1. William McDougall, *Psychoanalysis and Social Psychology* (London: Methuen and Company, Ltd. 1936), p. 31.
2. Sigmund Freud, "Three Contribu-

tions to the Theory of Sex," *The Basic Writings of Sigmund Freud*, p. 576. The use of the word "instinct" to translate the German word "*trieb*" has been questioned. I employ "instinct" as the most convenient handle. It is the process described that matters.

3. *Ibid.*, p. 576.
4. *Ibid.*, p. 605.
5. *Ibid.*, p. 605.
6. *Ibid.*, p. 611.
7. *Ibid.*, p. 611.
8. Sigmund Freud, "The Defense Neuro-Psychoses," *Selected Papers on Hysteria and Other Psycho-Neuroses* (New York: The Journal of Nervous and Mental Diseases Publishing Company, 1909), p. 121.
9. *Ibid.*, p. 122.
10. *Ibid.*, p. 123.
11. *Ibid.*, p. 123.
12. *Ibid.*, p. 123.
13. *Ibid.*, p. 124.
14. *Ibid.*, p. 124.
15. *Ibid.*, p. 127.
16. *Ibid.*, p. 132.
17. Sigmund Freud, "On the Right to Separate from Neurasthenia a Definite Symptom-Complex as 'Anxiety Neurosis,' " *Selected Papers*, p. 141 ff.
18. *Ibid.*, p. 141 ff.
19. *Ibid.*, p. 148.
20. *Ibid.*, p. 148.
21. *Ibid.*, p. 149.
22. *Ibid.*, p. 153.
23. *Ibid.*, p. 153.
24. *Ibid.*, p. 154.
25. Sigmund Freud, "The Defense Neuro-Psychoses," *Op. cit.*, p. 129.
26. Sigmund Freud, "On the Right to Separate from Neurasthenia a Definite Symptom-Complex as 'Anxiety Neurosis,' " *Op. cit.*, p. 150.
27. *Selected Papers*, p. 188.
28. Sigmund Freud, "The Psychotherapy of Hysteria," *Selected Papers*, p. 110.
29. *Ibid.*, p. 110.
30. *Ibid.*, p. 116.
31. Sigmund Freud, "Further Observations on the Defense Neuro-Psychoses," *Selected Papers*, pp. 156–57.
32. see "The Role of Sexuality in the Etiology of the Neuroses."
33. Sigmund Freud, "Further Observations on the Defense Neuro-Psychoses," *Op. cit.*, p. 157.
34. *Ibid.*, p. 157.

35. *Ibid.*, p. 158.
36. *Selected Papers*, p. 192.
37. Sigmund Freud, "Further Observations on the Defense Neuro-Psychoses," *Op. cit.*, p. 158.
38. *Ibid.*, p. 159.
39. *Ibid.*, p. 160.
40. *Ibid.*, p. 160.
41. *Ibid.*, p. 159 fn. This is true if we assume the Unconscious cannot borrow energy from the secondary ego. We will indicate later that it can.
42. Sigmund Freud, "The Role of Sexuality in the Etiology of the Neuroses," *Selected Papers*, p. 192.
43. *Ibid.*, p. 193.
44. Sigmund Freud, "Hysterical Fancies and Their Relations to Bisexuality," *Selected Papers*, p. 194.
45. *Ibid.*, p. 200.
46. *Ibid.*, p. 193.
47. Sigmund Freud, "On Psychotherapy," *Selected Papers*, p. 183.

NOTES TO CHAPTER V

1. Sigmund Freud, "The Interpretation of Dreams," *Op. cit.*, p. 368.
2. *Ibid.*, p. 369.
3. *Ibid.*, pp. 371–73.
4. *Ibid.*, p. 381.
5. *Ibid.*, p. 382.
6. *Ibid.*, p. 433.
7. *Ibid.*, p. 423.
8. *Ibid.*, p. 515.
9. *Ibid.*, p. 518.
10. *Ibid.*, p. 532.
11. *Ibid.*, p. 533.
12. *Ibid.*, p. 533.
13. *Ibid.*, p. 533.
14. But see the vexing wishes of children, *ibid.*, p. 223.
15. *Ibid.*, pp. 455–57.
16. *Ibid.*, p. 508.
17. *Ibid.*, p. 508.
18. *Ibid.*, p. 508.
19. *Ibid.*, pp. 505–506.
20. *Ibid.*, p. 503.
21. "The Interpretation of Dreams," *op. cit.*, p. 504.
22. *Ibid.*, p. 503.
23. *Ibid.*, pp. 513–14.
24. *Ibid.*, p. 234.
25. *Ibid.*, p. 446.
26. *Ibid.*, p. 446.
27. *Ibid.*, pp. 503–504.
28. *Ibid.*, p. 491.
29. *Ibid.*, p. 529.

30. *Ibid.*, p. 530.
31. *Ibid.*, p. 544.
32. *Ibid.*, p. 546.

NOTES TO CHAPTER VI

1. Sigmund Freud, "The Interpretation of Dreams," *op. cit.*, p. 256.
2. *Ibid.*, p. 259.
3. *Ibid.*, p. 294.
4. *Ibid.*, p. 532.
5. *Ibid.*, pp. 301–302.
6. *Ibid.*, pp. 297–98.
7. *Ibid.*, p. 305.
8. *Ibid.*, pp. 305–306.
9. *Ibid.*, p. 306.
10. *Ibid.*, pp. 229–30.
11. *Ibid.*, p. 230.
12. *Ibid.*, p. 231.
13. *Ibid.*, p. 298.
14. *Ibid.*, p. 297.
15. *Ibid.*, p. 297.
16. *Ibid.*, p. 297.
17. *Ibid.*, p. 311.
18. *Ibid.*, p. 294.
19. *Ibid.*, p. 294.
20. *Ibid.*, pp. 292–93.
21. *Ibid.*, p. 295.
22. *Ibid.*, p. 295.
23. *Ibid.*, p. 509.
24. *Ibid.*, p. 509.
25. *Ibid.*, p. 509.
26. *Ibid.*, p. 509.
27. *Ibid.*, p. 510.
28. *Ibid.*, p. 507.
29. *Ibid.*, p. 507.
30. *Ibid.*, p. 510.
31. *Ibid.*, p. 529.
32. *Ibid.*, p. 545.
33. *Ibid.*, p. 545.

NOTES TO CHAPTER VIII

1. Sigmund Freud, "Three Contributions to a Theory of Sex," *op. cit.*, p. 572.
2. *Ibid.*, p. 572.
3. *Ibid.*, p. 583.
4. *Ibid.*, p. 611.
5. Sigmund Freud, "Instincts and Their Vicissitudes," *Collected Papers*, IV, p. 66.
6. Sigmund Freud, "On Narcissism: An Introduction," *Collected Papers*, IV, pp. 33–34.
7. Sigmund Freud, "Instincts and Their Vicissitudes," *op. cit.*, p. 69.
8. Sigmund Freud, "On Narcissism: An Introduction," *op. cit.*, p. 36.

9. *Ibid.*, pp. 40–41.
10. *Ibid.*, p. 42.
11. *Ibid.*, p. 42.
12. *Ibid.*, p. 30.
13. *Ibid.*, p. 31.
14. *Ibid.*, pp. 44–45.
15. *Ibid.*, p. 45.
16. *Ibid.*, p. 46.
17. *Ibid.*, p. 45.
18. *Ibid.*, p. 47.

NOTES TO CHAPTER IX

1. Sigmund Freud, "On Narcissism: An Introduction," *op. cit.*, p. 50.
2. *Ibid.*, p. 51.
3. *Ibid.*, p. 51.
4. *Ibid.*, p. 52.
5. *Ibid.*, p. 53.
6. *Ibid.*, p. 51.
7. *Ibid.*, p. 55.
8. *Ibid.*, p. 55.
9. *Ibid.*, p. 57.
10. *Ibid.*, p. 59.
11. *Ibid.*, p. 59.
12. *Ibid.*, p. 59.
13. Sigmund Freud, "Mourning and Melancholia," *Collected Papers*, IV, p. 153.
14. *Ibid.*, p. 153.
15. *Ibid.*, p. 154.
16. *Ibid.*, p. 155.
17. *Ibid.*, p. 155.
18. *Ibid.*, p. 156.
19. *Ibid.*, p. 157.
20. Sigmund Freud, "Mourning and Melancholia," *op. cit.*, p. 157.
21. *Ibid.*, p. 158.
22. *Ibid.*, p. 159.
23. *Ibid.*, p. 161.
24. *Ibid.*, p. 162.
25. *Ibid.*, pp. 169–70.
26. *Ibid.*, p. 165.
27. *Ibid.*, pp. 165–66.
28. *Ibid.*, p. 167.

NOTES TO CHAPTER X

1. Sigmund Freud, "A Note on the Unconscious in Psycho-Analysis," *Collected Papers*, IV, p. 24.
2. *Ibid.*, p. 25.
3. *Ibid.*, p. 27.
4. *Ibid.*, p. 29.
5. Sigmund Freud, "Repression," *Collected Papers*, IV, p. 86.
6. *Ibid.*, pp. 86–7.
7. *Ibid.*, p. 87.

8. *Ibid.*, p. 90.
9. Sigmund Freud, "The Unconscious," *Collected Papers*, IV, p. 109.
10. *Ibid.*, pp. 109–10.
11. *Ibid.*, p. 110.
12. *Ibid.*, p. 111.
13. *Ibid.*, p. 112.
14. *Ibid.*, p. 111.
15. *Ibid.*, p. 113.
16. *Ibid.*, pp. 113–14.
17. *Ibid.*, p. 114.
18. *Ibid.*, pp. 118–19.
19. *Ibid.*, p. 119.
20. *Ibid.*, p. 122.
21. *Ibid.*, p. 123.
22. *Ibid.*, p. 122.
23. *Ibid.*, p. 124.
24. *Ibid.*, p. 125.
25. Sigmund Freud, "The Interpretation of Dreams," *op cit.*, pp. 505–506.
26. Sigmund Freud, "Metaphysical Supplement of the Theory of Dreams," *Collected Papers*, IV, p. 141.
27. *Ibid.*, p. 142.
28. Freud, "The Interpretation of Dreams," *op cit.*, p. 501.
29. Freud, "Metaphysical Supplement," *op cit.*, p. 140.
30. *Ibid.*, p. 140.
31. *Ibid.*, p. 140.
32. *Ibid.*, p. 141.
33. *Ibid.*, pp. 142–3.
34. *Ibid.*, p. 145.
35. *Ibid.*, p. 146.
36. *Ibid.*, p. 148.
37. *Ibid.*, p. 148.
38. *Ibid.*, p. 149.
39. *Ibid.*, pp. 149–50.
40. *Ibid.*, p. 150.

NOTES TO CHAPTER XI

1. Sigmund Freud, "The Most Prevalent Form of Degradation in Erotic Life," *Collected Papers*, IV, p. 213.
2. *Ibid.*, p. 213.
3. *Ibid.*, p. 214.
4. *Ibid.*, p. 214.
5. *Ibid.*, p. 215.
6. *Ibid.*, p. 215.
7. *Ibid.*, pp. 215–16.
8. Sigmund Freud, "Some Character Types Met with in Psycho-Analytic Work," *Collected Papers*, IV, p. 319.
9. *Ibid.*, p.319.
10. Sigmund Freud, *A General Introduction to Psycho-Analysis* (New York: The Liveright Publishing Company, 1935), p. 381.

11. *Ibid.*, pp. 382–83.
12. *Ibid.*, pp. 383–84.
13. *Ibid.*, p. 386.
14. *Ibid.*, pp. 376–377.
15. *Ibid.*, pp. 380–81.

NOTES TO CHAPTER XII

1. Sigmund Freud, *Beyond the Pleasure Principle* (New York: Boni and Liveright), p. 2.
2. *Ibid.*
3. *Ibid.*, p. 3.
4. The reader will note similarity between Fechner's view and Cannon's view of homeostasis.
5. Freud, *Beyond the Pleasure Principle*, p. 5.
6. *Ibid.*, p. 5.
7. *Ibid.*, p. 6.
8. *Ibid.*, p. 6.
9. *Ibid.*, p. 6.
10. *Ibid.*, pp. 6–7.
11. *Ibid.*, pp.11–13.
12. *Ibid.*, p. 13 fn.
13. *Ibid.*, pp. 13–14.
14. *Ibid.*, p. 14.
15, *Ibid.*, p. 15.
16. *Ibid.*, pp. 43–44.
17. *Ibid.*, p. 16.
18. See "The Defense Neuro-Psychoses," *Collected Papers*, I (1894).
19. Freud, *Beyond the Pleasure Principle*, p. 15.
20. *Ibid.*, p. 17.
21. Freud, *Beyond the Pleasure Principle*, p. 18.
22. *Ibid.*, p. 18.
23. *Ibid.*, p. 18.
24. *Ibid.*, p. 18.
25. *Ibid.*, p. 19.
26. *Ibid.*, p. 19.
27. *Ibid.*, p. 19.
28. *Ibid.*, p. 19.
29. *Ibid.*, pp. 21–22.

NOTES TO CHAPTER XIII

1. Sigmund Freud, *Beyond the Pleasure Principle*, p. 19.
2. *Ibid.*, p. 29.
3. *Ibid.*, pp. 31–32.
4. *Ibid.*, p. 32.
5. *Ibid.*, pp. 32–33.
6. *Ibid.*, p. 34.
7. *Ibid.*, pp. 34–35.
8. *Ibid.*, p. 35.
9. *Ibid.*, pp. 36–37.

10. *Ibid.*, p. 37.
11. *Ibid.*
12. *Ibid.*
13. *Ibid.*, pp. 37–8.
14. *Ibid.*, p. 38.
15. *Ibid.*, p. 39.
16. *Ibid.*
17. *Ibid.*
18. *Ibid.*, pp. 39–40.
19. *Ibid.*, pp. 44–45.
20. *Ibid.*, p. 47.
21. *Ibid.*, p. 46.
22. *Ibid.*, pp. 46–47.
23. *Ibid.*, p. 48.
24. *Ibid.*, pp. 48–49.

NOTES TO CHAPTER XIV

1. Sigmund Freud, *Beyond the Pleasure Principle*, pp. 49–50.
2. *Ibid.*, p. 50.
3. *Ibid.*, p. 49.
4. *Ibid.*, p. 49.
5. *Ibid.*, p. 50.
6. *Ibid.*, p. 50.
7. *Ibid.*, p. 47.
8. *Ibid.*, pp. 52–53.
9. *Ibid.*, p. 63.
10. *Ibid.*, pp. 63–64.
11. *Ibid.*, p. 64.
12. *Ibid.*, p. 67.
13. *Ibid.*, p. 67.
14. *Ibid.*, p. 68.
15. *Ibid.*, p. 67.
16. *Ibid.*, pp. 68–69.

NOTES TO CHAPTER XV

1. Sigmund Freud, *Group Psychology and the Analysis of the Ego* (New York: Liveright Publishing Corp., 1951), pp. 37–8.
2. *Ibid.*, p. 58.
3. *Ibid.*, pp. 115–16.
4. *Ibid.*, p. 116.
5. *Ibid.*, pp. 117–18.
6. *Ibid.*, p. 118.
7. *Ibid.*, pp. 118–19.
8. *Ibid.*, pp. 119–20.
9. *Ibid.*, p. 40.
10. *Ibid.*, p. 56.
11. *Ibid.*
12. *Ibid.*, p. 57.
13. *Ibid.*
14. *Ibid.*, p. 124.
15. *Ibid.*, p. 126.
16. *Ibid.*, p. 60.
17. *Ibid.*, p. 62.

18. *Ibid.*, pp. 62–3.
19. *Ibid.*, p. 69.
20. *Ibid.*
21. *Ibid.*, p. 70.
22. Freud, *Group Psychology and the Analysis of the Ego*, p. 69, italics ours.
23. *Ibid.*, p. 80.
24. *Ibid.*, p. 81.
25. *Ibid.*, p. 89.
26. *Ibid.*, p. 87.
27. *Ibid.*
28. *Ibid.*, p. 91.
29. *Ibid.*
30. *Ibid.*, p. 92.
31. *Ibid.*, p. 93.
32. *Ibid.*, p. 94.
33. *Ibid.*, p. 85.
34. *Ibid.*, p. 102.

NOTES TO CHAPTER XVI

1. Sigmund Freud, *The Ego and the Id* (London: The Hogarth Press, 1927), pp. 15–17.
2. *Ibid.*, p. 10.
3. *Ibid.*, p. 12.
4. *Ibid.*, pp. 17–18, italics ours.
5. *Ibid.*, p. 27.
6. *Ibid.*, p. 28.
7. *Ibid.*
8. *Ibid.*
9. *Ibid.*, p. 30.
10. *Ibid*
11. *Ibid.*, p. 32–33.
12. *Ibid.*, p. 32.
13. *Ibid.*, p. 40.
14. *Ibid.*, pp. 40–41.
15. *Ibid.*, p. 42.
16. *Ibid.*
17. *Ibid.*
18, *Ibid.*
19. *Ibid.*, p. 43.
20. *Ibid.*
21. Sigmund Freud, *Group Psychology and the Analysis of the Ego*, p. 60.
22. Freud, *The Ego and the Id*, p. 44.
23. *Ibid.*, p. 45.
24. *Ibid.*, p. 48.
25. *Ibid.*, p. 49.
26. *Ibid.*
27. *Ibid.*, p. 102.
28. *Ibid.*, p. 49.

NOTES TO CHAPTER XVII

1. Sigmund Freud, *The Ego and the Id*, pp. 61–62.
2. *Ibid.*, p. 64.

3. *Ibid.*
4. *Ibid.*, pp. 62–63.
5. *Ibid.*, p. 64.
6. *Ibid.*, p. 65.
7. *Ibid.*
8. *Ibid.*, pp. 61–62.
9. *Ibid.*, p. 65.
10. Sigmund Freud, *The Problem of Anxiety* (New York: W. W. Norton and Company and the Psychoanalytic Quarterly Press, 1936), p. 24.
11. *Ibid.*, p. 24.
12. *Ibid.*, p. 23.
13. *Ibid.*, p. 20.
14. *Ibid.*, pp. 17–18.
15. *Ibid.*, p. 19.
16. *Ibid.*, p. 39.
17. *Ibid.*, p. 61.
18. *Ibid.*, p. 19.
19. *Ibid.*, p. 98.
20. *Ibid.*
21. *Ibid.*, p. 102.
22. *Ibid.*, p. 105.
23. Freud, *The Ego and the Id*, pp. 71–73.

24. Freud, *The Problem of Anxiety*, p. 25.
25. *Ibid.*
26. *Ibid.*, p. 26.
27. *Ibid.*, pp. 26–27.
28. *Ibid.*, p. 27.
29. *Ibid.*, p. 62.
30. *Ibid.*, pp. 63–64.
31. Sigmund Freud, *Autobiography* (New York: W. W. Norton and Company, 1935), p. 71 fn.
32. Freud, *New Introductory Lectures in Psychoanalysis* (New York: W. W. Norton and Company, 1933), pp. 244–45.
33. See Hobbes's *Leviathan*.
34. Freud, *Future of an Illusion*, London (1928) p. 26.
35. Freud, "Civilization and Its Discontents," *Civilization, War and Death* (London: The Hogarth Press, 1939), p. 67.
36. *Ibid.*, pp. 66–67.
37. *Ibid.*, p. 67.
38. *Ibid.*, pp. 31–32.

INDEX

INDEX

269